Anthony deMello

The Happy Wanderer

ANTHONY DEMELLO
THE HAPPY WANDERER

BILL DEMELLO

Edited by Clifford W. DeSilva

ORBIS BOOKS
Maryknoll, New York 10545

Founded in 1970, Orbis Books endeavors to publish works that enlighten the mind, nourish the spirit, and challenge the conscience. The publishing arm of the Maryknoll Fathers and Brothers, Orbis seeks to explore the global dimensions of the Christian faith and mission, to invite dialogue with diverse cultures and religious traditions, and to serve the cause of reconciliation and peace. The books published reflect the views of their authors and do not represent the official position of the Maryknoll Society. To learn more about Maryknoll and Orbis Books, please visit our website at www.maryknollsociety.org.

Copyright © 2013 by Bill deMello

Published by Orbis Books, Maryknoll, New York 10545-0302.
Manufactured in the United States of America.

Library of Congress Cataloging-in-Publication Data

deMello, Bill, 1944-
    Anthony deMello, the happy wanderer / written by Bill deMello ; edited by
    Clifford W. DeSilva.
        pages cm
    Includes bibliographical references.
    ISBN 978-1-62698-020-4
        1. deMello, Anthony, 1931-1987. 2. Jesuits—India—Biography. I. Title.
BX4705.D2845D45 2013
271'.5302—dc23
[B]
                                                                    2012034279

CONTENTS

For my brother Tony.
For Frank and Louisa, our parents.
Also for Caridade, our grandfather,
with whom this story began.

ACKNOWLEDGMENTS

I HAD LONG DESIRED TO expand on my short internet biography of Tony. Finding the time and motivation to accomplish this task was daunting enough. Add to this the difficulty in obtaining accurate additional information about my brother and the task seemed well-nigh impossible. I wanted to provide much more than mere information on his family background and origins. If I was going to write a comprehensive biography of Tony I was going to need a mountain of information from various sources.

I asked myself where on earth I was going to find all this material. Tony and I had been separated so many years before, when he left home to join the Society of Jesus. Contact during the years that followed was limited to a few days in his company and our interaction was more of a personal nature. This was not enough to enable me to compile a comprehensive history of his life and his many achievements. I needed lots of vital information to which I was not privy.

There were many requests coming from correspondents asking me for more information about Tony. I was quite sure I could never find the answers to satisfy everyone. Moreover, if ever I did find the information I needed, how was I going to compile it all into a comprehensive book?

I was very close to giving up on the idea of rewriting his biography.

Then one day, a thought occurred to me. I remembered that I

had chosen the New Testament as one of my subjects in my final year at school. Not so much because I was religiously inclined as because I just found the story about Jesus so interesting and inspiring. It was the Bible, then, from which I drew inspiration to begin this book. I remembered Christ's Sermon on the Mount and loosely paraphrased his suggestions.

I began asking for information and to my amazement, it just poured in by the truckload.

I sought and I was delighted at the treasures I discovered through the generosity of legions of people.

I knocked and people opened not only their doors but lovingly also opened their hearts to me.

I owe thanks to scores of people who have continued to correspond with me, persuading me to persevere. It was on account of your mail that I decided that this book needed to be written. I hope you find the answers to all your questions and more in this book.

As intended before I started compiling all this information for my book, I have refrained (except in some cases) from ascribing names to quotes or experiences provided in the pages of this book. Some of you mentioned below will recognize your contribution(s) in the ensuing pages. Others will be pleased to see that you have pointed me in the right direction and that I have taken full advantage of your advice and guidance.

If I have somehow left someone out of the list given below, I beg your forgiveness. It will definitely not have been intentional. Please remind me to mention you in subsequent editions. To everyone listed below, I therefore extend my heartfelt gratitude.

I have to acknowledge there are a few people who deserve special mention. I am sure they do not desire any special attention. Nevertheless, I mention them because of their help and guidance, without which I would not have been able to complete this book.

I owe a very special note of thanks to Daphne and Dominic Gonzalvez. Dominic helped me by editing the e-biography of Tony which many people have read and enjoyed for many years. This led to all that correspondence and encouragement, accompanied by requests that I work on an extension of the short biography.

Were it not for Daphne hosting the first short biography on her webpage it would probably never have seen the light of day. She continues to graciously host the link on her web address and makes changes as and when I request them. Over and above, both of them have constantly encouraged and urged me on, in the course of my writing this book.

Multi-talented Daphne was responsible for "repairing" old family photos and rendering them as good as new. Besides this, she also arranged to convert very old audio cassettes into CDs from which I was able to extract so much valuable information.

Daphne and Dominic, thank you for being there at the right time and for devoting so much of your valuable time to helping me.

I would like to express my gratitude to my young artistic friend, Vlada Peterka. He wrote some months ago requesting a photo of Tony, so that he could draw a portrait of him. The beautiful portrait you see on the front cover of this book is a result of his skill and expertise. He is currently working with me to construct a website which will be devoted to Tony. Nothing I have asked him to do was considered difficult or cumbersome by him. Vlada, I thank you for your patience and for being ever so generous with your time.

It was my wish that someone special—a close friend of Tony's—write the Foreword to this book. Tony had a way of making everyone he came into contact with feel very special. Therefore, there were many very worthy and qualified people who would have done justice to the task. I, however, had no qualms about asking Fr. Joseph M. Feliu SJ to write the Foreword. He is one of Tony's oldest friends and I can plainly perceive when he speaks about Tony, the love, respect, and comradeship—not to mention the jokes and humor—he and Tony shared right from the time they were young scholastics in Spain. This relationship continued to the end of Tony's life.

When I first made my desire known to him, he politely declined on the grounds that he did not feel worthy of performing such an important task. I am so very pleased that I persisted, persevered, and insisted that it was he and he alone who should write the Foreword.

Fr. Feliu, I am very grateful to you for making precious time in your horrendously busy schedule to write the Foreword. It is beautifully worded and composed with so much love and sensitivity. It is a joy to read your tribute to Tony.

I could not complete this section of the book without some very special comments about my editor, Clifford DeSilva. In fact, were it not for Cliffie, I may not have been writing this section at all. He painstakingly (and I don't use this word lightly) read my work, corrected me where necessary, and complimented me when appropriate. At the same time, he graciously left the bulk of my writing untouched. His knowledge of the Society of Jesus was priceless. Being an ex-Jesuit, he was able to guide me through some of the very difficult stages of this book. Above all, his close association with Tony accounted for the deep knowledge he had about my brother.

The stories he shared with me about their close relationship caused me slight pangs of envy. At times I wished I too could have shared some precious times like those with Tony. There are things I would never have discovered were it not for Cliffie. His computer skills and literary and religious acumen helped me in areas where I would otherwise have floundered.

In addition to my own stories, various and numerous threads of information were coming to me from dozens of sources. Clifford helped me weave all that information into a smooth narrative.

Cliffie, words cannot express my sincere gratitude to you. You did a stupendous job of editing my work. Above all and most importantly, thank you for your patience, for being my friend and mentor and for lifting my spirits during those difficult times when I was troubled and dejected. You calmly and patiently guided and encouraged me to persevere when I almost gave up and abandoned the entire project.

I would like to express my very sincere thanks to Fr. Jerry Sequeira SJ, Director of Gujarat Sahiyta Prakash. Fr. Jerry, you were accommodating and cooperative from the very beginning when I wrote asking whether you would publish my book. You got it approved by the board of directors of Gujarat Sahitya Prakash in record time and thereafter you have always been helpful and generous with your time.

My sincere gratitude to Robert Ellsberg and the team at Orbis books for having faith in me and in particular in Tony. Robert, thanks to you, this book will be launched in the USA during the 25th year of Tony's passing. Where other publishers stalled and balked, you took up the challenge, recognizing the huge audience in North America who are eagerly awaiting the publication of Tony's biography. I am confident that thereafter, this book will reach the world at large.

A final note of thanks to everyone listed below—in alphabetical order:

Anil Sequeira, Aubrey Stanley, Augustus Mallier, Br. Mario Correia SJ, Catherine D'Silva (nee Castellino), Cedric Saldanha, Celine Castelino, Clifford DeSilva, Daniel Szajdek, Daphne Gonzalvez, Diamond Publications, Goa, Dominic Gonzalvez Dorothy Furtado, Dr. Lilly Rodrigues MD, Fernand Melder, Fr. Abel Fernandes, Fr. Alban D'Souza SJ, Fr. Albert Menezes SJ, Fr. Allwyn Nazareth SJ, Fr. Aurel Brys SJ, Fr. Errol Fernandes SJ, Fr. Fio Mascarenhas SJ, Fr. Francis de Melo SJ, Fr. Federico Sopena SJ, Fr. Hilario Fernandes SJ, Fr. Jerry Sequeira SJ, Fr. Joaquim Tellis SJ, Fr. Joe Rebello, Fr. John Misquitta SJ, Fr. Joseph M. Feliu SJ, Fr. Lawrie Ferrao SJ, Fr. Lisbert D'Souza SJ, Fr. Miguel Lafont SJ, Fr. Prashant Olalekar SJ, Fr. Ronnie Prabhu SJ, Fr. Thomas Reddy SJ, Fr. Tony J. D'Souza SJ, Fr. Vincent Banon SJ (Deceased), Fr. Vincent Vaz SJ, Francisco Nunes, Gerard Mascarenhas, Grace deMello, Ivan Dias, Joe Fernandes, John Arago, John D'Souza, Laureen Patrao, Leonie Miranda, Lise Kool, Marina D'Costa, Milton Vanderhyde, Noel Godin, Prof. Anand Nayak (Deceased), Richard Perkins, Rita Maloney, Roger Pereira, Sr. Isabel Martin SCJ, Sr. Ita Fernandes FDCC, Sr. Jessie Mendonça FDCC, Sr. Josita Myladiyil MMS, Sr. Margaret Rodericks

SCN, Sr. Olive De Silva FDCC, Sr. Rosalia Medeira MMS, Stanley Baptista, Tamar Crane, Vernon Braganza, Vlada Peterka

The help you all gave me so willingly and generously, the time you devoted and the promptness of your replies to my request for help is what made this book a reality.

Thank you all; thank you from the bottom of my heart.

—Bill deMello
(bill_demello@hotmail.com)
Sydney, Australia

FOREWORD

I HAVE KNOWN TONY SINCE the time both of us were in our early twenties. We were students of philosophy in a Jesuit college near Barcelona in Spain. We soon became friends and remained so until the end. From what I know of Tony since those early days, I can vouch that the pages that follow have succeeded in portraying him, his character, his freedom, his talents, and his spirituality fairly accurately.

Contrary to what often happens, especially when there is a blood relationship, Bill deMello seems to have managed to harmonically combine love with objectivity. The outcome is a book which is less a panegyric than a faithful portrait. True, if the personage written about is beyond the common stock of us mortals, it is not the fault of the writer of the book, who simply narrates what is truly extraordinary. The Tony whom I knew and whom the reader will find in these pages was indeed extraordinary, normal beyond what is normal, jovial to the extreme, and with a high degree of intelligence that showed itself more in his intuitive abilities than in discursive thinking. ʾ

Tony was indeed a theologian but only in the sense that he was familiar with God. He expressed himself via simple stories about the spiritual insights with which he was enlightened. He may have seemed to be a borderline Christian, but in fact he was a man who never crossed the line drawn by Jesus, assuming that the good Lord ever drew such a line. Tony was at the crossroads and frontiers of faith and had a unique vision of reality that many questioned because they did not share this vision. His spirituality was not constrained by creeds but all the same found both inspiration and expression very much within the Catholic Church.

Many of us owe a deep debt of gratitude to Tony beyond what mere words can express. Many who were walking now fly and to many who were simply obedient to the rule, Tony demonstrated that there is something higher than simple obedience, namely, the fulfillment one finds through the free acceptance of God's loving plan for each one of us. Finally, after the personal example of Tony, many have discovered the joy of working indefatigably and enthusiastically to the very end.

Joseph M. Feliu SJ
Mumbai, India

PREFACE

On May 31, 1987, Tony and I met at Fordham University and dined together. Later in the evening, I parted company with him, never to see him alive again.

During Tony's lifetime, I used to receive a complimentary copy of all his books, video, and audio recordings. I was thrilled to receive them but never thought for a minute to read or listen to his work. I just assumed they would all be about religion and spirituality in neither of which I had an interest.

Years after Tony died and when the internet became more easily accessible, I took great delight in searching for items of interest and finding instant answers to my questions. One day, just out of curiosity, I typed Tony's name into a search engine and to my amazement I saw more than a dozen sites devoted to my late brother. One thing led to another and I found myself subscribed to one of these sites. After a few weeks, I introduced myself to the site provider as Tony's brother. Following that, he persuaded me to write a biography so that Tony's life and death could be published not only for members of his website but for others as well.

So, in the year 2000, with the help of Daphne and Dominic Gonzalvez, I did write and post a short biography of Tony on the internet.[1]

The response to this biography has been phenomenal. I have re-

---

[1] Bill deMello: http://users.tpg.com.au/adsligol/tony/tony1.html.

ceived and continue to receive mail from people of all religions, from agnostics as well as atheists from all over the world. They thank me for the biography, tell me how Tony changed their lives and ask for more information about this remarkable man. Until now, however, I had been preoccupied, getting on with my life and thinking that besides what I had written in the short biography there was not much more to tell.

Then early in 2010, one of my correspondents wrote and told me that she lived in the same city as I and that she was in the process of making a short documentary on Tony's life. Would I be prepared to meet her and be interviewed for her project? I did meet this young woman and was struck by the sheer happiness she exuded. When I commented on this to her, she said, "This happened after I discovered your brother's *Awareness* Conference. After I listened to him, my life has changed."

I told her that some years before, when I myself was going through a particularly difficult period in my life I had read and devoured that book several times and it had only left me more confused. She said, "Bill, by all means read Tony's books, but 'listen' to the recordings as well; it makes a world of difference."

You know, ever since that last meeting with Tony, I could never summon up the courage to listen to his voice recordings. The very thought of "watching" any of his video productions sent shivers down my spine. As I said, correspondence in response to the short biography clearly indicated that Tony's works were inspiring and changing many people's lives for the better. I have not received a single negative message over all these years. And yet, here was I, with a treasure in my possession and I had chosen to bury it rather than benefit from it. No wonder therefore that while the lives of so many people had been changed and enhanced by him, mine had remained sluggish—as it had been for years!

A few months after meeting this young woman, two audio cassettes privy to very few of Tony's inner circle of friends came into my possession. Until they were presented to me by my sister Grace (who had copies) I had no idea they even existed. I had once discussed with her the possibility of my writing another—extended—biography of Tony and now she thought the tapes might be useful for my research. What a pleasant surprise I got when I listened to them.

One is a set of meditations very similar to his *Awareness* Conference, probably recorded by a participant in Lonavala. The other is a tape recording of the Mass he celebrated on his fiftieth birthday. In this cassette, I hear Tony getting very emotional, surrounded by his closest friends, showering him with love and kindness. I was so very touched when I listened to that tape. It revealed so many of his inner thoughts of which I was totally unaware. I transcribe part of this tape here:

> I am talking aloud and singing a lot but I'm finding it very hard not to cry. (*Here he pauses for forty-five seconds, obviously fighting his desire to cry, then continues.*) It began this morning when I went to the dining room and saw how beautifully you had arranged everything and how much trouble you had taken. Then, when you began to sing "Happy Birthday," again I had to make an effort not to cry. I was about to cry and I controlled myself—against everything I teach you in Sadhana about control. Because when I was looking at you I was also thinking of so many people who would be thinking of me today, praying for me and loving me. I had thought: what would I say during the Mass? I thought I would prepare a nice sermon, but then, there was nothing to say. I am so moved and I am so grateful to God, to all of you. I felt like a spoiled child of God. God who gave me so many blessings, so many gifts, so many graces, so much happiness, so much love, so many insights, I could hardly believe it. It was too much to take in, so undeserved, so totally undeserved; I suppose that is what grace is.
>
> Then, when you were lighting those flames, those five flames, I was thinking: each of those flames represents one decade of my life. The first when I was aged 1 to 10, 10 to 20, then 20 to 30,

30 to 40, and 40 to 50, and all these scenes kept flashing through my mind. How different I am today, how different I was during those periods; something like an intensive journal in a short time—how much I have changed, how much I have grown.

The other day, I told you about that letter I received, written ten years ago and looking at that letter asking myself, "Is that really me?" So different but all through, always sheltered by God, protected and loved by him. And guided by him and then I thought: The two greatest things that God gave me, by far the greatest gift, the most precious of all has been the grace to *create people;* to look at them and get insights into them and help them and love them and see them come alive and see them become free and see them grow. No human being can ask for a greater grace than this. There is nothing I can conceive of as greater than this; and all along I would not look at it too clearly. Yes it's there, it's alright, let it be. But during these past few days, I have been reflecting on this and thinking: what greater gift could God give to a human being than that he would use him to bring life and power and freedom and grace into the lives of others? So, the greatest of all possible gifts has been given to me. God gave it to me so lavishly, so freely, so undeservedly. So naturally, I am so grateful to him for that.

Then, the second greatest gift is that I have been surrounded by love, such beautiful love, so undemanding, so unconditional, so loyal, always there; a love which has created me, which has changed me, which has made a prince out of me; a love which is symbolized by all of you present here this morning. What more can a man ask for? God's grace coming to him in love, God himself coming in that love, because God is love; so there it is. What more can a man desire?

After listening to these two recordings, I summoned up the courage to not only *listen* to the *Awareness* Conference but also to unearth a couple of his videos and *watch* my brother in action, delighting and enlightening his enraptured audience. I started listening attentively to Tony delivering his *Awareness* Conference. His voice, at times soothing, at times loud, at times laughing boisterously and delivering his message about waking up to myself; and suddenly the penny dropped!

In that *Awareness* Conference, Tony says, "When the Sage points to the moon, all the idiot sees is the finger." Prior to "listening" to him, I was the idiot. I was in such a hurry to read the book and "get on with it," that I had totally missed the point. Not everyone is sensitive enough to extract wisdom from only reading a spiritual book. Now that I have my brother's voice to guide me, I can go back to his books and better understand the message from which many thousands have benefited.

I then started writing to some of my correspondents and telling them that I could feel a change coming into my life as well and that I was beginning to now realize what they meant when they had written and told me, "Your brother changed my life." Many of them suggested that I extend the first biography and convert it into a detailed chronological book about Tony's life and to share with the world how he had *created* people and changed their lives.

So I did decide to write this extended biography, to share whatever information I could garner from my own memory and from that of others who knew Tony and who personally interacted with him. When I conveyed my decision to some of Tony's friends and to some of my correspondents, one correspondent who knew Tony well replied:

Bill, so wonderful to hear you are writing an extended biography. What always amazed me about Tony was that he was so human. That such an ordinary humble man could be so brilliant and have such insight into human nature and such a deep understanding of spirituality in the midst of all his humanity was what made him so very lovable to so many. Please hasten to write that biography; we need to know the truth.

In the pages to follow, you will indeed have the truth and an accurate account of my brother's life.

When I began writing this book I did not imagine, in my wildest dreams, the things I would discover about my own brother. After he joined the Jesuits we rarely had the chance to meet and discuss things at any great length. In the course of writing this book, however, a vast array of people have come forward willingly and shared their innermost thoughts and the experiences they had had with Tony. It is through them that I have re-discovered a brother who left home when I was so young, one I had thought I had lost forever on that fateful night in 1987.

This book is a tribute, not only from me but from many others, to a brother whom I love and admire and finally came to understand, thanks to so many who found his message of peace, happiness, love, and freedom and shared it with me. I want to share their experiences and my new found discovery so that many more people can attain freedom and happiness.

PROLOGUE

UNTIL RECENTLY, EVERY TIME I revised this chapter, it would bring back painful memories of the last meeting I had with my brother. I had been listening to Tony's *Awareness* Conference again and again on the DVD player in my car. With all the distractions, I somehow missed things to which I should have been paying attention. So one day, I went for a long walk by the sea, very near where I live. It was very early in the morning and there were hardly any people around. I sat down on a deserted bench, inserted the earphones of my MP3 player, and started really "listening" to him. I could vaguely hear the waves crashing on the shore and the occasional screech of a seagull or two in the background. But otherwise it was peaceful and I was able to focus on what I was listening to. I suddenly realized that there was a clear message for me there. Tony was telling me not to cling to past memories; to cherish them as much as I wish but a time must come when I should begin living in the present.

I made a discovery that day. I now understand what Tony means when he says, "If you love me will you not let me be free? Will you not let me go?"

I have received correspondence from some of Tony's closest friends who have shared their feelings—and, in some cases, letters— which Tony wrote to them. One such letter is of particular interest because it was written and posted from New York on the day before he died, to a close friend, a religious Sister who received the letter only after she had heard of his death. It gave me so much joy to read what this Sister sent me:

Dear Bill,

I am happy to share my memories of your brother with you. Before I proceed, I would like to tell you that on the day before he died in New York, he wrote me a very touching letter. Part of that letter was about you and I transcribe his words here for you. He wrote, "I am eagerly awaiting Bill's arrival. Some business to attend to and then I want to spend as much time as possible in his company, talking and joking and laughing and relishing some of the old memories." He was eagerly looking forward to this meeting with you. I wonder whether he had the slightest knowledge that this would be the last time both of you would meet here on earth?

Tony and I did meet the night before he died but the laughter was limited for reasons that you shall see later. I guess, with the limited time available, we talked about things as best we could. We did laugh a bit but there were no jokes and during my visit it soon became apparent that Tony was in no mood to listen to or share any. Time flew by fast and before I knew it I had parted company with Tony on that night, May 31, 1987, never to see him alive again. I did not have the slightest inkling that he would suddenly pass away. Years would go by before I could come to terms with reality and accept that he had indeed been called up so early. I remember another meeting I had had with Tony, fifteen months prior to this. Unlike our last coincidental meeting, the earlier one was planned.

I had met Tony in early 1986 under rather sad circumstances. Dad had passed away in January that year and I was required to go to Mumbai to personally sign certain documents relating to his estate. Tony was expecting me for a day visit at St. Stanislaus Villa, Lonavala. We sat outside on ancient deck chairs, within the grounds of the old dilapidated holiday-home, which the Jesuits occasionally used. It was then still serving as the base of Tony's famed Sadhana Courses, awaiting the construction of a building better suited to the needs of Sadhana.

Lonavala is a pretty hill-station nestled in the hills of the Western Ghats—a two-and-a-half-hour train journey from Mumbai. Once in Lonavala, you leave the hustle and bustle and chaos of the city and enter into tranquil serenity. There are beautiful tall trees full of birds everywhere. The Villa is within walking distance of Lonavala train station.

In this peaceful setting Tony and I settled down and reminisced about Daddy. Tony told me how, a few months before Dad died, it had become necessary to accommodate him in a residence for aged persons because he was becoming very difficult to care for in his own home. Tony had experienced firsthand Dad's nonchalant attitude to walking on the road instead of on the sidewalk and realized that he needed constant care. So Tony spoke to the nuns who ran Nirmala Home for the Aged in Nashik about 160 kilometers northeast of Mumbai and they arranged to accommodate Dad there.

At first Dad was quite apprehensive about the arrangement but he soon settled in nicely when he realized he was surrounded by several other aged persons in similar situations. All the nuns at the Home knew and loved Tony and cared for Dad as if he were their own father; in fact they all called him "Daddy" just like we all did. Dad told someone (who later told me) that he was being treated like royalty and that he was very happy there. But of course he would have been treated like royalty by the nuns. The way they regarded Tony, Dad would have been treated like God the Father! Sadly, he did not enjoy this care for long. A few days after he entered the home, he passed away peacefully. One nun in particular, who was a very close friend of Tony's, was with Dad when he died and it was comforting to know that he died among his adopted family.

Tony and I continued talking, pausing occasionally to listen to the call of a bulbul[1] or some other bird and at regular intervals the sound of a rooster from a neighboring village. It is one of those nostalgic sounds I carry with me to this day. After lunch, Tony and I continued to talk, after which we walked along a beaten path in the woods, to the beautiful lake he so loved. I recall it was the month of April. The monsoon rains had not yet arrived and the lake was not as full as it would be a few months after the monsoons. The sun was setting on the horizon casting a shimmering glitter on the surface of the lake and I took some pictures of this beautiful, natural tapestry. When I turned back to look at Tony, I noticed he was gazing serenely into the distance as if in a trance. For a while we were both silent and at peace, absorbing as much of this natural wonder before the sun would finally set behind the hills in the distance. With dusk fast approaching and croaking frogs signalling nightfall, we made our way back to the Villa.

As we walked back I told Tony about my progress at work and described the changes we were planning to our new home. I encouraged him to visit us again and assured him that when he did, he would not recognize the old place he had been to earlier. I shared with him a particular problem I was facing with one of my sons because I seemed to be clueless as to how to deal with him at the time. He was going through a phase of rebelliousness so common to youth; and I was going through the consequent helpless phase that all fathers go through in times like that.

Poor Tony must have had a thousand things on his mind. Nonetheless, he listened patiently and said with much tenderness, "Bill, don't worry about him, he will be fine; he is a good boy and he will eventually sort things out on his own. Don't press him too hard. Support and encourage him, now that he is still young and vulnerable." I held my tongue but that answer did not satisfy me because I wanted him to give me an immediate solution on how to deal with the problem. It never struck me then that Tony

---

[1] An Indian songbird.

had refrained from reminding me about an incident that had occurred many years earlier—an encounter involving Tony, my own
parents, and me. I was the rebel then. All these years later, I can
see what he meant and he was right. My son did settle down and
has a family now and probably a couple of his own "rebels" to
contend with.

Tony then told me about his work and that he was now giving
his *Awareness* Conferences not only to clergy but also to lay people.
Tony was scheduled to give another conference in the USA a few
months after our meeting. At that point in time, I had no idea what
his work involved except that he was a very well-known Jesuit and
that when he visited us in Australia he had conducted retreats there
for the Jesuit community. Other than that, I did not know what
the content of the retreats or his programs were. Tony and I made
a detour to visit the site of the new building which was due to be
completed very soon and he asked me whether it would be possible
to visit again toward the end of the following year with my family.
He assured me that apart from offering us better, more spacious living quarters, he would also be able to give us much more time as he
would be taking a break during the Christmas holidays and would
be unhindered by any work commitments.

The prospect of being with a Tony with lots of time to spend
with my family was too good to resist. I told him that as soon as I
returned to Australia I would make my plans for a visit.

On this occasion, I was visiting on my own and I was particularly
disappointed to see that the day had flown by without either of us
realizing it. Tony and I had thoroughly enjoyed the day, as he would
say, "in present moment freshness," and before I knew it, the time
had come for us to part company.

We decided to walk to the train station, so that we could continue
to share each other's company. It was, as usual, sad to say goodbye
to my brother whom I hardly saw often enough but this time there
was hope of yet another meeting in December 1987 and it held the
promise of being an enjoyable, memorable one too. Little did I know

that I would be meeting Tony sooner than I had anticipated and that it would be our last meeting.

Early in 1987, I received a letter from Tony to say that he would be in New York to give another of his conferences in the month of June. In March 1987, my employer in Australia advised me that they wanted me to attend a conference in the USA. Imagine my delight, then, to discover that my commitments in the United States would most likely be scheduled for late May that year—in New York!

It was impossible to contact Tony in Lonavala by telephone and since I had to plan my trip in order to be in New York at more or less the same time as Tony, I called Fr. Frank Stroud SJ in New York who was responsible for organizing Tony's Conference. Frank told me that Tony's arrival was confirmed for late night of May 30, and that he would have a very busy schedule thereafter. Nevertheless, he assured me Tony was not due to start his conference before June 2, and that left enough time for a meeting. Frank assured me he would facilitate this meeting and that I was to call him after my arrival in New York. I could scarcely contain my excitement. Since Tony left to join the Jesuits in 1947 our meetings had been brief and rare. Any additional occasion to meet Tony, however briefly, was a great source of pleasure and excitement for me and that excerpt from the letter I have quoted above confirms that Tony shared similar sentiments about me.

I arrived a week ahead of Tony and made contact with Frank who invited me to dinner. I had to postpone my initial intended meeting with Frank by a couple of days because of a very painful gastric ailment I had had, probably owing to dodgy airline food. Colleagues at work suggested a good dose of Pepto-Bismol which relieved the problem a day or so later.

I had met Frank before, on one of my trips to India when he was doing a "Maxi-Sadhana" with Tony in Lonavala. I remembered him as a genial, friendly, outgoing man, pleasant to talk to and I noticed he had not changed. Over dinner the conversation naturally veered to Tony and Frank delighted in telling me that this time the deMello *Awareness* Conference would not be restricted to a single venue with a capacity of two or three hundred people; instead, this conference was to be broadcast via satellite to over six hundred universities throughout the United States, reaching thousands of people!

He was upbeat and excited. So was I, not so much because of the conference but because I was going to meet Tony in a couple of days. Frank expressed some concern for Tony's wellbeing at having to give such a taxing conference immediately after his long journey from Mumbai. But he assured me that Tony was in good shape, having had a complete check-up by an eminent physician earlier that year. Frank told me that this physician was none other than ex-President Jimmy Carter's cardiologist. Frank personally knew this cardiologist and he told me Tony came out of that check-up with a clean bill of health; he would be ready for action.

I would have liked to have been with Frank to greet Tony on his arrival, but transport from Manhattan to JFK airport and back would have been a problem. So Frank suggested I call Fordham University late afternoon on the day of Tony's arrival. He assumed that Tony would be jet lagged and that he would almost surely need to catch up on his sleep. Frank told me he himself would only be back at Fordham very late on that night. He quipped that in this case, I could have Tony all to myself for the entire evening.

On the morning of May 31, I attended work as usual and kept watching the minutes tick away on a clock which seemed to move at snail's pace. By 3:00 in the afternoon I could contain myself no longer and decided to take a chance and call Fordham to see if Tony was ready to see me. When he answered the phone he said, "Bill, where have you been? I have been waiting all day for your call." I told him about Frank's instructions and we both laughed, agreeing that Frank was playing the protective mother hen. I then told Tony that if he was refreshed enough I would come over straightaway and he said, of course, he could hardly wait.

It was already past 5:00 in the evening when I arrived at Fordham. Tony and I spent a few minutes talking and exchanging information about common acquaintances after which Tony suggested we dine in the cafeteria. It was a bit early in the evening for dinner but Tony was concerned about the cafeteria staff having to work later than their normal shift. That was typical of Tony—always concerned about others and never wanting to inconvenience anyone.

I noticed Tony did not eat much but I never thought of asking him why. He appeared in good spirits and during dinner we kept conversing. After we had finished our meal, he suggested we retire to a room within the building so that the staff could clear up and go home. We went to a room and began talking about a number of things. He asked me about my plans for the forthcoming visit to Lonavala later that year and I assured him that I had followed up on my commitment to him and that our tickets were reserved, needing confirmation of plans. We then continued talking about *his* plans and he told me that this conference was the biggest he had ever undertaken and that he intended to start giving bigger conferences upon his return to India. He planned on including lay people in the conferences, just as he was doing in the United States.

During the course of our conversation, Tony started burping and complained of severe pains in his stomach. Of course, I immediately put it down to dodgy airline food! What else could it have been? I asked him if they had any Pepto-Bismol on the premises. He said he would go and check, left me for what seemed like only a few minutes, and returned to say they did not have what I had recommended. However, someone or other had given him an Alka-Seltzer and he was feeling a bit better.

I had my doubts about that and expressed them, telling him this could only cause more gas in his system and make him feel worse. I offered to go downtown and find a drugstore and get him a bottle of Pepto-Bismol to which he agreed. I remember thinking on my way out of the University campus that Tony's condition must be really bad because, under normal circumstances, I had never known Tony to complain. He was generally loath to put anyone through any trouble on his behalf.

It took me over half an hour to get back from the drugstore. I found Tony sitting exactly where I had left him. I instructed him to take a dose of the liquid immediately and thereafter follow the instructions. I assured him it had done me much good and that I was sure he too would get relief almost immediately. It surprised me to see how readily Tony obeyed my instructions—big brother taking instructions from his kid brother! He must have been suffering a great deal of pain and prepared to try anything to ease his discomfort. We talked some more. I was expecting to spend at least another hour or so with him; but he said he was now indeed feeling a bit tired and thought it best if he retired. So together we walked to the exit, gave each other a huge hug, and he said, "Bill, I'm sorry I was not in the best of moods today; but we are going to meet again in December and will have plenty of time to talk. I am so looking forward to meeting Rose and the boys again too."

I reassured him that it was alright. Having suffered the same ailment as he, a few days earlier, I knew what he was going through. Reminding him to take another dose of the "miracle potion" I bade him goodbye and made my way out of the campus, back to my hotel in Manhattan. I was so sure he would be fine by morning.

On the morning of June 1, I was in the office of one of my colleagues when his phone rang.[2] He fielded the call and told me it was for me. I answered the phone and heard, "Bill, this is Frank Stroud." My first words to him were, "Hey, Frank, how's Tony feeling this morning?" I really expected him to say, "Thanks to you, Bill, he is feeling much better. That Pepto-Bismol really did the trick." Instead he said, "Bill, I have some bad news."

OK, my next thought was, "Oh God, it was worse than I thought and Tony has probably been hospitalised."

I waited for Frank to speak and he said, "Bill, Tony is dead! I went to wake him this morning and found him motionless on the floor of his room, curled up in a fetal position." He then broke

---

[2] Tony died in the US on June 1. Time-wise, India is ahead of the USA. In India his death day is regarded as June 2.

down and sobbed. My reaction to this news was utter disbelief. I remember a chill running through my entire body. Then another thought, probably quite silly in retrospect, flashed through my mind. I asked Frank if this was some kind of joke he was playing on me. He then collected himself and said, "No Bill, I am not joking; it's true and I am devastated. Be brave, we will take care of everything. His body has been moved to the hospital morgue and I will inform you about funeral arrangements sometime today. Oh, by the way, Sergeant So-and-So [I do not recall the name] from the Bronx Police Department may want to interview you and ask you a few questions, seeing as how you were probably the last person to see Tony alive."

I realized what a state of shock I must have been in when my colleague came up to me, placed a hand on my shoulder, and took the phone from me. Frank had by then already hung up. My colleague asked me what the news was about. After recovering my composure I told him my brother had died during the night. It was no secret at the office that Bill deMello was meeting his brother from India the previous evening. I had told everyone who was prepared to listen what a great coincidence it was that we brothers were meeting. They had all been delighted for me and some of them had even heard about Tony and his Conferences. One in particular offered to bring me an article from a newspaper which discussed the Conference. Unfortunately, I never did see that article.

What happened next is still a blur. I remember being woken up the next morning by the hotel phone. It was Frank, asking if we could meet that evening for dinner and discuss funeral arrangements. I had the entire day to myself and I dreaded it. In order to while the time away, I went for a long, meandering walk around Central Park which was not far from my hotel. Occasionally I sat on a bench and pondered on the events of the last twenty-four hours, thinking over and over again that this had to be some kind of joke, that it simply wasn't true. Sadly it was and whereas only a few hours earlier, I was so elated, I now felt completely desolate. I felt utterly alone and more than anything I wanted to get back home to my wife and sons, to share my grief with them, to feel their comforting arms around me, telling me all would be well.

I kept my dinner appointment with Frank and he discussed the state of affairs telling me that no one from the police department wanted to talk to me after all. He did not specify why and I did not think of asking him the reason for this. I was still in a state of shock and I did not feel like discussing anything related to Tony's sudden death with anyone. I think I was in a state of denial then and the idea of his death had not fully sunk in.

Frank told me he wanted Tony buried at Fordham since he considered Tony would feel it was his home away from home. I was in no emotional condition to discuss Tony's funeral arrangements and did not want to be involved in any decision-making. Besides, when Tony left home, aged sixteen, to go to the Jesuits, they became his "primary family" and I would have considered it normal for the Jesuits to take things in hand.

Tony himself was like the Master in one of his books who claimed that it made no sense at all to define oneself as Indian, Chinese, Hindu, Christian, or Muslim, for these are mere labels. If you had asked him his identity he might well have replied like that Master, "Nothing."[3]

Something that demonstrates this point is an incident that Tony himself mentioned to me. This occurred in the early 1980s, when he was making frequent trips to the USA, conducting conferences in that country. Being an Indian citizen involved getting a visa for the USA for every trip and he was sometimes making more than one trip per year. With his busy schedule, Tony found it increasingly time consuming to present himself in person each time at the US Consulate in Mumbai.

It is at this point that Frank Stroud achieved something that demonstrated the reach of his tremendous influence. He suggested

---

[3] *One-Minute Nonsense,* p. 109.

that Tony apply for a "green" (Permanent Resident) card. For some Indians, a green card is the equivalent of the Holy Grail. Tony in his usual nonchalant manner told Frank to go ahead and obtain the card. He was thinking only of the convenience of having one. But Frank went one step further. When Tony next arrived in the States, he received a call from the US Citizenship and Immigration Services (USCIS) requesting his presence in so-and-so city to attend his citizenship ceremony!

Frank had actually wangled American *citizenship* for Tony! Needless to say Tony politely declined. This was not because he had anything against America. He just did not want the "additional attachment" that is associated with being a citizen of X or Y country. In his Awareness tapes he declares, "Boundaries and countries were drawn up by stupid, avaricious politicians. I salute the human race not national flags." I often think he and John Lennon would have had a lot in common, when I hear the latter's "Imagine." He was simply saying that he did not need any labels. He was "Indian" only by accident of birth; his label was "nothing." To Tony, it would not have mattered where his mortal remains were laid to rest.

Eventually, the Provincial of Bombay (now called Mumbai) Province at that time, Fr. Lisbert D'Souza SJ, and the Provincial of New York mutually agreed that his body be sent home for burial in his own home town.

Frank told me that since Tony was to be buried in India, he had organized a memorial service in the Chapel of Fordham University and I refused to attend if Tony's body was to be on display. I just could not bear the thought of seeing his dead body after seeing him and hugging him when he was alive just a few hours earlier. He assured me that this would not be the case and that I had no need to fear anything. Accordingly, the next morning, I made my way to the Chapel at the appointed time. So many thoughts and emotions were coursing through me when I entered the Chapel. Thoughts of anger . . . Why did he die like that without telling me? Feelings of utter grief . . . I will never see him again. Of guilt . . . I should have known better and alerted someone to get a doctor. Mostly feelings of shock, while one thought kept repeating itself again and again in my head: How in God's name could he have died of a heart attack when, just a few months earlier, he was checked out by an eminent US heart specialist?

With all these horrid thoughts engulfing me, imagine my utter shock then, when upon entering the Chapel I walked straight into a coffin with Tony laid out in it, eyes closed as if in a deep sleep. Knees trembling and now fighting to prevent myself from breaking down and shaming myself by crying, I made my way to a pew and sat down, with head bowed, struggling to keep my emotions under control. Frank made a small speech and someone made an attempt at what I thought was going to be a eulogy. I did not look up to see who it was, but he started by saying, "Tony never complained. All the years I have known him, he never ever complained." I shall never know what else he wanted to say, because soon after, he broke down sobbing. How true those words were. I remember thinking, if only he *did* complain more often, he might still have been alive. . . .

There was total silence for a few minutes and then I heard one of the most powerful, resounding baritone voices singing "Amazing Grace," one of Tony's favorite hymns. That voice—and *that* hymn in particular—was all I needed to break down and the emotional flood gates opened. I sobbed and sobbed and eventually had to leave the Chapel before the service ended.

Ever since that day, I could not bear to hear this beautiful, meaningful hymn either sung or in instrumental form. It was only a few months before I started writing this book, when I had summoned up the courage to once again listen to Tony's *Awareness* tapes and those intimate audio cassettes, that I was delighted to hear Tony himself singing that very hymn. He was accompanying himself on the guitar he had purchased when he visited Australia in 1981.

Frank generously offered me accommodation and some counselling if I felt the need to avail of this. But I declined his offer. All I could think of then was of leaving the scene of my angst and stress. I could think only of returning to my family in Australia, to seek their comfort and understanding. I wanted to be as far away from the scene of Tony's death as possible. Accordingly, I did not even consider attending his funeral which was held at St. Peter's Church, Bandra on June 13, 1987.

TONY'S TIMELINE

1931, September 4:	Tony is born.
1947, July 1:	Joins the Society. Novitiate at Vinayalaya, Andheri.
1949:	Takes his First vows.
1949-1952:	Juniorate.
1952-1955:	Philosophy at San Cugat, Barcelona
1955-1956:	Regency at St. Mary's High School, Mazagaon.
1956-1958:	Regency—teaching the Juniors English at Vinayala, Andheri.
1958-1961:	Theology at Papal Athenaeum (JDV), residing at De Nobili College, Pune.
1961, March 24:	Is ordained priest.
1961-1962:	Fourth Year Theology at Papal Athenaeum (JDV), residing at De Nobili College, Pune.
1962-1963:	Tertianship at Hazaribagh.
1963-1964:	Completes M.A. Pastoral Counseling at Loyola University, Chicago.
1964–1965:	First Year of Postgraduate Degree in Spiritual Theology, at Pontificia Università Gregoriana, Rome.
1965, February 2:	Makes Final Vows in Rome.

1965–1966:   Apostolate and Marathi Studies at
               Catholic Ashram, Nashik.

1966, April 10:   Superior of Manmad/Shirpur Mission

1967–1968:   In addition, Consultor of the Province
               and District Superior.

1968–1972:   Rector of Vinayalaya.

1972–1979:   Director, Sadhana Institute,
               De Nobili College, Pune.

1979–1987:   Director of Sadhana Institute housed at
               Lonavala.

1987, June 1:   Dies suddenly in New York, USA.

PART I

THE JOURNEY TO SADHANA

CHAPTER ONE

FAMILY BACKGROUND AND THE EARLY YEARS

Who was this man? Where did he come from? What was his
background? How did he turn out to be such an erudite and
influential speaker? Was he always like this? What influenced him?
What moved him? What made him tick? If he was from India how
did he come to have a name that has a decidedly Latin flavor?

THESE ARE THE QUESTIONS I have been asked repeatedly by my
correspondents.

To answer these questions it is necessary for me to delve briefly
into the context and backdrop against which to read this story.

In 1498 Vasco da Gama succeeded where Christopher Co-
lumbus had failed. With the former's discovery of a sea route
to the East came colonization. The Dutch, French, Portuguese,
and British all occupied and colonized various parts of India,
importing their culture and religion with them. The British, who
departed in 1947, were the last but one to leave. The Portuguese
left last—in 1961. Their colony in India comprised Goa, Da-
man, and Diu.

Goa is a tiny state on the west coast of India, some 650 km
south of Mumbai. Since Goa is relevant to my story let me give a
brief history of how the Portuguese came to be in Goa. After Vasco
da Gama first landed at the southern port of Calicut in Kerala, the
initial interest of the Portuguese was trade. They carried silk fab-
rics and porcelain from China. These they traded with the inhabitants of Calicut in return for spices and other condiments. However,

like the other European nations, they soon realized that colonizing was the way to go. Eventually they turned their attention to Goa, realizing the importance of this strategic port. After defeating the ruling Bijapur kings, they colonized the territory in 1510. They continued to rule this important territory for roughly 450 years until 1961.

With the Portuguese came priests. With the priests came conversions to Christianity. This was initially achieved with the assistance of the ruling Portuguese authorities. They enticed local leaders with grants of land (which belonged to the local populace in the first place but was now usurped by the invaders) and positions of authority in the administration. Once the local leaders converted, members of their entire community followed and this resulted in large numbers willingly or unwillingly converting to the Catholic faith. In some areas where bribery failed coercion and brute force were used. Some succumbed to these. Others fled to neighboring states to escape being enslaved to a religion they simply did not want.

Goa is the tiniest state in the Indian Union. Its unique red soil is in striking contrast to its verdant hills. And its sandy beaches and blue sea make it a tourist paradise. Goa was once described as "a pimple on the face of India." That was in a political context, with two countries jockeying for advantage in their claim to possess it. In fact it is more apt to describe Goa as a beauty spot on the face of India. It is in this land that my story has its origin. Somewhere in this scenic land called Goa my ancestors were born.

Over the years, I have often been asked about the origins of my family name and I am quite sure Tony would have faced the same question. When I travelled to Europe in 1968, Europeans were quite intrigued by the fact that I came from India and spoke fluent English and that I had a European name and surname. They wanted to know how this came about and why it was that I did not have an Indian name and surname. It still is confusing to some.

One letter I got from a perplexed correspondent shows his level of intrigue:

> Why is Tony so American fluent in his writing style? Why does your family have English names like Grace, Frank, Tony, Bill? If your parents were Portuguese, why do they look completely Indian?

My ancestors were not Portuguese and they certainly were not Christians. It is not known whether they were Hindu or Muslim or of any other religion. For that matter I do not know whether they embraced their new faith willingly. What is obvious is that somewhere along the line they converted to Catholicism and were baptized.

When my ancestors converted, it was the custom at the time to give all the converts of that particular day a Christian name and surname. All of them would get the same surname. The surname usually came from a powerful Portuguese family. In some cases they were given the surname of the priest who baptized them. There then, is where the surname deMello originated. The day my ancestors converted there must have been a fresh lot of folk answering to the name "deMello" in Salvador do Mundo, my ancestral village in Goa.

Is it typical, I wonder, for a woman to retain details about her family history and pass them on to her children, whereas the man tends to not discuss his family background as much? There is a wealth of knowledge available about my maternal grandparents, passed on by my mother to my sisters and maternal aunts.

Such is not the case with my paternal grandparents. I have asked both my sisters and other surviving members of the deMello clan for information relating to my paternal grandparents. To date I have drawn a blank. I have just a few details. Our paternal grandfather Miguel Antonio do Casuo deMello married Sofia Eulalia Mariauinha da Silva. They had four children, the eldest being our father Francisco Cristino (Frank). Grandpa Miguel was a bailiff of the high court and a land owner. In fact the village of Salvador do Mundo was at one time called "deMellovaddo," vaddo meaning a ward within a village.

Now comes an interesting and important story. There was a man named Caridade Castellino from Goa. Caridade's father lost his first wife and remarried. Both marriages produced a boy and girl each. Caridade's half-brother stayed home to help his father run the family business. Caridade was "offered" to the Jesuits in Goa and began studying to become a priest. In those days in India (and even later, in the time of my parents), it was considered a signal honor if at least one of their children chose to join the priesthood or enter a convent. In fact, some families had more than one child who joined a seminary or a convent. Some families actually coaxed their child to go to the Church.

Providence played a hand in Caridade's life when his half-brother died suddenly. His father was no longer a young man and relied on his surviving son to take over the business from him as well as continue the lineage. Finding himself in this dilemma, Caridade's father approached the Jesuits and requested he be sent home to replace the son they had lost.

Caridade was not yet ordained. Dutiful son that he was, he reluctantly abandoned his vocation and obediently followed his father's instructions and returned home. He would have been considered a very eligible bachelor and, as was customary in those days, his father sought a bride for him. In Caridade's lifetime, arranged marriages were the order of the day—a custom which still prevails in India. The social network consisting of housewives would meet after Sunday Mass and exchange information about eligible bachelors and prospective brides. It was the Facebook of those days—and perhaps a trifle more effective and definitely safer!

Selecting a life partner for their children probably depended on status and wealth as well as caste, education, and especially the future prospects of the male provider. Caridade's father owned a thriving bakery and wine shop which he intended handing over to his son and this would have weighed heavily in his favor with the mothers of prospective brides. Who came forward were the parents of a young woman called Leonildes. They were land owners and clearly saw the potential in this union between their child and Caridade. When told she had been selected to marry the son of a wealthy business owner, Leonildes expressed her reluctance to marry. She was after all only sixteen years old and was not interested in marriage. But her parents convinced her to accept the proposal, with the promise of new clothes and shoes and reminded her of the other weddings she had witnessed where the bride was carried on the shoulders of four men on a beautifully decorated palanquin called a *machila*.

Leonildes' parents were nice enough in convincing her to accept the proposal. There were many reluctant brides literally dragged to the altar whether they agreed to the marriage or not. In those days, once parents agreed to a union between their children, the marriage went ahead. And so it came to pass that Caridade Castellino married that comely young bride called Leonildes Menezes. They had six children. The third of these was my mother Louisa.

I recall Mum telling us about poor grandma Leonildes' wedding day. She had not laid eyes on Caridade until the day of her wedding and being all of sixteen was terrified. When she arrived at the church with her father and walked down the aisle with him, she looked up to see two men at the altar. On the right was a dour-looking, burly individual. On the left was a gentle, kindly-looking man. Of course Leonildes had no idea which of these two was the bridegroom and which the best man. She only remembered trembling as she prayed, "Please God, let it be the man on the left." Her prayers were answered!

When Leonildes married Caridade she was not just leaving her home but also her country because Caridade's family business was in Bellary, right across the breadth of Karnataka at its eastern point, 400 kilometers away from Panjim which was Goa's capital. Grandma Leonildes told of the time she and her husband went to

live in Bellary. When they settled into their home, she started sorting things out. She was quite perplexed and disturbed to discover
a few well-laundered, neatly-pressed cassocks in Caridade's travel
case and asked him whom they belonged to and what they were
doing there.

That's when he told her his story. Having packed in a hurry after
the wedding, he had forgotten to discard the cassocks! Prior to that,
Leonildes had no clue about this and in fact knew very little about
her husband. Caridade had reportedly smiled and said to her, "I may
have been called away from God; but someday, a son or grandson of
mine will become a Jesuit." His prophecy came to pass when Tony
joined the Jesuits. And what a Jesuit he became!

On the other side of the land, in Salvador do Mundo (7 km from
Panjim), Miguel and Sofia deMello's four children were born and
raised in Goa. Frank, our father, had completed his education in Goa
under the Portuguese educational system; but English would have
been encouraged by those great educators, the Jesuits, and Frank
succeeded in obtaining good school grades. He was now ready to
enter the work force to earn his own way.

Since job opportunities were severely limited in Portuguese
Goa, young Goans usually migrated to British Bombay to seek
employment. Frank was no exception. He was a Christian, had
good command of English, and was eager to work hard. He easily found employment in the British Indian Railways as a trainee
clerk. A few years later, he decided it was time to marry and raise
a family.

Once again, the social network went into action and a bride was
soon identified and pointed out to Frank. Louisa's father, Caridade
had died suddenly some years earlier, and she had travelled to Bombay to study for a nurse's certificate. She was considered to be a very
suitable match for Frank and they accordingly met and were later
afforded the privilege of either accepting or rejecting the proposal—
unlike their parents who had had no such choice. They must have
liked each other because they mutually agreed to the union.

Frank and Louisa were married on September 27, 1930. They set up home in a suburb of Bombay called Santa Cruz. Some years later, they moved to Byculla and later returned to live in Santa Cruz Railway Quarters after Frank received a promotion, entitling him to a subsidized bungalow as family quarters.

THE EARLY YEARS

ON SEPTEMBER 4, 1931, Tony was born.

There were no trumpets blaring, no sign from heaven to indicate that someone who was destined to be great had just joined the ranks of India's teeming millions. Tony must have yelled his head off like any other newborn till he was comforted by Mum.

He was baptized on September 20, 1931, at Holy Cross Chapel (which would become Sacred Heart Church later). I thought my parents did me an injustice when they christened me with three names. One would have been sufficient. Tony's baptism certificate has a list of names as long as one's arm. The poor fellow inherited what looks like the names of the entire deMello and Castellino forebears! My parents must have thought they might not have another child and so gave Tony the whole lot. Of his given names, Caridade was Mum's choice, without a doubt!

Mum would give birth to four more children: Grace, followed by Merlyn, who died in infancy, Marina, and last of all me. With her nurse's training, Mum was capable of seeking gainful employment but decided to stay home to run the household and care for the children.

Tony makes a touching remembrance of her in the recording of his fiftieth birthday celebration Mass, with several long emotional breaks in his narration:

When I woke up this morning, I thought of my mother [Mum had passed away in October 1980]. She was always very proud of me and still is I'm sure and from somewhere, some way, she is so happy for the grace to be my mother; to have given birth to me and to be such a powerful influence in my life. She would have been happy to be alive today and I would have been so happy to have her here today on my fiftieth birthday. She's probably happier where she is now.

Indeed, Mum was very proud of Tony and why not? He was not only well-known and highly-regarded by so many people during her life time but also well loved and respected by everyone. Like the rest of the family, she had every reason to be proud of him.

Mum was not without her faults but she influenced, inspired, and was proud of all of us in whatever we did, always encouraging us to try as hard as we could and accept the outcome as our destiny. She was the rock of the family and although a strict disciplinarian, had a heart of pure gold.

On the other hand, Dad was an easy going, soft-spoken, humorous, gentle soul who wouldn't hurt a fly. Where Mum expressed her pride in us verbally, Dad showed it in physical ways, with few words but his expression always displayed his pride in all his children. Mum did not spare the rod. Dad was a different matter. I am told that whenever my older siblings misbehaved and needed to be disciplined, Dad would pretend to find the cane, thus giving the offender plenty of time to get away. I am the only one on whom Dad used the cane. I hasten to add, I deserved every bit of his wrath. Dad also had the beautiful capacity of forgiving and never ever carried a grudge around with him. Whenever it became necessary, Dad sprang into action in defense of his family. But once action had been taken the incident was set aside and Dad moved on.

This mixture of discipline, good humor, and gentleness is where we all got our sense of fairness and acceptance of others, qualities which abounded in Tony.

He inherited Mum's determination and resolution and Dad's gentleness and capacity to readily forgive. So it was at home, when he was growing up, that his training in human relations was nurtured by both our parents.

It was from Mum though, that we all inherited our resilience and determination to see a task through, no matter what the consequences. Tony would have also first made contact with his religious faith through Mum. We children all feel Mum was born way before her time. She thought about religion and God differently from others.

Grace recalls an incident when she told Mum that she would go to church on Sunday and pray for an intention and Mum said, "Why wait till Sunday, why don't you pray to God right now, right here?" Grace asked her, "Is God here now, Mum?" Mum replied, "Yes he is; he is here right now with you and me. There is no need to go to a church or temple to find him. He is everywhere and sees everything." This almost sounds like Tony speaking!

The local parish priest might have considered this mildly blasphemous, given the era in which she lived but it did not deter Mum from speaking her mind. She was religious in her own way. She followed her faith in accordance with Church rules but she was practical about her religious devotion.

Mum got her religious inspiration from her father Caridade. She often recounted her childhood and adolescence to us and one of the things which she often discussed was that her family shared their home with an uncle of her mother who was a diocesan priest. It appears there was constant discussion and argument between this priest and her father. Caridade was an ex-Jesuit who took great pride in the fact that he was a liberal thinker. He was critical of his uncle-in-law for being narrow minded and cloistered in his thinking. He singled out the Church's attitude of currying favor with the rich while ignoring the plight of the poor.

This would explain Mum's advice when Tony expressed the desire to become a priest from an early age. I am told that Mum said, "Tony if you ever become a priest, become a priest for the poor, not a priest of the rich."

I have a letter written by a Spanish Jesuit, a dear friend of Tony's who has now passed on. He is responding to my e-bio of Tony on the net and writes about our family and about Mum in particular:

Dear Bill,

Your narrative gives the reader insight into a Tony who was unknown and therefore offers rich material to the biographer of Tony. It is generous of you to diminish yourself the way you do. It is done very naturally and spontaneously; but obviously you also reflect the stuff of which the deMellos are made. I have personally admired your whole family, you too as a lovable kid but especially your mother Louisa. She stands before me as a very distinguished lady! She chose to be cremated, the first Catholic as far as I know, to do so in Mumbai. I was at the crematorium with Tony (quite a vivid experience). Your mother had style.

Mum often described her father as a kind-hearted, gentle, and considerate soul. But she also spoke of him as a revolutionary, forward thinker, who was not afraid to speak his mind even if it meant getting himself in trouble with Church authorities. Mum, of all her siblings, became such a person herself and passed on her philosophy to all of us. Tony would have been listening and absorbing all she said.

Some of Tony's friends and close associates describe him as a rebel, a revolutionary, saying that he delighted in shocking people. Another close friend has described him as "the good soil" waiting for the seeds. Those seeds were sown at home at a very early age in the company of his parents: seeds of consideration for others, kind-heartedness, and humor as well as that seed of revolution and rebellion against unfairness.

In another chapter of this book, I have transcribed accounts from people who knew Tony well and they testify that he did indeed become a priest of the poor but he was inclusive of everyone and that included all human beings no matter whether they were rich or poor, law abiders or thieves, believers or non-believers. Tony followed Jesus Christ's teachings and lived his life as a true follower of Christ.

With a few exceptions, most people who came into contact with Tony described him as gentle, understanding, and compassionate; a humorous individual with a contagious laugh that filled the room he was in. People have said that they knew Tony was around somewhere when they heard his laughter from way down the hall.

While I will not dispute this, having myself experienced all of the above, his other siblings tell a different story about him when they were growing up. Tony was considered "bossy" and sometimes quite the obstinate individual; but always well-meaning, gentle, and fair-minded. His siblings would find it very hard to win an argument with Tony. He was apparently a very good debater.

Before I was born and when my siblings were still very young, World War II was raging and India, as a British colony, was involved in every aspect of the war. The deMello family, like every other family in India at that time, faced great hardship with restricted electricity, oil shortages, and food rationing. Even though our family was entitled to the famed ration card for commodities such as rice, sugar, flour, and oil, making ends meet would have been tough indeed. Mum, as custodian of the pantry, ensured that the children were always well-fed and clothed.

I was born in July 1944—a month after D-Day in Europe. War continued to rage in the Pacific until atom bombs were dropped on the cities of Hiroshima and Nagasaki and Japan surrendered in August 1945. While restrictions and rationing were still in place, I was too young to remember having experienced any difficulty when growing up. My sister Grace looked after me for most of my childhood since Mum did not keep very good health after I was born. I am reminded to this day by my siblings that I was a mischievous, spoiled brat. I admit this was true. I was the youngest in the family and after the war ended everyone experienced a great burden being lifted from their shoulders. Our parents would have been more relaxed after having raised three children under very difficult circumstances. I was therefore not subjected to the same rigors as my siblings and got away with a lot.

I remember that my early childhood was a very happy one, wandering the neighborhood, climbing trees and doing everything that a naughty boy could dream up. I don't recall having had any negative interactions with Tony except for one occasion. This was to leave me with a lasting remembrance of him as a tyrant. I would recall this before an interlude with him several years later. Overall, he was a studious, pious individual who buried himself in his books and studies and served daily Mass as an altar boy.

Tony went to St. Stanislaus High School in Bandra, two suburbs away from where we lived. He was a brilliant student, an avid reader and was academically inclined from a very early age. He never gave our parents cause for concern. Corporal punishment was the order of the day in schools then. I, for one, never reported it when I came home for fear that I would get a double dose of the same punishment from Mum. Other boys my age would do exactly the same with their parents. In those days, we were conditioned to believe that the punishment fit the crime and we expected to be punished for whatever (so-called) misdemeanors we had committed.

Mum was a strict disciplinarian and trusted the teachers and superiors at school to dish out the punishment, knowing the type of mischievous fellow I was. In Tony's case it was a different story. He was so well-behaved that when he came home with both his palms swollen one day, Mum asked him what had happened. At first he refused to tell her. She persisted and he eventually told her. His teacher had used the cane on his palms because she thought he was responsible for talking in class, thus disrupting the other students' concentration.

Mum immediately went to the school, demanded to see the principal and told him that if her son was not immediately transferred to another class, she was taking him out of the school and enrolling him in another. The principal investigated the incident and found out it was not Tony after all but another boy who had disrupted the class when the teacher's back was turned. Tony had not revealed this to his teacher and had not denied her allegations. He had accepted punishment rather than reveal the identity of the real culprit.

His devotion to studies and reading to expand his knowledge were mistaken for absentmindedness. Mum told us of the time she sent him to buy their daily quota of milk and Dad asked him to buy the daily newspaper as well. On the way home, Tony had the bottle of milk tucked under one of his arms while reading the newspaper. Perhaps he knew he would have to relinquish it to Dad when he got home. Having finished reading the front page, he flipped the page over, completely forgetting that the bottle of milk was still under his arm. He arrived home with the paper and no milk.

I, on the other hand, was an excellent and ready errand boy. But I was also a wayward truant, never interested either in studies or serious school work or, I might add, in religion. I never got down to learning the prayer recitals in Latin necessary in order to be an altar boy in those days. I knew the first few words and mumbled the rest. How I got away with that I will never know. I suspect the priests probably made allowances because I was Tony's brother. Maybe they thought that with a brother like mine, there was still hope for me.

I remember the times when Tony accompanied Mum and me with the rest of the family to church and during the Elevation, when everyone was supposed to bow their heads in reverence, my eyes would be wandering all over the church, observing the latest trends. Then I would sense a pair of eyes boring into the back of my tender head and turning around, I would see Tony glaring at me with a look that would have scared Satan. This was followed by a very painful pinch from Mum just to make sure the stare had had its proper effect!

When Mum was pregnant with me, she and Dad went to see a movie about the exploits of Buffalo Bill Cody, that character from the American Wild West. Mum must have been impressed by the actor because she told Dad that if the baby was a boy, she wanted to call him Bill. I was indeed named Bill (William) and more than lived up to the antics of my namesake. In fact the things I got up to probably made Mum rue the day she decided to name me after that character. I also got away with most of my mischief because, as I said, Mum was not in very good health and could not keep up with me. I often wonder whether I was responsible for the heart condition she developed later on in her life but Grace has assured me she was unwell even before I was born.

Years later, I heard from a very close friend of Tony's that whenever he spoke to him about me he was always full of pride and love for me but he always sounded concerned for my welfare. Poor Tony; the stories he had heard from my concerned parents must have made a big impression on him.

Tony, from what I can remember, besides playing with and reading to me, never interfered with my upbringing except once. I was three and a half years old and, in a few months, Tony was to leave for the Novitiate. I had got into a scuffle with one of my siblings who, being older and bigger, might have roughed me up a bit. Because I could not retaliate physically, I called her a "bloody swine." Tony was within earshot and he called me to him and said, "What did you say? What did you call her?" I innocently repeated what I had said and, much to my shock, he put me over his knee and spanked me and said, "Don't you ever use bad language again with anyone." I was immune to the pain of those slaps, having received quite a few from Mum. What hurt was the humiliation and surprise at his not taking my side in the issue. I mean, up to that moment, he had always taken my side in any skirmishes I had had. So this unusual reaction from him surprised and scared me. I reminded myself to give this tyrant a wide berth in future and to swear only under my breath.

I have heard from Mum, as well as several family members, that ever since he was a young lad, Tony had expressed the desire to become a priest. Grace recalls an incident when she was probably six or seven years old. She and Tony were playing with two of our cousins who were visiting. They were role playing what they wanted to be when they grew up. They all had their own childish ambitions and Tony's was to become a priest.

He encouraged my cousin to make a "confession" to him and solemnly "absolved" her of her sins. Later, she is reported to have cornered Tony behind a shed and when Grace came upon them, she saw that the cousin had a rope around Tony's neck, saying, "If you ever tell my Mum what I told you in confession just now, I'll strangle you." Tony, in all earnestness, replied, "Don't worry, I'll never tell anyone what you told me. Priests are not supposed to tell anyone what they hear in the confessional."

On another occasion, a couple of years later, my parents, along with Dad's brother and his wife wanted to go to a local function where children were not allowed. They decided to leave all the children at our home in the care of Tony, who was the oldest cousin. He was left with instructions to supervise the other children and serve them their dinner and to be gener-ally "in charge" of things. During the course of the evening, a couple of the younger ones started misbehaving and refused to obey Tony. He warned them that if they persisted, he would re-port them to their respective parents. This meant they would receive the expected dose of punishment which generally meant the cane. They settled down after the warning and Tony went about his tasks while the others continued their games. At some point in the evening Tony brought down a jar of chana (roasted chickpeas). To this day it remains a favorite snack in India. In wartime India, even a cheap snack like that would have been budgeted for and children as well as adults treated everything as precious. Tony began peeling the skins off the chana and eating the roasted cores when the two recalcitrants mentioned above approached him for some. He reportedly told them to eat the discarded skins! When they complained he said, "That's what you get for misbehaving." Grace tried to intervene on their behalf and said, "Tony, don't be mean, give them some." To which he replied, "No, let them eat the skins. The skins have all the nourishment these two need to get some sense into their heads." This left the two offenders livid with rage but there was nothing they could do. He already had them over a barrel with his threat to report their misbehavior when the parents returned home.

Later, he relented and gave them a share of the chana; but only after they all agreed to attend his "Mass" and listen to his sermon. Knowing what Tony was like as a young man, before he returned from Spain, I can well imagine what that sermon would have been about. Grace does not recall the exact words but they would have contained words of fire and brimstone, with the threat of eternal damnation if they were not well-behaved.

When, however, the parents returned home later that night and asked Tony if the children were all well-behaved, he did not report any of their misbehavior and said that everything went smoothly and that they were all well-behaved. I guess he must have been quite pleased with himself for handing out his own punishment, in his own way, without having them subjected to the cane.

Talking about fire and brimstone, years after this incident, when I was just about old enough to understand a proper conversation, the cousins were all together at a function. Tony was getting ready to join the Jesuits then and everyone was discussing something or other about the sermon given by the priest on Sunday. I can't remember the sermon myself (I never paid attention to them anyway). It surely must have had something to do with the infallibility of the Pope and one of the younger ones said, "Who is the Pope to tell me what I should do? He is a human being just like me" or words to that effect. At this, Tony rose to his full height—which was considerable even then—and pontificated, "If you talk like that, your ticket to hell is already booked." Whoever it was that made the statement quickly backed down and that was the end of the discussion.

Tony thought long and hard before he decided to join the Jesuits.[1] My parents might have harbored a wish that one of their children would go to the Church. However, as Tony grew older and expressed his wish to become a Jesuit, Mum started having qualms about his choosing the Jesuits specifically.

Everyone had heard of the strict regime Jesuits followed: during the first two years of their training, they were not allowed home at all and contact with their families during this period was limited.

In fact before Vatican II, Jesuits were not allowed to spend time at home at all; that is, they were not to spend the night away from their Jesuit residence. Later, after they had completed their training, they might have been allowed a day visit; but never more than that. Therefore Mum started dropping subtle hints that maybe Tony should reconsider his future career.

Tony, however, was determined to become a priest and Mum then suggested he consider becoming a diocesan priest instead of a Jesuit. Tony is reported to have told her that in that case he would rather not be a priest and would opt for other studies.

Mum then tried another ploy and said she had heard that the Jesuits took the vow of poverty and that everything they earned, they shared within the Jesuit community. They were not allowed to contribute to their family's welfare, unlike the diocesan priests. In this case, she asked him, who would care for her and Dad during their old age? You see, in India even now the daughter of the house goes to live with her in-laws after marriage. The son, when he married, would have his wife staying with him and, accommodation being quite scarce in those days, would have his parents living with him and his family.

I am quite certain that Mum would not have been serious and would have mentioned it tongue-in-cheek. You will read, a bit later, a testimony to this from Tony himself. Moreover, knowing the type of person Mum was, I believe she would have been putting Tony to the test, to see if he was as serious as he said he was about becoming

---

[1] *Ah! These Jesuits! Going My Way,* pp. 64-66.

a Jesuit priest. Neither Mum nor Dad would ever have stood in his way if he seriously wanted to become a Jesuit.

Tony, however, took her comments seriously and said he would pray that God would give her another son and if this were to happen, would she then consent to his joining the Jesuits? Mum was at an age then when she would never have expected to have another child and she readily agreed. A few months later, much to everyone's surprise, not least her own, she did become pregnant. During her pregnancy Tony never once brought up the topic of her promise to him.

The day I was born, Tony was at school and he was unaware that Mum had been taken to the hospital. When he arrived home from school, a neighbor called after him and said, "Tony, your Mum has had the baby and is in Khar hospital. She wanted you to bring her a couple of pillows as soon as you got home."

Tony, as he often said, was not an athlete. But that day he grabbed the pillows and ran all the way to the hospital which was at least a few kilometers away. At the hospital the nurse would not let him in to see Mum. When Mum discovered he was outside, she asked the nurse to let him in and he entered the room, placed the pillows on her bed, and said, "Is the baby a boy or girl?" When Mum told him it was a boy, he must have had the widest grin in the whole of Bombay. "My prayers have been answered," he shouted gleefully. "Now I can go and join the Jesuits."

He was a little over twelve years old then and Mum still thought this was a passing fancy and that maybe he would soon get over it. What she did not realize was that he was very serious about his vocation and determined to become a Jesuit and nothing else. Being a twelve year old when he extracted that promise from Mum, he would have been comforted by the fact that Mum and Dad now had their assurance of being looked after in their golden years by a sturdy responsible successor to him. Mum was not quite convinced that Tony knew for sure that he had a vocation. She was adamant in her belief that he was not only too young but also too inexperienced in the ways of the world before going and locking himself away.

A few months before he left she gave it one last try. She and Dad took him to the New Year's Eve dance, hoping he would have a great time dancing and interacting with young girls. Instead, Tony stayed out at the gate with an uncle, selling raffle tickets. The next morning when Mum asked him whether he had enjoyed himself and had he met any interesting young girls, Tony replied that he was not interested in dancing or girls. I firmly believe that for all Mum's objections to Tony's joining the Jesuits, she secretly harboured a wish that he would indeed join them. All the objections she put were actually her way of testing him to see if he really meant what he said and whether he really had a vocation.

She would have told him the same story she told all of us, about her father who almost became a Jesuit priest himself were it not for fate playing a hand in his having to leave before he was ordained. Mum would have been thrilled that in the end, it was Tony, her son, who fulfilled her father's prediction that one of his sons or grandsons would become a Jesuit. What is more, it was Tony himself who made the decision to join, without being coerced or persuaded to do so by anyone else.

Three and a half years after I was born, Tony left home to join the Jesuits. Ironically, there was another twist in the tale. Events that ensued some years later did not quite fall into place as anticipated. I, the son who was supposed to care for my parents in their twilight years, left home for France in 1968. There I lived with my wife and young son till 1974 when we migrated to Australia. Mum and Dad were quite independent and really did not need a benefactor in the form of a redeeming son. They managed quite well on their own, with the help of Grace. And it was Tony who was always close at hand in India and frequently visited them whenever he was in town.

On July 1, 1947, Tony entered the Jesuit Novitiate where he was to start a remarkable journey. It would be a journey into the priesthood and also an exploration of his "Easternness." It would be a journey that would end in an extraordinary blend of the spirituality of East and West; a journey that would produce an unusual mystic.

Chapter Two

THE NOVITIATE

As Jesus walked by the Sea of Galilee, he saw two brothers, Simon, who is called Peter, and Andrew his brother, casting a net into the lake—for they were fishermen. And he said to them, "Follow me, and I will make you fish for people." Immediately they left their nets and followed him.—Matthew 4:18-20

As the day approached for Tony to leave home, the mood in the family turned from somber to gloomy to depressing. Everyone, including Tony, looked serious and preoccupied. If Mum, Dad, and my sisters looked sad, so did Tony. I was too young to understand much at that time. I was mostly given this information later on. But I have flashes of memory here and there. I remember that no one had told me that Tony was leaving home permanently. I was perplexed, to say the least. I was always being left out of the loop.

Dad had ordered a Victoria for the journey to Andheri. A Victoria was a horse-drawn carriage similar to a phaeton which served as taxicabs in those days. In Bombay the Victorias were open but had an accordioned canopy in case it rained. They were the first convertibles! There were four passenger seats, two facing forward and two back. There was also a seat next to the driver if one wanted to climb up there and I was always an eager volunteer.

The time finally arrived for Tony to leave. Did I imagine that Tony's eyes were moist when he picked me up, gave me a hug, and kissed me on the forehead, without saying a word? I vaguely remember the next part but have heard about it enough of times. Tony then picked his case up and descended the stairs to the waiting carriage. We children stood on the veranda looking over the railing and waving. Mum was crying and Dad had a stony look on his face as they got into the carriage with Tony. The driver cracked his whip and the horse took off—slowly at first, then broke into a canter. My sisters were crying and, because I could "feel" the sadness of the moment, I too began sobbing. I do not remember much of this scene. But I do remember that on every other occasion that Dad had ordered a Victoria, prior to our departure, I was allowed to pat the horse and climb up next to the driver. This time no such antics were permitted. My sisters ensured that I stayed alongside them on the veranda. They were surely following instructions from Mum and Dad as requested by Tony.

What I do remember as clearly as if it happened yesterday is that Tony waved to us just once and then sat facing forward. And he did not look back!

That, for me, is the most symbolic thing about Tony. Looking forward was the only option he considered.

For months after he left, there was a void in the house. Everyone looked colorless and dejected. Mum in particular seemed the most affected. It took many months for everyone to come to terms with the fact that a son and brother had left home.

We were all distraught. What about Tony? What were his feelings and thoughts on leaving home?

In 1959, a series of promotional booklets published by the Jesuit Vocational Bureau appeared in Catholic book stores and school libraries. It was generally rumored that Tony was the author of this series. After his death, this series was revised and brought out under a new title.[1] In the Introduction it is candidly revealed that "the Bombay Jesuits commissioned a group, led by the late Fr. Tony deMello, to bring out some booklets which would give some idea of how a vocation to the Society of Jesus develops."[2] Since these book-

---

[1] *Ah! These Jesuits!*
[2] *Ah! These Jesuits! Going My Way,* p. ii.

lets were written anonymously at the time they were first published, the authors could have been describing their own situations. Now that it is revealed that Tony was the main author one can presume that many of the sections are autobiographical.

In the promotional booklets Tony describes the feelings of "Bertie" at having to leave home and the upheaval it caused in his life. Bertie's situation would have not been far different from Tony's. He speaks of being sad at having to leave home, his "parents, two sisters and little brother." After reading those booklets, I understood the stress Tony would have been undergoing and that was probably why he had reacted the way he had and spanked me; the sadness and stress must have gotten to him. I have spoken to close associates of Tony who expressed shock when I told them about the spanking. All of them were unanimous in declaring that Tony did not have a violent bone in his body, that they had never known him to raise his hand in anger. So he would have been under enormous strain to have lost his temper with me—for something which I considered rather petty. In those days "bloody swine" was not an acceptable term, but it was hardly "foul language!" He was, after all, human, like all of us.

It would also have been a tremendous sacrifice to leave his friends—especially one in particular. I cannot remember him too well but I have heard countless stories about him from Grace. Tony and he used to get up to a lot of mischief and they were inseparable. In particular, they delighted in antagonizing an elderly gentleman who lived in their building complex.

Tony was also disappointed at having to leave behind a girlfriend. Oh yes, that big brother of mine was quite a romantic! Mum told me of the time when they were together at a family gathering and Tony, who was probably very young at the time, had said to his cousin, "When we grow up, I am going to marry you and make you a wedding dress with every star in the sky." Later, he must have realized that marrying his first cousin would not be permitted and so he turned his attention to "Elsie," mentioned in one of the booklets. He deliberated for hours on how best to tell her he was leaving her to join the Jesuits. He eventually wrote her a goodbye letter which he never posted.[3]

Tony would write home once a month. All his letters were addressed to Mum and Dad, who took turns at reading them to us. I used to listen attentively to these letters but much of the content made no sense to me. He took the rules seriously and I understand that were it not for his Novice Master Fr. Nubiola's insisting he write home at least once a month, Tony would have refrained from doing so altogether.

When Tony left for the Novitiate, it made no sense to me that my older brother had to leave home just so that he could become a priest. I missed him a lot even though, before he left home to join the Jesuits, I spent most of my days wandering the neighborhood and getting up to mischief and did not see him during the day at all since he was at school himself. It was another matter when he was at home on the weekends and he used to spend a lot of time with me, playing with me and patiently reading to me. Of course, I don't remember a word of what he read since my mind was always wandering to the next bit of mischief I could get up to. In time, I got over his departure and got on with what I was best at— mischief—at times terrifying Mum with my antics. Like the time when I was about five years old and tried to ride my brand new tricycle down a flight of stairs. Somehow, I managed to cling on to the bannister and save myself. I'm afraid the tricycle did not fare quite as well.

The Jesuits are one of the few Orders that have a two-year Novitiate instead of the regulation one year. (They face a good deal of ribbing from members of other Orders who insist this extra year is because Jesuits are "slow"!) In the Novitiate, Jesuits go through a training period and are not, under normal circumstances, allowed frequent personal contact with the outside world. Things have

---

[3] *Ah! These Jesuits! Going My Way*, pp. 91–92.

changed with the times; but in Tony's day as a novice, the rules were strict and were rarely bent.

The promotional booklets are well written, amusing and informative. The second one describes life in the Novitiate but it does not tell the true "inside story." These are promotional books, obviously published to attract men to join the Society. The booklets are accurate in that they give the daily routine and training structure of the young novices. But the finer points have been painted over to make life in the Novitiate sound easy and happy, making those novices the envy of every young man.

I have spoken to several Jesuits over the years who have described what life really was like in the Novitiate. Some of the rules and regulations were stringent to the extreme. To endure and obey these rules, a young man would indeed need a very strong vocation. I cannot, however, recall Tony ever speaking of his life in the Novitiate as being hard. In fact he covered up most of the hardship and never complained about a thing. These must have been extremely determined men, intent on following their calling to serve Jesus Christ.

Here is what one ex-Jesuit has to say about the state of affairs when he joined:

> The first shock I got when I joined, along with the nagging feeling that I may have bitten off more than I could chew, was when I realized on Day One that there was to be silence at all times except for an hour of recreation each after lunch and dinner and during games which was after tea. I said to myself, "What have I let myself in for? How am I going to survive?" Thoughts of not unpacking my trunk were running riot in my mind, believe me. Just to give you an idea, the timetable was as follows:
> 5:30 Wake up!!
> 6:00 Meditation
> 7:00 Mass
> 8:00 Breakfast
> 8:30 English class

11:00 Conference (this was explanation of the Constitution of the Society etc.)

12:50 Examination of conscience

1:00 Lunch (eaten in silence while someone read a book out loud—exceptions were on Thursdays and Sundays)

1:30 Recreation

2:00–2:30 Siesta (I never took this as I could not sleep for just half an hour. On days I did sleep I would wake up at 4:30 and once I was woken up by the "Socius" (Novice Master's Assistant) himself!

2:30 Spiritual reading

3:00 Speech and Voice Therapy followed by Salvation History class

4:00 Tea followed by either work or games on alternate days

6:00 English classes

7:00 Meditation

7:50 Evening prayers in the chapel

8:00 Dinner (in silence while read to)

9:15 End of recreation

10:00 Bed. From 10pm to 8am was the Magnum Silentium or Great Silence and there was to be absolutely no talking in this period except in case of war, strife, natural calamity or death.

Games were on Tuesdays, Thursdays and Saturdays. On the three other week days there was "Manualia" or manual work, which involved sweeping and swabbing the corridors, rooms and toilets, digging holes, levelling ground, gardening, etc. etc. On Sundays we went out to teach Catechism. I used to constantly ask myself how I was going to survive this. I was a carefree happy go lucky guy with not a care in the world but wait till you read what some of the manual work involved and tell me if I was unjustly worried.

When cleaning the toilets we had to clean inside the bowl, including below the waterline—with our hand and a scrubber with soap powder on it. These were modern flush toilets. In Tony's time the toilets were the old type which had a metal box at the bottom. They had to go behind the toilets with long brushes and a hose and clean them out.

This was the time table years after Tony joined the Jesuits; during his stay in the Novitiate, it was much harder and with much less time for games and recreation. And they had to wear their cassock—a khaki one—even when playing football!

Visiting days and the amount of time the novice spent with his family were restricted to three days per year—his birthday, Christmas day, and family day; and they became family outings which I looked forward to. On the second visit I got quite a surprise when Tony entered the room. We arrived and were admitted to the parlor by a young novice who said he would go and fetch Tony. When Tony arrived, I got the shock of my life to see him in a cassock. I had once asked an elderly priest (and got a clip behind the ear from Mum for my impertinence) why priests dressed in long dresses like ladies. I was told that priests wore cassocks to distinguish themselves from lay people. In my mind I set an image of cassock-wearing priests as funny-looking elderly gents who were somewhat different from all of us. And here was my brother in a crisp, starched "dress" looking quite proud of himself! I remember Tony laughing at the look on my face and then raising his cassock a bit to reveal a pair of trousers underneath, much to my relief.

When we visited, after the initial formalities, I was allowed a free run of the property to explore the farm they had at the back, where they bred chickens, pigs, and a couple of milking cows. I remember Tony always being very serious at that time and his big smile had all but disappeared, at least for the first few visits. I guess he was playing the part he thought he was expected to play: the serious novice, studying to become a priest, extending the house rules to his family as well.

People often visited our home and inquired after Tony. They would tell Mum stories they had heard either from idle gossip or rumors about what life was like in the Jesuit Novitiate. Naturally, what she heard would have worried her. For example, she did hear about the manual labor and Grace recalls a visit to the Novitiate which confirmed Mum's fears. Says Grace:

> Tony came to the parlor and met us and while, usually, he was very animated and gesticulated a lot with his hands, this time he sat with hands folded. At some point during the conversation, Mum asked him if something was wrong and why he sat with his arms folded. Tony denied anything was wrong; but Mum persisted and asked him to show her his palms. When he did eventually display his palms to her, she saw he had nasty blisters on both of them. She was shocked and asked him how he came to get these. He eventually revealed that the previous day, he had been allotted gardening duties and he had the job of digging up a new garden patch in which they were to plant some vegetables. Mum then said, "Tony, how can they make you do such things? How can they force you to do such hard labor that you have ruined your hands like this?" Tony replied, "Mummy, I am not the only one here who does this kind of work; everyone has to share in all the work that needs to be done and we all do it willingly. No one forces us to do anything. In fact, I volunteered to do the work myself. So please set your mind at rest and understand that if I am to serve God's children in the future, I must learn to first serve my brothers here in the Novitiate."

Tony may have considered this the end of the matter but it did not satisfy Mum. In fact it only served to confirm those rumors she had been hearing about the hardships the novices had to endure. Tony was not given to performing household chores like sweeping floors or cleaning the toilets when he lived at home. India had— and still has—a very large domestic work force which is used effectively to everyone's advantage. Before Tony went to the Novitiate he would not have known the difference between a toilet scrub and a dishcloth. So it's just as well Mum never found out that her son was on his knees scrubbing the toilets or else she would have made a trip to the Novitiate and demanded that the person in charge relieve her precious son from these demeaning duties. Tony's case was not unique. Every novice would have been expected to take turns at performing these tasks and kept these facts from their families. It is true that some of the tasks they undertook in the Novitiate would have been considered beneath the dignity of most people of that era. Those jobs were normally allocated to the domestic staff and no one would have contemplated performing these tasks in their homes even for a moment.

I am told the idea was to toughen a person up so that he would be able to undergo hardships later in life. It was similar to boot camp when one joins the Armed Forces.

There were a lot of rules. Here is what one of my correspondents writes about some of the rules. He went through the novitiate many years after Tony did and he adds that during Tony's time the rules would have been much stricter:

> There were certain rules in the Book of Common Rules. I mention a few of interest:
>
> The Rule of Touch. We could not touch each other at all. For example, we see friends walking about with their hands on each other's shoulders. This kind of thing was not permitted.
>
> Modesty of Eyes. Generally when we moved about we were expected to look down—not up and about and everywhere. No roving eyes.
>
> No Particular Friendship. No one was allowed to have a "special" or "best" friend. Of course it is natural to like some person more than another but in no way was this to extend into a special relationship where the two of us could spend quality time with each other. These rules were not only for novices but across the board, so to speak, for all Jesuits.

All the novices had to take turns to serve at table and eat only after everyone else had had their meal. In this particular incident, Tony tells of the time when it was his turn to serve at table:

I wonder if waiters in hotels feel shy when they go about their job. I did, the first time I served in the refectory. It was at supper. I somehow had the feeling that all the brethren had their eyes on me to see how I'd come off in my first trial. (As a matter of fact they did have their eyes on me—they were trying to draw my attention to the fact that I had forgotten to serve the potatoes.) I tried to look the other way, [Modesty of Eyes at work?] which made me drop the gravy on Fr. Raser's lap.

Serving at table, take my word for it, is rarely a pleasure. In all my thirteen years of formation as a Jesuit, I never quite got used to it. The main difficulty is that one has to do it on an empty stomach. But what first class training it is! Service to others, with a smile to disguise your hunger and a cold meal after everyone has finished.[4]

Mum had heard that the young novices practiced self-discipline in the form of silence, fasting, and, most disturbing of all, physical self-punishment. This practice was encouraged in the early years of the Church and there is a brief mention of this too in one of the booklets, without great emphasis on the type of self-punishment they practiced. I do recall in my early years being encouraged to repent for my sins by saying the rosary with outstretched arms. This was a very painful experience indeed. So if mine was repentance lay-person's style, one can only imagine what the Jesuits expected of a future priest.

Novices were trained to practice the vows they would eventually take. One of them is Obedience. In order to be able to obey their Superiors, they needed training in humility. Their training also involved stretches of helping slum dwellers; cleaning the streets, clearing up garbage, and providing clean drinking water to the inhabitants of the surrounding slum. This was supposedly part of their training, to make them understand what life was like for the very

---

[4] *Ah! These Jesuits! The Man in the S.J. Mask*, p. 25.

poor and marginalized, in order that they learn how best to serve these people. When I first read about this in one of the booklets, I was skeptical. I thought there had to be a hidden agenda underlying this act of apparently thankless charity. I was convinced the Superiors wanted to show slum dwellers that Catholics with their acts of charity were pure of mind and heart while their agenda would have been to attract them to embrace the Catholic Church. I later found out that my skepticism was quite unjustified. Knowing Tony, I am sure he would not have questioned the motives behind the exercise; he would have flung himself into the task wholeheartedly.

Here is an amusing but telling transcription which describes their venture into spreading the Word:

> The villages surrounding our Novitiate simply swarmed with little children; but if you looked too long at them, chiefly at their hands and faces, you had to take care to give your eyes a good long rest later. It was to these lively kids that we were sent. Catechism centers were established and volunteers called for. Everybody volunteered.[5]

The section goes on to describe how difficult it was to get these kids to concentrate on what the novice was trying to say to them and the message he wanted to deliver. They are noisy, distracted, and seem to know nothing about what the novice is talking about:

> You couldn't be strict because one or the other of the girls was sure to cry and would probably not come to class the following Sunday. You couldn't be lenient either because that was sure to make the boys unbearable. I just tried to ignore the noise, yelled out the lessons I had prepared and left the rest to the Holy Spirit. . . . And so we went grinding along. They seemed to know nothing but their own names and even this bit of personal information they seemed to give very reluctantly and in such a low voice that

---

[5] *Ah! These Jesuits! The Inside Story,* pp. 31–32.

you had to ask at least five times before you caught it. If you wanted them to answer anything you had to make sure you told them the answer first or you were sure to spoil the show.[6]

Here is the part which indicates the type of person Tony was—serious about what he was doing but nevertheless, understanding enough to accept that those kids were not to blame for his failure to deliver:

> That evening you would have found a very desperate novice in the Chapel. That novice was me. He had gone out to conquer the world and had come back to lick his wounds, defeated by a bunch of children and he was saying something like this to our Lord in his heart: "Look Lord, I can't teach catechism to those children. They are noisy and besides what's the use of my teaching them when they don't listen to a word I say?" That novice has grown to be a good deal wiser since then I hope. I learnt in time that those poor dirty children were just the type that our Lord has a special love for; that if they didn't listen to me it was because there was something wrong with me, not with them. I had just got them together and lectured them like a college Professor. That was not the way.[7]

Another vow that Jesuits take is that of Poverty. Anything they are given, even their personal possessions, are not considered their own but given for their use. St. Ignatius insisted on detachment and he did not want any "inordinate attachments" to anything.

I remember one of the family visits to the Novitiate a few months after Tony went there. It was on his birthday and while he would not have taken any Vows yet, like all the novices, Tony had started to practice them. It was a very special occasion just three months after he had left home. We were allowed a special visit only because

---

[6] *Ah! These Jesuits! The Inside Story*, pp. 33, 34.
[7] *Ah! These Jesuits! The Inside Story*, pp. 34, 35.

it was his birthday. Mum had gone through a lot of trouble to bake him his very special favorite cake. We arrived and were admitted to the parlor by a young novice who said he would go and fetch Tony. I remember the disturbing silence which prevailed; all of us sat whispering to each other with Mum constantly correcting me on my irritating habit of touching everything; probably afraid I would break something or other. After a while, Tony arrived and greeted all of us rather seriously, thanked Mum and Dad for the cake and placed it on a nearby table. I recall his being rather stiff and formal; not the Tony I was used to at home, ever ready to give us a hug. After a few formal questions and answers, Mum asked Tony to fetch a knife to cut the cake so we could all sing "Happy Birthday" for him but he said that no such thing was allowed at the Novitiate. (That shattered my personal dream of getting at that cake.) He said it would be shared by everyone in the Refectory later. That got Mum worried and thinking in that case should she have baked a larger cake? She also shared her concern with Dad on the way home saying she was now really worried as to what kind of establishment Tony had entered where he was not allowed to share his birthday cake with his own family. Tony makes it very clear, in one of the booklets, that he had left mother, father, sisters, and brother in order to do God's work and that the Jesuits were now his family. Grace narrates an incident which occurred during one of these visits and this gave Mum a clear vision of how devoted her older son was to his vocation:

> We all went to visit Tony once and Mum met a lady there who was visiting *her* son. Mum mentioned that we were there to see Tony and that it was a pity that visits were restricted to only three a year. The lady in question was quite adamant about visiting her son whenever she felt the urge to visit him and said that having given her only son to the Jesuits, she was not going to be restricted on when to visit him. She would visit him whenever she pleased! When Tony came to meet us, Mum mentioned this to him and wanted to know why she could not do the same as that lady and

he said, "Mummy, I have joined the Jesuits and their rules are three visits a year. I am not about ready to bend these rules and if *you* insist on my bending them, then I'd rather go to my room, pack my bags right now and come home with you."

A response like that can be a bit of a conversation stopper. Mum never brought the topic up again.

Tony was not exceptional in what he did in the Novitiate. All those young men, when they first joined the Society of Jesus were following a vocation to serve other people at the cost of their own benefit. When young people join the armed forces or, for that matter, any other establishment they all go through a tough time at first and start at the bottom of the ladder and rough it out. Consider though, that all those young people expect to one day reach the top of the ladder and benefit from all the years of hardship they endured. Jesuits, however, take the vows of poverty, chastity, and obedience. They do not aspire to any high post. They lay claim to absolutely nothing material or worldly when they finish their training and throughout their lives as Jesuits. All they lay claim to is a life of service to God and their fellow human beings. Tony, as I said earlier, took his Vows very seriously and obeyed the rules of the establishment. In fact he imposed those rules upon himself with rigidity and would not bend them for anything.

I was too young to remember the exact details but Tony once had to be coerced by his Superior to bend that rule of restricted visits and, in fact, stretch it further. Grace remembers the incident well and tells me that he was literally forced to come home when I received my First Holy Communion—such an important occasion in the life of all Catholics. After the Church ceremony, my parents had organized a big party and invited all the relatives and close friends and they were very keen to have Tony's presence at the party.

By now Mum knew her son well so she cleverly invited his Novice Master, Fr. Nubiola for the occasion and innocently asked if he would bring Tony along. Tony must have known exactly what Mum was up to. He refused, saying that if all the other novices obeyed the House rules he had no right to break them. Fr. Nubiola convinced him that this was a very special occasion which called for a bit of leniency and that Tony should accompany him to the First Communion. Tony eventually agreed but said he would only go to the Church and not to the party.

All of us young Communicants were required to make our first confession with the aid of an adult and Tony volunteered to help me make my first confession. I remember some of this; but being very young at the time, I was more interested in the party and what gifts I would receive. I do remember being dressed by Grace in white from top to toe, my hair neatly combed and, I suppose, looking like a little angel disguising the devil within. That and the anxiousness to come to the party was all I could think of at that time. The actual sacrament did not occupy my mind at all. For me, it was a necessary ritual which I had to undergo and I wanted it finished and done with as quickly as possible.

> Grace recalls this incident: Tony took you to the church for your first confession and was supposed to instruct you on how to make your confession to the priest. He told you that you had to tell the priest all your sins and that you would then be absolved and be free of sin, pure enough to receive Christ for the first time in your life. You were not sure what to tell the priest and asked Tony what you should say and Tony asked you if you remembered the Ten Commandments and when you said yes, he asked you if you had broken any of these, like for instance stealing or being rude to Mum and Dad etc. You instantly said, "Yes I did steal sweets." So Tony told you to tell the priest this. When it was your turn to go to the priest, you knelt down and told the priest that you stole sweets from the cupboard. The priest must have asked you how many times and you then came back to Tony and said, "He wants to know how many times; do I have to tell him how many times?" And Tony, controlling himself from laughing, told you to say five times. You insisted that you had stolen sweets more than

five times and Tony said, "Never mind, just tell him five times and that will be enough to get you absolved." Later, after you had received your First Communion, Tony was laughing when he told us about this. I guess he must have realized how innocent you were then.

He may have laughed but I didn't. In confessing that I had stolen sweets from a cupboard which was kept under lock and key by Mum, I had to then reveal my secret. With my small hands I had found a gap behind the cupboard through which I had managed to steal them. After that, Mum had that gap sealed!

Two years after being in the Novitiate, the young men decide whether they want to continue with their priestly studies and if they decide they do, they write to the Jesuit Provincial requesting permission to be formally admitted into the Society. Tony too wrote such a letter to his Provincial.

It could have been like the one he mentions in the booklet:

My dear Fr. Provincial,

Within a month it will be exactly two years since I entered the Society of Jesus. I have gone through all the experiments of the Novitiate, I have read the Constitutions of the Society and I have come to the conclusion that I have a vocation to be a Jesuit.

I solemnly declare that this decision I have made is a free one. I have not been forced into it by anyone.

I therefore ask for the favor of being allowed to become a Jesuit by being admitted to the perpetual vows of Poverty, Chastity and Obedience, if your Reverence judges me fit.

Yours sincerely,[8]

Tony goes on to describe how worried he was when after a few days he had no reply to his letter to the Provincial. At an audience with his Novice Master, he explained the cause of his worry, tell-

---

[8] *Ah! These Jesuits! The Man in the SJ Mask*, p. 4.

ing him that maybe he was not worthy to become a Jesuit and Fr. Nubiola advised him to write another letter to the Provincial. So he did write again and this time he got a reply from his Provincial saying: "Vows granted. Congratulations and welcome into the Society." I guess Tony was still the absentminded young man when he joined the Society that he was at home. A few days later, he put on a freshly washed cassock and discovered that he had left his first letter in one of the pockets!

It is amusing to read this segment where Tony openly confesses to his absentmindedness at a time when his mind was racing ahead and forgetting the most mundane of things. This, coming from a man who went on to give a world-famous conference which was later published as *Awareness!* He had obviously learned to deal with his absentmindedness and focus on the present, as he advocates in this book.

Once a Jesuit novice has taken his First Vows he is accepted into the Society. He is a Jesuit and has the privilege of adding the initials "SJ" after his name.

The next stage in his formation is called the juniorate. The Novitiate is grounding in spirituality, humility, perseverance, ability to undergo hardship, and so on. The Juniorate—which could be anything from one to three years—is meant to train the new entrant into the Society in "mundane" studies. During the Juniorate the "Junior" would be taught English, Latin, and a bit of Greek as far as languages go. This was in Tony's day. He would also be given a general appreciation for the arts and have subjects as varied as History of Art and Architecture, History of Literature, World History, and other general subjects. The Juniorate was the equivalent of a college degree. This is partially what enabled the Jesuits to emerge as accomplished men of ability and learning.

The booklets mention "Sundays off." It's probably training like this that made Tony such a good story teller and prolific writer:

You've probably heard it said that Jesuits are inveterate writers. "A Jesuit seems to think that he will not enter heaven unless he has written at least one book in his lifetime"—that's what a writer of our time has exaggeratedly said of us. Now if all the books and all the writings of all the Jesuits were to be placed end to end, I would not be able to tell you how many times they would go round the world. What I can tell you is that the majority of those books owe their origin to the Juniorate Sunday.

For Sunday was Composition Day. This meant that we were given most of the day, plenty of paper and all the ink we wanted; with these ingredients, we sat down and wrote, wrote, wrote. We wrote essays, poems, short stories, articles, sermons, speeches, addresses, and letters. That looks easy enough. Yes? Try it I beg you. Apart from facing an audience from a pulpit, there was nothing I dreaded more than facing a blank paper on a Sunday morning. A great writer has said that the most difficult profession in the world is the writer's profession. If he passed that statement around, every Jesuit Junior would sign it!

The difficulty was that either I felt "inspired" or I did not. If I was not inspired, I spent most of the day scratching my head in the hope that that would bring on the inspiration. If I was inspired, I'd produce something like this:

"Hardly had the twittering birds departed on hasty wing to their pretty homes on the giant tree-tops in the glowing west while that majestic king of heaven, the Sun, had just lowered his diademed head beyond the flaming horizon, when the gigantic shadows lengthened and night stalked stealthily to occupy the throne left vacant by the departing day."

How do you like this? It is an extract from my essay on "Politics Today." I thought it the best thing going since Milton. Fr. Beamish unfortunately did not. He thought it was meaningless trash—and he said so when he corrected our compositions. When I got my composition book back there was a red line running right across that paragraph and the following comment: "This is not a sentence. It is a sausage." Paragraph two had a red line and a comment too: "When you can say something in two words, don't use twenty." Paragraph three earned this one: "What on earth are you driving at? Be simple and you'll be understood!" And so on and so forth.

Fr. Beamish has long since gone to his rest; but his memory is held in benediction among his former pupils. He had the rare virtue of being straightforward in his criticism. He taught us to write (I won't say he succeeded), to "have something to say, say it quickly and then shut up."[9]

Hopefully I can take a page out of Fr. Breamish's instruction manual when compiling this biography of Tony!

Tony had three years of Juniorate. By the end of these he, along with his fellow Juniors, was ready for the next stage in his formation.

Tony's journey through the stages of his life as a Jesuit was not without sacrifices, the biggest being having to leave home and his beloved family. This would have been as true for him as for every other Novice and Junior. Again the booklets come to my aid, describing Family Day:

At last, the great day arrived. The invitation card said distinctly that the function started at 5:00 p.m. My good parents were models of punctuality. They turned up at a quarter past three! And who can blame them? They pretended that they were looking forward to the tea-party, that they were keen on the entertainment but it wasn't true. What they wanted a million times more than any tea or play was to be with their son once more, and they knew that if they came two hours before the show began, they would have me all to themselves in a corner of the parlor. They literally feasted on my company for those two hours.

I have always been convinced that Almighty God has given me the best parents in the world. I know my brother-Jesuits will claim their parents are the best in the world. Let them. Nobody

---

[9] *Ah! These Jesuits! The Man in the SJ Mask*, pp. 41–43.

will ever make me change my mind (or make them change theirs, for that matter) on the subject. I remember the day I decided to become a Jesuit and broke the news to my mother. She had always secretly wished, I knew, that God might call me to be a priest. But a Jesuit? But why a Jesuit? Her only difficulty to that was a difficulty of the heart. If I became a Jesuit, I would have to leave home—and her. Why not become a diocesan priest and be able to live near her and come home for the holidays? In spite of her difficulty, neither she nor my father put the slightest obstacle in my way. They had always said they wanted their children to choose their own careers in the world. And they were as good as their word, although I chose a career that was going to cost them most.

I never told my parents so, but I don't mind confessing that if there was one difficulty I had in becoming a Jesuit it was the thought that I would have to leave them. It is very, very difficult, believe me. It takes a whole vocation to make the sacrifice of the type of vocation that is embodied in our Lord's words: "He who loves father or mother more than me, is not worthy of me. Whoever leaves father or mother, brother or sister or land. . . . for my name's sake shall have a hundredfold in this world and life eternal in the next."

I have experienced this hundredfold that Our Lord spoke of. For every brother I left I have found hundreds who make up our Jesuit family. Instead of parents, God has given me superiors who have been father and mother to me. For the little wealth I might have had, God had given me a whole Society that looks after all my needs. For the career in the world I sacrificed, God has chosen for me a vocation which is truly noble.

God has mysteriously arranged that, through sacrifice, love is perfected; and I know I love my parents a thousand times more now, than before I became a Jesuit. As for them, some of their sons are out in the world with wives and children and careers of their own, but they know that the one who loves them most disinterestedly and undividedly, is the son they "gave to the Jesuits." Strangely enough, in giving him they kept him more securely for themselves.[10]

Those last words were to be prophetic.

When pondering how best to close this chapter I drew inspiration from the story in *The Song of the Bird* where *one* monk was needed in a monastery in the South. The monastery in the north wisely sent five. Why? One by one they dropped out along the way in order to do useful and worthwhile work. Only one reached the destination.

Tony ends the story with, "I have always dropped out for the best of reasons: to reform the liturgy, to change Church structures, to update the study of scripture and to make theology relevant. Religious activity is my favorite escape from God."[11]

Like the last monk, Tony remained a faithful son of the Society of Jesus. The training he received in the Novitiate was his foundation for life after he left home; it was in the Novitiate that he was taught to practice the vows of poverty, chastity, and obedience. The Novitiate trained him to keep his Vows and he remained faithful to these to the very end. The Juniorate and the rest of his Jesuit formation gave him the freedom to explore his talent as an orator, a story teller and a writer who inspired thousands, if not millions around the globe. Eventually, even in death, he became a very well-known Jesuit and Master of Spirituality, his books and audio and video conferences encouraging so many to change their lives.

Tony was indeed the head of the group that wrote the promotional booklets but the contents could be applied to every young man who entered the Society. There are other Jesuits who have also scaled great personal heights and gone on to become eminent Jesuits themselves, prominent and well known in their fields. In fact

---

[10] *Ah! These Jesuits! The Man in the SJ Mask,* pp. 47-50.
[11] *The Song of the Bird,* p. 94.

the way they are trained, every Jesuit attains his very own personal best performance, no matter what he undertakes. Some go on to be world famous like my brother; others get on with their jobs, unobserved and unrecognized and unsung; but serving humankind nonetheless.

I include in this group the ex-Jesuits as well; those who, like the monks in Tony's story, found they did not have a vocation to the Society and left. I know quite a few of these gentlemen who have gone on to become community leaders and prominent citizens outside the Society of Jesus, nonetheless helping their fellow citizens.

After completing three years of Juniorate Tony got ready for the next step in his formation. This step was one that would have been exciting for any Jesuit, as will be seen.

CHAPTER THREE

PHILOSOPHY IN SPAIN

"To the Jesuit Order that I feel so proud and so unworthy to belong to."
—DEDICATION IN *Wellsprings: A Book of Spiritual Exercises*

IT WAS CUSTOMARY IN those days for the Bombay Province to send a few scholastics to Spain every year to get their degree in Philosophy. In Jesuit parlance this is called "doing" one's Philosophy. In 1952 Tony, along with two other Indian Jesuits, was selected to do his Philosophy at San Cugat, the Philosophate in Barcelona, Spain.

To go to Spain is the most exciting place that any Jesuit can aspire to. For the Society of which Tony was so proud was founded by a man from Spain.

Born in 1491, Ignatius of Loyola, a Basque born into nobility spent a good deal of his youth courting fame and fortune. He was a good battle commander but he was hit by a cannon ball in the Battle of Pamplona against the French. The wounded Ignatius was taken to Loyola, where one of his legs had to be broken and reset. One leg, however, remained shorter than the other and an unsightly bone protruded below the knee. So vain was he that he ordered the surgeon to saw off the offending bone and to lengthen his leg by systematic stretching. He bore all this pain without complaint at a time when there was no anaesthesia. During his long recuperation he looked for reading material.

What he wanted was romantic or adventure novels. What he got was *Life of Christ* by Ludolph the Carthusian and *The Golden Legend*, a book on the lives of saints. Instead of being bored he felt inspired by these stories. He reflected that if these saints could do so much for Christ then he could do likewise or more. He began to seek how he could do more for Christ. This idea of "more" (*magis*) remained with him throughout his life and is something he instilled in the members of his Society. In the course of his spiritual development he laid down his sword before Our Lady at Montserrat, the "black Madonna." He then went to Manresa where he would spend seven hours a day in prayer in a cave he discovered there. Eventually he founded the Society of Jesus in September 1540—a Society that was to lead the Counter-Reformation and would be known as the shock troops of the Church.

The Spiritual Exercises written by St. Ignatius are considered his greatest contribution to Western spirituality. Every Jesuit undertakes the Exercises by way of a thirty-day retreat in the Novitiate and another before his Last Vows in the Tertianate.[1] Every year a Jesuit undertakes an eight-day retreat which is the Spiritual Exercises in shorter form.

The prospect of going to Spain must have been exciting for Tony and his companions. They may have harbored the secret hope of seeing Manresa and Montserrat and even—if they were lucky—the Sanctuary of Loyola in Azpeitia, built over Ignatius's birthplace!

For their families it was a matter of pride. I remember how proud our entire family was when we heard that Tony had been selected to go to Spain. By now, the deMello family had gotten used to the fact that Tony was not coming home. The Novitiate-Juniorate years had flown by so quickly. Everything we had heard about Tony was positive, in fact quite flattering. The day he was to leave for Spain,

---

[1] The two-year Novitiate ends when a Jesuit takes his First Vows. Before he is finally accepted by the Society he goes through an additional probationary period known as Tertianship, usually about 14 years after joining the Novitiate. After this he takes his Final Vows.

Dad hired a private car (which was a country mile ahead of the Victoria in which they had left for the Novitiate) and we all went to the Mazagaon docks where Tony and his companions were to board the ship. Whereas there were tears when he left home the first time, there were back slapping and smiles all round on this occasion. We were all so proud of Tony.

I am sure the families of the other two young Jesuits felt just as proud.

Tony and his companions from the Mumbai province sailed for Spain in 1952.

When Tony left for the Novitiate, we were all crying and after he waved once, he never looked back again. This time, we were all smiling and happy. When the ship cast off and began moving away majestically from the dock, Tony, accompanied by his companions, stood on the deck waving to us and their families.

Another journey had begun for Tony, another chapter in his life. For us, his family, it was the beginning of great expectations from him.

One of Tony's companions describes the boat trip:

> It took 13 days. . . . It was nice. Only towards the end of the journey one got stale food. . . . The ship stopped at Aden, also Cairo. In fact some people even went on a tour there. . . . We were not so fortunate.

It appears Tony was always light hearted, telling jokes and making the trip most enjoyable.

At San Cugat there were 80 to 90 philosophers; about 30 in each year. According to Tony's companion in Spain:

> Most of the lectures were in Latin. We had to talk Latin. We had Latin even in our recreation—one or two days in the week we had to speak in Latin. Our Disputation where a philosopher has to expose a topic—give the presentation, then questions keep coming up and he has to defend his proposition . . . all in Latin.

About these Disputations, another companion of Tony's remarks about Tony and his two companions from Bombay:

> We used to have the Public Disputation of Philosophy every year where presentations were made and then defended. These three from Bombay were often selected. And they were exceptional. So much so that the Professor of Cosmology, Fr. Puigrefagut said, "If all the Bombay Jesuits are like these then we stand nowhere." These three were head and shoulders above most and Tony especially was brilliant. He did not mean to be more brilliant. He just was.

While Latin was the medium of study it also served as a common language for Jesuits to communicate with other Jesuits from around the world. Why, then, did Tony and his companions have to study Spanish when they went to Spain? As a Spanish companion of Tony's who met him for the first time in Spain aptly puts it, "Our studies were in Latin but life was in Spanish. Besides, some subjects such as History of Philosophy, Physics, and Cosmology were taught in Spanish."

Prior to leaving for Spain, Tony and his companions had learned basic Spanish. That was what Tony was doing in his third year of Juniorate. They had to build on this when they got to Spain. One of his companions comments that Tony had a gift for languages and became quite fluent in Spanish. He was a "natural" and spoke the language fluently with the local accent, delighting his hosts in Spain. I do not think that was only talent. He worked at it. I am told he improved his Spanish by reading Spanish literature. He would read Cervantes,in his spare time. Perhaps he read of the exploits of Don Quixote, the Man of La Mancha in the original Spanish?

Doing one's Philosophy makes the Jesuit an all-round person. It is a maturing process. In three short years he learns to debate, to question, to thrust and parry verbally. He develops the thinking and reasoning skills he will require later in the pulpit or the classroom or any stage upon which he cares to venture.

Tony's interests went beyond merely getting a good grounding in Western Philosophy. He also became deeply interested in Spirituality. At the time that Tony went to Spain there was a recognized expert on the Spiritual Exercises who was the Spiritual Director at San Cugat. This person who was to influence Tony tremendously was Fr. Calveras SJ. Tony seemed to have been fascinated by him. According to Fr. Miguel Lafont's website, Tony often insisted that his own spiritual director was Fr. Calveras.[2]

Fr. José Calveras had already written a book on the subject of the Spiritual Exercises (*The Harvest-field of the Spiritual Exercises of Saint Ignatius*, Bombay, St. Xavier's College, 1949). Tony had the opportunity of making an eight-day retreat under him. This may have been the launching pad on Tony's path to spiritual fulfillment. He would eventually learn from these retreats, designed exclusively for Jesuits and write his own book of spiritual exercises called *Wellsprings*, which after Sadhana, is regarded as a masterpiece of spirituality, not only for Catholics but as a Note at the start of the book suggests, "for persons of all spiritual affiliations—religious, a-religious, agnostic, atheistic."

The very close friend of Tony's, the Spanish Jesuit I spoke of earlier, says that he loves and admires Tony for many things. I requested an interview to be conducted with him to better understand his views on Tony and to find out what it was that Tony learned from Fr. Calveras, that remarkable retreat director. Here is what this close friend has to say:

> Tony showed great interest in Fr. Calveras because Tony knew how to strike gold. . . . I do not know how often they met. . . . Fr. Calveras and Fr. Nubiola, who was Tony's Novice Master, were like Formula One drivers. . . . Fr. Calveras was in the Manresa House where the retreats were conducted, sometimes also in the House in Barcelona. Tony was interested in Calveras because of the latter's knowledge of the Spiritual Exercises.

Many of my respondents recall Tony telling them the following

---

[2] See *Sophia*, #2.

incident mentioned on Lafont's website:

> Tony related with feeling the following episode about him
> [Calveras]. On a certain occasion in the course of their meeting
> Calveras said to Tony, "Tell me how you pray."[3] Tony was
> perplexed. However, after pondering deeply he gave him the
> desired answer, whereupon Calveras after listening carefully
> responded, "You have still not had an experience of prayer."
> Thereafter he taught Tony the third of St. Ignatius's three
> methods of prayer, and suggested he do as follows, "Take a deep
> breath and recite the Lord's Prayer (per anhelitos)." Tony did
> so, and later recalled that it was only then that he had his first
> experience of prayer.[4]

Before Tony joined the Society there was the incident at home of
Tony and the discussion on the Pope's infallibility. After his return
from Spain, however, there was a change in his "strict" attitude and
discipline. I have often wondered what caused a change in Tony's
thinking. I was to personally experience this change in an incident
which occurred at De Nobili College a few years later.

After hearing about Fr. Calveras and his expertise in the Spiritual Exercises, I thought that maybe these retreats had the effect of
"changing" Tony from a rigid dogmatic to becoming liberated in his
thinking.

Tony's Spanish friend countered my thinking as follows:

> Tony never really "changed." He was good soil and the plant
> took its time but it grew. . . . I did not feel there was a change
> in Tony—not a big change—the structures were always there in
> place. They took their time to mature after Tony gave them time.
> . . . Tony was beyond teaching in a school; he was a master of life.

---

[3] The text of the Spiritual Exercises for this method reads: "With each breath
or respiration one should pray mentally while saying a single word of the Our
Father . . . in such a way that from one breath to another a single word is said."
The Spiritual Exercises of St. Ignatius, p. 73.

[4] Sophia, #2.

He was not a man of structure. We need structures but, as St. Paul says, when he was a child he needed certain things which he did not need once he became a man. . . .

Tony was a free man. . . . He was in the structure when he was a philosopher and beyond the structure when he was in Lonavala as Director of Sadhana etc. . . . I believe there was no big change in Tony. The seed was always there. He was always open. There was more of an evolution. It was a difference of degree rather than one of kind or of substance. . . .

This view is confirmed by another companion of Tony's who was asked the same question about Tony and change. At first this companion wanted to know what was meant by change. After it was explained he said:

Tony was very exceptional—in the sense that he was very intelligent and he could perceive how things function. He could get a grasp of the situation. That is why he could "change" because he saw that the situation required another way of presenting the faith or the Spiritual Exercises . . . because he was very sharp. He could penetrate the minds of people and the nature of the situation. . . .

I think by nature, Tony was open . . . open to change, open to understanding. But what happened was, in the Society at that time, from the forties to the fifties—the Old Society—we were very strict. And given a Novice Master like Nubiola . . . So contrary to what you might think, it was the Society that imposed on him this "disciplinarity"—I would not say he was a stickler for rules. Formerly the rules were insisted upon: the way we walked, modesty of eyes, rule of touch, no particular friendship . . . all of this was emphasized.

Even in school during his Regency, you must have got that impression; he was fairly strict. It's because we had that sense of discipline imposed on us. Now, of course, it is different. Once he had finished formation and he had to face new situations, new kinds of people, then his original character came into play.

... The change in Tony was already before Vatican II.

I have corresponded with close friends of Tony's, some of whom are still Jesuits, others who aren't. From this correspondence I pick up the common notion that while Tony was constantly implementing change in his life, he was born with a soft, gentle heart and a determination to pursue his vocation within the Society. He was constantly seeking the truth on how better to serve God through serving others.

During the summer holidays in Spain Tony was assigned a special duty. Spanish Jesuits who had volunteered to go as missionaries to India or other English-speaking countries had necessarily to learn English. Tony's Spanish friend was one of those destined to go to India later and this is what he recalls of his English classes:

> Every summer we had an "English House" for those who would be going to English-speaking countries as missionaries. The only rule was that everyone had to speak only English. There would be one or two professors from England. Then there would be a few from Spain—in all eight professors and twelve students. I was one of the students and Tony was one of the professors. So I took my first steps in English with Tony. Tony was hilarious. He never had formal classes. He was always inventing stories. I still remember he invented this girl called Nataki Nataka. He would start a sentence about her and we students would have to add sentences to make up the story as we went along. Tony would force us to give vent to our imagination. We could not use a sentence that had been used before. For instance he would say, "Nataki Nataka sat on the lion's back." Someone would say, "The lion wanted to eat her." I would say, "No, Nataki Nataka wanted to eat the lion!" It was a lot of fun. And without realizing it we learned to speak English. ...

I remember Tony accompanying a couple of the new arrivals from Spain to our home in Bandra one year after he had returned from Spain in 1955. These young Spaniards faced a number of difficulties. Apart from being in a new country and adapting to different cultures and food, they also had to cope with speaking and making themselves understood in their new homeland. Tony was appointed as their guardian and English teacher when they first arrived.

I recall when Tony was studying in Spain, Mum had written to him and asked him to get her one of those beautiful Spanish lace veils which were so popular. In those days, men took their hats off and women covered their heads when entering a church. We all wondered why Mum wanted the veil because she dressed exclusively in a sari and used a part of the sari (as all women in India do when necessary) to cover her head.

The veil, I discovered, was not for her. She gifted it to my class teacher in school, no doubt, to "curry favor" with her on account of my bad grades. I remember passing with flying colors that year. Not so the next year, when I inherited a male class teacher!

To get back to the Spaniards, Tony told Mum that he had not actually bought the veil himself; that it was in fact the mother of one of the young Jesuits from Spain who had bought it and gifted it to Tony for Mum. This young Jesuit was present that day when Tony visited and Mum thanked him and asked him to tell her more about his family.

The poor man blushed; firstly because he was obviously embarrassed by Mum's gratitude, when he himself knew nothing about the veil. Secondly, he was literally at a loss for words and stammered, "Well, my mother, *he* did not tell me that *she* buys that veil and so I cannot tell *him* thank you from you."

Quick to spot his mistake, Tony pounced on the sentence and said, "Now [name withheld] make up your mind, is your mother a man or a woman? Is your mother therefore a *she* or a *he*?"

The unfortunate young man, now looking like he wanted a hole to appear and swallow him, said, "No, no, my mother is *she* not *he*." Tony replied, "So in that case make yourself clear, tell my mother that your mother is *she* not *he*."

The way I narrate it this story may sound cruel and insensitive but coming from Tony's lips and his style of delivery, it was hilarious and made everyone laugh, including the hapless young Jesuit. Tony had a way with words and a very nice way of making a joke at someone's expense, without belittling the person.

I end this chapter with the words of Tony's Spanish Jesuit friend speaking of their time together in Spain. He speaks from his heart and his words serve as a perfect appraisal of Tony's nature:

Tony was extremely lively, kind and a very-very good companion. At that time we could not go for meals to our family. I could take him to my house only for tea. . . . Tea was like an excuse so that between meals we went over. But that tea was so loaded it was like a meal! I was thinking of coming to India and I took the three of them to my house—more than once. My mother was in love with Tony. The three of them spoke Spanish very well . . . but Tony was so lively! He would make us laugh. He was always like this even later though he had come down a bit. He enjoyed people and he came across as a very good-hearted man. . . . Mischievous but never malicious. Always teasing people but up to a certain level . . . not to hurt them.

CHAPTER FOUR

REGENCY

*The master could be quite critical when he thought criticism was
in order. But to everyone's surprise he was never resented for his
reprimands. When asked about this once, he said, "It depends on how
one does it. Human beings are flowers: open and receptive to softly
falling dew, closed to violent rain.*

—*One Minute Nonsense*, P. 2

THE TERM "REGENCY" is an interesting term. What is "Regency"
as understood in the Society and why is it called so?

The first part of the question is fairly easy to answer. St. Ignatius
wanted the men who joined the Society of Jesus to be trained wisely
and well. So he prescribed a special—and extended—period of training and preparation prior to their ordination. The training period to
become a priest in the Society of Jesus is perhaps the longest compared to other Orders and Congregations—a minimum of thirteen
years. Ignatius wanted Jesuits who had a feel for the real world and
who could understand and empathize with the people they served.
So it came about that Jesuit scholastics have to take a break between
their philosophy and theology studies to work "in the field," often
teaching in an educational institution run by the Jesuits. This period
which could be from one to three years is called "Regency."

The second part of the question is more difficult to answer. *Why*
this period is called "Regency" seems to be unknown. The Jesuits
and ex-Jesuits I have interviewed just take the word for granted and

when I asked them why the word "Regency" they were unable to answer. I can only assume it was coined to refer to the fact that traditionally a regent was someone who was in charge of certain things under his watch. So it may have been with the Jesuit Regent. Generally the Regent would be assigned to a school where he would look after the boarders if any and also teach in the school. The Regent served also as a model for the young boys and many a young man joined the Jesuits because he was impressed by the dedication and idealism shown by the Regent in his school.

Being of help in a school is only one of the appointments that might be given to a Regent. The Regent might be assigned elsewhere. St. Ignatius had the motto "AMDG"—seen in every Jesuit institution. This stands for *Ad majorem Dei gloriam—For the greater glory of God.* The Jesuit does anything that will serve the greater glory of God. This is why one sees Jesuits in a variety of professions and vocations. So the Regent could be assigned to get a college degree from a regular University in the sciences or arts or engineering or medicine or whatever would promote the glory of God. Or he might be sent to assist at a mission station. Sometimes, because of a shortage of personnel the Regent might be assigned the double duty of looking after the boys in a boarding school as well as getting a college degree. It is all part of the toughening process AMDG—for the greater glory of God.

Coming after the hard years of Novitiate and Juniorate and differently difficult two (or three) years of Philosophy, Regency—however tough—is a welcome respite for the Jesuit scholastic. Now, he would be occupied with a more hands-on, personal, human approach with other individuals, without having to take care of the kind of tasks expected of him in the Novitiate or the studies in the following years.

Tony's first year of Regency was at St. Mary's High School, Mazagaon. This involved looking after the boarders there as well as teaching in the school. The boarders came from different backgrounds and places and studied in the school and were lodged in a hostel. Normally, the boys went home for the holidays to their families but if their families were stationed away from Mumbai or were overseas, they had no choice but to stay in the hostel on weekends and other holidays.

The varied characters of these boys often stretched the patience of the Regent who cared for and looked after them. It was not an easy task and I can say this with a degree of authority. I attended the very same boarding school as these boys who were in Tony's care. This was after Tony had finished his tenure there though.

At times we intentionally tested the Regent's patience to see just how far we could go. We paid the price for it: corporal punishment or, if we were lucky, detainment and/or forfeiting privileges such as weekend outings. We had an instinctive ability to suss out the character of the Regent. Each one was quite different from the other. Some of them had short tempers and very little patience when it came to misbehavior.

Apparently Tony was not one of these. Among Tony's many duties, the primary one would have been twenty-four-hour accountability for a large group of red-blooded boys whose sole aim in life seemed to be discovering new ways to torment the Regent—or so it must have seemed to the latter. This was a challenging assignment. Imagine being the full-time guardian of a rowdy, boisterous group of boys ranging from eight to sixteen years of age from dawn to dusk—and often beyond.

Having been in that school I know what life was like as a boarder and can only now imagine what a Regent must have been going through in fulfilling his duties. I have received correspondence from an ex-Jesuit who describes his own Regency. The school was not the one I attended. The era and location are different but the situation is amazingly similar in all aspects:

> I spent two years of my regency getting a Bachelor of Arts degree and then had a year in a school where I was the Boarding Prefect and also taught English Grammar, Marathi, History, Geography and Civics in the school. My two college years were

a cakewalk compared to regency proper—which can be very stressful.

I had to wake up and complete my hour of meditation and then wake the boys up at 6:00 a.m. and make sure they stayed awake. Considering how difficult waking up was for me, my heart would go out to those poor lads. The youngest were barely six years old and were away from home for the first time. But they all had to be treated with the same discipline. They had to do an hour of studies which I would supervise before they attended Mass, followed by breakfast and then school. It was not possible to make them study. All I could do was stop them from talking or being distracted or distracting others.

I would have my breakfast after they went to school. While they were at school it was a huge relief for me because then they were someone else's responsibility. I had a full teaching workload which I did not mind at all since I have always loved teaching.

Once school was over, I had to take charge of the boarders again—seeing that they had lunch without too many potatoes or other articles of food being flung on others, coping with petty complaints and seeing that the younger lads were not surreptitiously ditching their spinach out the window or diddled out of their dessert by the older ones. They then had a break before putting in an hour of studies again, followed by some tea and buns and then games. Games were as much a break for us Regents as for them. We played basketball, volleyball or football with them and they used the opportunity for a little rough play with us and get a bit of their own back.

After games there was communal bathing—well almost. There were individual shower stalls with doors but there was a common valve that opened all the showers at once. Yours truly handled this valve. The valve was opened for a while and then closed. Everyone had to soap themselves when the valve was closed. The valve was opened again and they had to finish their shower by the time I closed the valve again. Then it was time for the next lot to go for their shower. There were the usual panic-stricken yelps of "Wait, Father . . . Not finished, Father" from the littler ones who had generally dropped their soap and had spent the rest of the shower time trying to pick it up. I used to go and help soap the younger ones, especially on the neck and around their ears. These little fellows really needed caring and dearly missed a mother's touch. There were the daily problems here of someone's soap missing or stolen, another person's towel being thrown into the wet shower stall and so on. The commonest problem was the fight to get into the first round of showers. Dealing with these boyish pranks—which seemed so fantastic when I was a kid indulging in them—was now a major headache.

After another hour and a half of studies, they had dinner, free time and then half an hour of studies before bed. Then the boarders' day would come to an end.

Not mine. I would have classes to prepare, papers and tests to mark, prayer to be done, books to be read and rounds to be done. (Don't let anyone fool you into believing that tired as they are, young boys will go to bed when bidden.) Sometimes I would be sorting out a pillow fight half an hour after lights out. I would often get a few of those pillow blows "by mistake" but it was all taken in good spirit. Occasionally I would resort to corporal punishment. This could be anything from making them sit in a corner to kneeling in a corner to a resounding slap on the cheek to a couple of "cuts" with a cane on the palms of the hand. The boys would test you right from day one to see what you were made of. If you were a softie they would take advantage of you for the rest of your stay there. If you were too strict they would get back at you in sneaky ways—trip you while playing football, elbow you at basketball and worst of all give you a most appropriate, accurate and scathing nickname. Such a nickname would be the toast of the entire school. The senior Jesuits in the House generally had an idea of how the Regent was setting with the boarders from the nickname he was given. Mine was a fairly uncomplimentary one that referred to my body size. I don't think I was quite in the same popularity league as Tony.

Apart from the tension of having to look after the boarders as well as do a full teaching job in school, the Regent generally feels as if he is living in a glass cage—under the scrutiny of all the senior Jesuits who seem to him to be on the lookout for the tiniest weakness in him. After some time he begins to get a little paranoid because he imagines that all the senior Jesuits are conspiring against him. In my case I knew that most of this was just the product of my overripe imagination but it was difficult to shake off nonetheless.

While regency in the boarding/school is a very trying time—I wanted to make up on sleep whenever I could—it had its ups. While in a house of formation—Novitiate, Juniorate, Language Year, Philosophy or Theology—a Jesuit lives in a kind of hothouse. He does not have much interaction with lay persons. In the regency years he is thrown out into the real world so to speak. Every day he meets new people, people with real difficulties and problems—parents of boarders come to visit, parents of school children, the teachers and staff in the school, the people who come for Mass. For someone who has spent nearly seven years in one or other house of formation, the regency years come as a great break.

As a Regent you are a role model for the students. I remember when I was a student we used to admire the Regents. In fact I found them fascinating and I think the first stirrings of joining the priesthood started when I saw the Regents at work and play. I think this is another reason why the Jesuits prescribe regency. The Regent is not yet a priest. He is older than the boys but not so old as to be considered "old" by them. He joins them in their games and is generally better at them than the students. He is younger than the priests and seems to understand the boys much better than the priests do. The Regent is a really cool guy for the boys. He might be a disciplinarian but he is also their confidant and friend, their mentor and guide. He talks to them about their home and family, understands their problems, is in loco parentis to them and is a rock in their unstable and growing years.

Regency is also a time for a Jesuit to size himself up, to see if he will be able to cope with this life in the priesthood. It is a time for him to decide what sort of ministry he is going to pursue. It is a time when the Society too can assess him (hence the semi-paranoia on his part).

Army recruits are given their training in warfare and then just before they are sent to the front the young soldiers go through war games with live ammunition. They will really have had to learn to keep their heads down or this would be curtains. Occasionally a soldier is hurt or even killed in such exercises.

The Jesuit regency is this kind of live exercise. The Regent is certainly given a baptism under fire. Sometimes a Jesuit who does not quite have it in him decides to leave at this stage. The regency is arguably the stage at which one finds the most "drop outs" from the Society. One way or the other regency is the best opportunity for a Jesuit to discover himself, his strengths and his true calling. Many a Jesuit who has left at this stage has gone on to do great things and live a rich, satisfying life.

From a boarder's perspective, life at times was just as stressful. He was away from home, without his family, and had to cope with his own set of problems be they academic or emotional. By the time I attended this boarding school, Tony had (unfortunately) already moved on to Vinayalaya, teaching English to juniors there. My reason for being there was, in fact, quite unique. I was there by my own request! However, most of the boarders I knew were there due to unavoidable circumstances. One such boarder who experienced Tony's regency told me that his father worked in the Railways and was constantly being transferred from one area to another. Because he wanted academic stability for his son, he enrolled him in the school as a boarder. These boys, besides having to cope with the rigors of daily school life, had to also cope with the whims and moods of not only other boarders but those of their Regent as well. I recall, not all the boarders were angels and I count myself in those ranks too. I had my moments of anger and despair and I sometimes took it out on others.

I think it is appropriate to introduce my non-Indian readers to a commonly used term in India to describe someone who "seeks favor" with those in authority. *Chamcha* literally means "spoon" in Hindi. The figurative meaning is quite amusing. Until the British and other Europeans arrived in India, Indians ate their food exclusively with their fingers. Indians still do. It is considered much more hygienic. One washed one's hands before and after meals. On the other hand, if not properly washed, cutlery was considered unhygienic. The British introduced cutlery and those Indians who followed them in their eating habits were seen as sycophants. They were scornfully called *chamchas*. In India *chamcha* is a "bootlicker."

In the "boarding" anyone who sought favor with the Regents was immediately labelled a chamcha. He was labelled more quickly and with greater venom if the Regent was not liked. There was a lot of friction within the boarding school and Regents were called on to break up quarrels which could sometimes lead to blows.

My friend who gave an account of his regency above says that the boarders sometimes got their own back by pushing and shoving the Regent on the playing field. He is quite right. In fact in our group we had other ways of getting back at the Regents we disliked, without physically manhandling them. Many of us were fifteen- and sixteen-year-olds who were growing and some of us were quite robust and bigger in size than the Regent. I remember we had one Regent who was quite a nice fellow in my opinion. But he was disliked by others because he was very strict. This guy was academically inclined and had a brilliant mind. He was intelligent, articulate, and studious but not inclined toward sporting activities and physical feats. As can be imagined, on the games field he was a complete misfit. He probably felt obligated to "join in" with us boarders when we played. I suppose he just wanted to be accepted by the boys.

When the soccer game would start, a few of the boys would connive to make sure he got the ball, regardless of which side he was on. Then, without warning, two or three boys from the opposing team would converge on him rather menacingly, with great speed. Members of his team would then shout at him to pass the ball or make a move. This guy, petrified to see the three aggressors descending on him, would panic and instead push the ball out of play. This brought hoots of delight from the boys. This used to cause him enormous embarrassment and eventually he stopped playing with us. For those who disliked him it was mission accomplished!

On the other hand, we had another Regent, a Spaniard who, while only 5'2" off the ground, was aggressive and enthusiastic about his soccer. He was a very well-liked Regent, liberal in his thinking and a very kindly man. He always had a good word for us and plenty of time to deal with any problems we wanted to share with him. We loved this guy and were very disappointed when we did not see him on the playing field with us. We were split into four groups under different colored "Houses." This Spanish Regent was free to join any House he pleased on the playing field. I was in the Green House and dearly wished he would join my team. But I was not alone. Every boy of every house fervently wanted him on their side. Diplomat that he was he would wisely switch houses every other day!

Life in boarding school was full of ups and downs. There were moments of happiness and I, for one, consider those three years as some of the happiest in my life. But they were not without problems, sometimes associated with home sickness, sometimes just plain petty issues between individuals. It was not by any means a life of leisure.

The routine has already been provided by my correspondent and I cannot add any more to this except to say that some minor details may have varied because of the location and structure of the school itself. That and the fact that Regents are also human and they all had their plus and minus points which we boarders had to either benefit from or contend with. I liked the routine myself because everyone had rules to conform to and we *all* had to do things whether we liked them or not. Studying, playing on the field after school, eating, bathing, attending Mass at the chapel every morning were all done communally. If for some reason one of us did not feel inclined to participate in any of these activities, we reported sick to the Regent, who promptly sent us to the Infirmary to be examined by the Infirmarian. This wise man would immediately prescribe a stiff dose of quinine. This bitter potion was considered the best form of fighting infection and a safeguard against malaria. In fact, gin-and-tonic, which contains quinine, was concocted in India as a way of giving the British troops a pleasanter way of consuming quinine. It was all very well for those soldiers. We boarders had no gin with our quinine to help it go down. We hated and dreaded that bitter dose. It was definitely the best antidote for faking illness. We only opted for the Infirmary if we felt really ill.

I managed to contact some ex-boarders a couple of years older than I, who came under Tony's regency. They have given me their opinions about Tony as a Regent. Here is a letter I received recently:

I remember Fr. Tony deMello very well. He was my prefect in the years 1955-1956. I was a boarder since age seven from 1949 until 1958. So I had many prefects through those years. Most of the prefects, both Indian and Spanish, were really cruel, especially to boarders they disliked. I was one of the recalcitrant ones and so I suffered many beatings, knocks to my head, and even caning. Rest assured, Bill, your brother was not one of them and if I remember him well, it is because he was the kindest Regent I ever had. He was most even-handed and fair in his dealings with us, and never once raised his voice or his hand to any of us. He was really conscientious about taking care of the kids entrusted to him, not only physically, but emotionally as well. He must have known how difficult it was for us to be there without family and confined for three months at a time within the walls of St. Mary's. He was the only Prefect I remember who made it a point to take his boarders on an outing every week (usually on Sundays). He would take us fishing to Mazagaon Docks, or to the Mazagaon Gardens. We were all so happy under his care.

When I was a boarder I had Regents who had their favorites and allowed them to get away with misbehavior, while others were punished for deeds which to us boarders were really not serious at all. My correspondent goes on to say:

> Tony never showed any favoritism towards any particular boarder, unlike all the other Prefects I know. I'm sure he may have liked some of us more than the others, but he never revealed it either in word or deed. We all felt like one family under him. I feel in my heart that he was fond of me particularly as he sensed my emotional need. Once when a bigger boy punched me in the face, he turned his face away as if nothing had happened. But before he did, I saw the look in his eyes. It was as if he were telling me, "Fight back, be a man!" Maybe if I did, he would have come to my rescue, who knows? He was just a great guy and a wonderful Regent to have. I wish the other Regents had learned a thing or two from him!

I can well imagine a Regent being reluctant to take his charges on an outing outside the confines of the school walls. He would have had to cope with an assortment of characters and personalities in wide open spaces and be accountable for their safety and behavior when in the company of outsiders. I clearly recall one such outing which Tony organized where he brought some of those boys to our home to sample Mum's home cooked food and to enjoy the company of our family. I could clearly see they relished the food and I had a great day in their company.

The following letter comes from another ex-boarder who had Tony as his Regent:

> I remember Fr. Tony very well because he was the only Regent who was well-liked by *all* the boys. In fact we could not wait for school to finish so that we could be with him. He always

had a smile on his face, was always calm, cool and collected. He never got angry and never ever raised his hand to any of us like some of the other Regents did. To them, it was license to assert their authority by way of corporal punishment. Tony had a way about him which made the boys want to do things for him. So we all realized that we had to behave well because it would ease his burden. Of course, when we misbehaved or broke the rules, he told us off but in a manner which did not deprive us of our dignity. He told us we were doing the wrong thing but he never demeaned us in any way. He showed us he was in charge but did it on a give and take basis. He never exerted his authority in a way that made him look good and us boys bad. He was the best Regent I ever had and I can say that with a good deal of authority since I spent my entire school life at St. Mary's boarding school and had a number of Regents. None of them compare in any way to Tony. Bill, he was the best Regent I had.

Tony must have enjoyed his regency at St. Mary's. He loved kids, their spontaneity and laughter, their energy and enthusiasm for life. It was a tough task to balance maintaining discipline while yet connecting with the young ones and encouraging them to enjoy learning, sport, and group activity. It was also exhausting—as any parent who manages a couple of young kids will testify, never mind looking after some twenty to thirty as in Tony's case.

If this responsibility were not enough, Tony was also assigned to teaching classes, mainly teaching English in middle school. The classes comprised of both day scholars as well as boarders. This brought Tony into contact with yet another group of young boys—some non-Christian—all of whom came gradually to adore him.

Why did the boys adore him? Why were they so happy in his company? Why did they rarely give him any trouble? From reading the answers sent to me by his ex-boarders I think I know why. Tony treated everyone with respect and dignity.

I received a letter from a schoolmate of mine. He was not a boarder but a student in one of the English Literature classes. This young friend went on to join the Jesuits soon after he finished school and later left the society. Here is what he has to say about his early encounters with Tony as his English teacher. Tony's English classes have the flavor of his "Nataka Nataki" English classes in Spain:

> I was thirteen years old, a rough-and-tumble 8th grader in St Mary's High School, Bombay with essentially no interest in academics. School was basically a huge bore if not an irksome burden.
>
> There was however an exception—the English Literature class. Tony was our English Literature teacher and this class was by far the most popular. Tony's broad smile, infectious enthusiasm and warm reach out to every student, made learning really fun. He found ingenious and creative ways to get every student interested and involved even in mundane English grammar. Five minutes before the close of each class he'd shut the books and launch into a joke-sharing session. This was heresy in the pedantic and doctrinaire teaching approach in India. But that was typical Tony—breaking boundaries in helping those in his care to live, laugh and learn.

The Tony I remembered before he went to the Novitiate was a strict, dogmatic, and categorical person. The person I encountered after his return from Spain was quite different. I wondered where Tony picked up this manner of dealing so gently and with so much understanding with his young charges, never giving them cause to complain against him. I had always thought it was because he had read a book called *Summerhill* which he mentions in the *Awareness* tapes but a friend sent me a letter from Tony which shows he read this book only in 1973.

When I read that letter, I knew that Tony already had, very early in his life, the makings of an understanding human being, respecting everyone with whom he came into contact. Moreover, he must have had a very open, clear-sighted mind in order to deal with youngsters in his care with such delicacy and understanding. Tony must already have nurtured the same ideals and philosophies on the subject years before he even laid eyes on Summerhill. He was in fact practicing in 1955-56, what he was advocating from a book he would read years later!

A little story I heard recently demonstrates the innocence and wonder of children and I can just hear Tony roaring with laughter, were he to have heard it himself.

A woman was driving along a freeway with her little six-year-old son in his child restraint in the back seat, when a woman in the convertible ahead stood up and waved. She was stark naked! The mother is reeling from shock, wondering what her little six-year-old is thinking when he shouts, "Mommy, that lady is very bad. She isn't wearing her seat belt!"

Such is the innocence of children and Tony must have understood this quality when he dealt with the boys in the boarding school.

Tony left St. Mary's after a year, perhaps much to the disappointment of his wards. For the next two years of his Regency (1956-58) he was assigned to teach English Literature at Vinayalaya to the Juniors.

In his Foreword to one of Tony's books, the late Fr. Paramanand Diwarkar SJ gives us a vivid word picture of how Tony functioned during these years:

> The first image of Tony deMello that I cherish goes back thirty years—and precisely to Lonavala, to the very house that much later became the home of the Sadhana Institute.
>
> Tony was then a Jesuit student, but engaged in teaching the young men who had just finished their novitiate. The whole group had come up to St Stanislaus' Villa for a brief holiday. I remember Tony with a batch of Juniors, as we called them, sitting under the trees outside the kitchen and cleaning vegetables for the day's meals, whilst he regaled a very receptive audience with his inexhaustible fund of stories.[1]

---

[1] *The Prayer of the Frog–I*, pp. xvii-xix.

We have already seen how Tony conducted his English classes in Spain as well as St. Mary's. I would believe that in these two years Tony got better and better at it. He believed in making learning fun. I see this fun element even later on when he is giving his *Awareness* or *Discovery of Life* Conferences. It would seem that wherever there was Tony there was laughter—and serious learning disguised as fun. There is no doubt of his exceptional ability as a teacher.

So it comes as a surprise, refreshing in its way, to find someone who did not quite like Tony as a teacher. This Jesuit writes:

> I was not a Junior whenTony was a Regent in Vinay, having joined in June 1957. But for a whole year, Tony gave us Novices (some 52 then!), a weekly evening hour's class in English. And it was at the beginning of those classes that my relations with Tony could scarcely have had a worse start. I couldn't stomach what appeared to me as Tony's put down of various guys who made mistakes in grammar and pronunciation, and my way of showing displeasure was by guffawing exaggeratedly whenever Tony made any one of his innumerable cracks at their expense. It was a return of compliment that Tony couldn't stomach me either. We also had a weekly essay to write for him, and I had filled my essay-copy book with what I thought were lovely ornate doodles, with caricatures of Hazlitt and the like. That copy book was shown in annoyance by Tony to the Novice Master. That gave the Novice Master an opportunity to ground me and grind me into humility; but this only made the distance between Tony and me much wider.

He must have truly got under Tony's skin if he could get Tony to complain to the Novice Master. One would believe that the antagonism between the two would be life-long after an incident like that. This Jesuit continues:

> End of that scenario. In June 1960, after the Novitiate and a year of the Juniorate, I went to De Nobili College for Philosophy, and Tony was still there after his ordination for the fourth

year of Theology. We rarely met, because of the then prevalent "separation of communities," but whenever we did I can only remember that, despite the past, it was always with cordiality.[2]

It is a tribute to both of them that their antagonism did not survive. In fact, some years later, one of them would do the other a historic good turn.

It is possibly during these two years of his regency that Tony and his team wrote those little promotional booklets on life in the novitiate. A close Jesuit friend of his tells me that he was the one who printed the booklets for Tony and "they sold like hot cakes." He is not sure why Tony did not continue writing more of the same type of booklets but he thinks that maybe Tony felt he had explained the situation well enough and wanted to move on to other chapters of his life.

This, in fact, is exactly what Tony did.

---

[2] In the "old" Society there was "separation of communities." This meant that Novices could not mix with Juniors, Philosophers could not mix with Theologians, Juniors could not mix with Theologians, and so on.

CHAPTER FIVE

THEOLOGY

THE PAPAL ATHENAEUM IN Pune founded in 1883 was origi-
nally located at Kandy in Sri Lanka. It was meant to cater to
the formation needs of priests for the whole of India. After India's
independence in 1947 it became increasingly difficult to go to Sri
Lanka. So in 1955 the Athenaeum was shifted to Pune. Later it
came to be called Jnana Deepa Vidyapeeth (JDV).

JDV is a huge campus. The JDV buildings are in the center of the
campus surrounded by the various Houses—Papal Seminary, SVD
Fathers, De Nobili, etc. Religious from various Orders and Congregations, and seminarians from all over India come here to read
Philosophy and Theology.

De Nobili College is the Jesuit House attached to JDV. It houses
the Philosophers as well as the Theologians. Jesuits from all the
Provinces in India come to JDV for their studies. So De Nobili
serves as a kind of cosmopolitan House where people from various
cultures, backgrounds, and—in Tony's time—countries rub shoulders with each other. In fact in Tony's time the foreign students/
missionaries were aplenty. It was a great place for broadening one's
horizons. De Nobili College is where Tony resided when he came to
do his Theology at JDV in 1958.

A Spanish ex-Jesuit who was Tony's close friend at the time
writes:

All my Jesuit formation ran parallel to Tony's, since we both
joined in the same year. I reached Bombay from Spain, only one

month after taking my First Vows. I was then nineteen. Tony and I studied Latin, Greek and Marathi together in our Juniorate, to which I had to add English because when I arrived Bombay I knew hardly any English. Tony was responsible for teaching the new arrivals from Spain English and his classes were most enjoyable besides being instructive. He made learning fun and we Spaniards soon picked up the basics of the language with no stress at all. Besides that, there is very little to report about those early days because they were uneventful. The next step in the formation is Philosophy. Since he was one of the brightest in the Juniorate he was sent to Spain to study Philosophy. I continued my studies in India.

We met again in Theology and studied together for four years. As usual he was outstanding. In the second year he was chosen to be the Beadle (Official-in-charge) of the entire Theologate. At that time it was full: there were a number of Spaniards, some belonging to Bombay Province, some to the Gujarat Province. There were Australians (for me the best-balanced group), Americans from the Patna and Jamshedpur Province, Belgians from the Ranchi Province and Maltese from the Santal-Parganas area. There were many Malayalis and Tamils from the South Indian Provinces. Also a few Germans and more Belgians from Calcutta, a couple of Frenchies also, not counting all the Indians from Bombay and Gujarat (I was forgetting those for the Belgaum-Goa Province). So, to be a Beadle of this humanity, wasn't very easy, but he did very well for himself.

As for Theology as such, he was the usual brilliant student. We had few but interesting meetings. In them he already showed his more human approach to morals. I will always remember one particular discussion on whether masturbation could be understood without calling it a sin. He managed to come out with some intelligent proposition that the Professors did not want, or wish to contradict.

To fully understand Tony you have to have a good perspective of his whole life. Tony did brilliantly in his exams and could definitely have gone on to become a professor of scripture but he was destined for other things. With Tony's brains, it could be very normal that he would be picked up to be a Professor, normally of Theology. Why wasn't Tony chosen to be a Professor? He had the brains, he had the push, and he had all the qualities. But, according to me, this was not meant to be. It was not the path in which Tony would bring about all that was in him, and that would come with the Spiritual Renovation of the Church and Christians.

My Spanish correspondent says that Tony did brilliantly in his exams. I thought it might be good to give the reader an idea of what kind of subjects they covered in Theology. Of course, I had no clue about these matters. But my trusty Jesuit/ex-Jesuit correspondents came to my aid here. One of them kindly sent me the following information:

Here are some of the subjects that are done in Theology: Study of Old Testament and New Testament. There are specialized subjects within the study of the Bible. For example the Wisdom books (Psalms, Ecclesiastes, etc.) are studied separately. So also the Prophets form one subject, Minor Prophets another. St. Paul is studied separately (Pauline Theology) as is John's Gospel and Letters (Johanine Theology). Moral Theology and Ethics are important subjects as is Canon Law. There are also Church History, Marian Theology, Homiletics and Doctrine. This is not a full list of the subjects. I merely mention them to give an idea of the kind of studies the Theologian pursues.

These are highly specialized and technical subjects and most lay persons would have difficulty in pronouncing some of them (e.g., Phenomenological Studies and Hermeneutics), leave alone understand what they mean.

My correspondent from Spain continues:

The examinations were mostly Vivas with just a few written examinations. Many considered oral exams unfair since not everyone is able to express themselves verbally. But that is how it was. The priest was after all going to be expressing himself verbally throughout his priestly life anyway.

Perhaps the most difficult exam to clear was the "Ad Auds." This was the exam that qualified a person to hear confessions. For this he needed to have a thorough knowledge of morals and the stance of the Church on all moral matters. This called for very comprehensive knowledge of a vast number of issues—what exactly constitutes or does not constitute a sin, how grave is the sin, are there extenuating circumstances and so on.

Tony's Spanish companion quoted earlier describes the Comprehensive Orals that came at the end of the fourth year of Theology:

> If you have crossed successfully all the exams, still there is a final hurdle. At the end of the 4th year Theology, just before you leave the study house, there is a Broad Final Exams, lasting two hours, in which you have to defend all the philosophy and all the theology you have studied along the career. In fact this exam is called "Ad Gradum," to obtain the possibility to be a professed. And, some poor fellows who have crossed all the hurdles, sometimes in this last Exam, they fail, or "are failed." In these cases the feeling can run quite high.[1]

From all the accounts I have received, Tony was as popular in the Theologate as he was everywhere he went. He attracted many friends and companions and most of those whom I have spoken to have remarked on how he attracted people to him like a magnet. He had a way about him, a charisma which made people want to be in his company. The same Spanish friend continues:

> Tony had a wonderful way of talking. After lunch and after supper

---

[1] Failing this exam meant the concerned Jesuit would not be granted the Fourth Vow. Apart from vows of poverty, chastity, and obedience, Jesuits take a Fourth Vow of "special obedience to the sovereign pontiff in regard to [the] missions, according to the same apostolic letters and the Constitutions." This is taken with Final Vows. In the old days, and in Tony's time, not all Jesuits were permitted to take this vow—only those of exceptional promise.

Jesuits have a period of recreation. Each one picks up those he wants to talk to and, normally, in De Nobili, some went round and round the inner courtyards. Others (Tony was one of them) would go up and down a fixed area: moving forward and backward. Tony would have the largest group of ups and downs. You could hear his laughter; he controlled the situation, though most probably he did not mean to. He just attracted people to him.

In Theology some started moving, in a small way, to do some social work, around the place, or in town. I am not aware that Tony belonged to any of these groups. This is not for or against him. He had his way and I believe it is important to keep this in mind to fully understanding what life was leading him to.

While Tony was occupied with his studies at JDV, I was in school. I was generally a very poor student and paid scant attention to my studies or to anything other than having a good time. During this period, an incident occurred in my life which led to an encounter between Tony, our parents, and me.

My parents were constantly extolling the virtues of their eldest child and suggesting that I learn from and emulate him. I may have given them the impression that I was listening attentively to them. But it was only an impression. Their words went in one ear and out the other, without registering in my brain. I heard much the same in school from the Jesuits. They were interminably reminding me that I had such a brilliant brother, headed for big things within the Society. I should follow his example in behavior and academic achievement.

I was extremely proud of my brother but I was never tempted to emulate him. To do that was too much hard work. I preferred the easy life. Moreover, whenever we met, Tony was always very careful to play down his own brilliance and never admonished me for my "underachievement" in studies or my lack of religious fervor. That approach from Tony sounded like music to my ears, but it probably encouraged an undesirable degree of complacency within me. While I was in awe of Tony, I was also somewhat cautious of him. That childhood spanking and his fanatical discourses on the Church and the Pope had left their mark on me.

My parents were at their wits end. They had one son who was a high achiever while the other seemed to be the class dunce. It was becoming evident to them that in a competitive world their youngest child was headed for a disastrous future.

By now I had turned truancy into a fine art and Dad was constantly getting notes from my teachers complaining about my disruptive behavior. To add to this when I was around fifteen years old, I also found I was developing an interest in girls like all young adolescent boys my age. In those days the closest thing to a thrill that we could aspire to was to be allowed to hold hands with a girl. Anything else was the stuff of dreams.

I discovered to my delighted amazement that there were a few girls from a convent school who were happy to join my accomplices and me in cutting classes and accompany us on our wanderings. On one such occasion, one of the girls handed me an envelope with strict instructions to open it in private. When I got home I opened the envelope and found a note and a couple of photographs of the group which were taken by one of the boys. This girl and I featured prominently next to each other in those pictures. When I read the note my heart skipped a couple of beats. She said she really loved me and thought I was the best guy she had met. There were other innocent statements of love and a promise to meet again soon.

All these delightful sentiments and I hadn't even got to hold hands with her! Common sense told me I should destroy the note and the photographs immediately. My ego dictated otherwise. There was no way I was going to destroy this treasure. And who could blame me? Here was a girl saying that she loved me and preferred me to all the other boys. I decided to keep this note as testimony of her love for me.

The house we lived in was not large and I did not have any particular hiding places to stash my treasure. The only place I could think of was under the mattress of my bed. A few days later, the maid was cleaning the house and discovered the envelope. She innocently handed it over to Mum! A few days earlier, I had received my year-end report card which stated that I would have to repeat my class. As if this news was not bad enough for my parents, there now was this "love note" to contend with.

When I got home from school, Mum and Dad were waiting for me. This time, I could see that Dad was not himself. The look on his face told me that he was about to make me the exception in the family and he did not spare me when he dished out the cane. I took the punishment manfully since I was conditioned to believe that I had done something wrong. I had not effectively broken any of "the rules" but the note must have caused a great deal of concern. This non-achiever son was now venturing forth with young girls within school hours. Whatever next!

After Dad had finished with me it was my turn to make a statement. This I did. I told them that if I was to concentrate on my studies and change my ways, I wanted to be enrolled in a boarding school. I told them that it was not possible for me to concentrate on my studies when my sister's friends kept coming over just when it was study time. Besides, after being "exposed" I knew that word would soon go around that the note and photos had been discovered by my parents. Boarding school was my only escape and I was determined to go there to avoid the discomfiture of facing my friends and That Girl in particular.

Blaming my sisters for my underachievement was a lame excuse and I knew it was. I expected my parents to jump at my suggestion so that they would not have the responsibility of supervising me and controlling me. But my parents had other views and announced they were going to get Tony to talk some sense into me. The trip was three days away. I don't believe I slept in all that time, worrying about what Tony would say to me. I knew he would not, could not, spank me now. But that would have been preferable to his lashing out verbally at me. I imagined the disappointed look on his face and dreaded meeting him. I looked up to this guy and the last thing I wanted was to face his disapproval and scorn.

The day finally arrived and I remember the anxious train ride to Pune during which not a word was spoken. We arrived at DeNobili College and were admitted into the parlor by Fr. Vincent Banon, a close friend of Tony's. Tony entered the parlor and my knees buckled when I saw the serious look on his face. I remember wondering whether my parents had somehow already contacted him to give him a preview. Mum began by narrating everything she knew about my antics. (I could have told her a few more things she was unaware of but I was not about ready to be lynched.) Then, to my utter embarrassment and fear, she handed over the letter and photographs to Tony.

He listened patiently, put the package containing the damning evidence into his pocket, and said, "Very well, Mum and Dad, you stay here, Fr. Banon will keep you company. Bill, you come with me, we are going to take a walk in the garden."

We walked in silence along a path bordered by some very beautiful rose bushes in full bloom and then Tony found a bench and we sat down. Tony looked at me with what I imagined to be accusing eyes. I cringed, bracing myself for what was to come next. Words can sometimes hurt much more than the cane.

I loved him dearly and felt so ashamed that my behavior had merited a lecture from him. Instead, in such a gentle voice that my heart swelled with emotion, he said, "Bill, Mum and Dad are concerned about you and I can understand the cause of their worries. You are a bright boy and could do so much better in school. All they want is for you to do your best and I am quite sure you can do better than you are right now." His voice had a touch of softness to it and it took me completely by surprise. Where was the brother who had spanked me for swearing at my sister? His gentle voice caused me to relax a bit. I went on to repeat what I had told my parents about the distractions at home and that I really would perform better if I went to a boarding school. I had decided to stick to my lame excuse to see if it would get me out of trouble with Tony.

I distinctly remember that when Tony spoke to me about doing better, the gentle tone of his voice made me immediately resolve that I was indeed going to do better and perform to my full potential, whatever it was. He was not pontificating or patronizing. He was talking to me man-to-man and it made me feel good about myself. It was almost as if I had done nothing wrong but that I had to correct my ways for my own good.

Tony tried to talk me out of going to boarding school. I knew he was the Boarding Prefect at St. Mary's High not long before so this response surprised me. I told him I wanted to get as far away from the scene of my "crimes" as possible —to make a fresh start. I suggested that I go to a boarding school quite far away to the north of Mumbai. I had heard many interesting things about that school. Tony pointed out that life in a boarding school, no matter where, was far from pleasant. That it was instead a lonely life away from family and friends and that the routine was rigid.

While I was pondering this, he pulled out that "dreaded" envelope with the letter and photographs and said, "Alright Bill, we will discuss that a bit later. Let's discuss this letter and photographs which Mummy gave me."

My eyes were on that envelope and I recoiled in horror at the thought he might open it. I was mortified enough when Mum read the letter and I felt terribly ashamed at the thought that I was to be exposed twice in a few days. Instead Tony said, "Bill, Mummy has given me these. They are not mine to read or look at. They are yours. What would you like me to do with them? Do you want them back?" My head nearly fell off my shoulders—I was shaking it so violently—as I protested, "No, no I don't want them back." Tony was calm when he said, "Bill, Mum tells me that this girl says she loves you. Do you love this girl?"

Now, to tell you the truth, I had not even thought about whether I loved this girl or whether I was simply attracted to her because she was to me. I would gladly have denounced her just to get out of my current predicament. My reply was an emphatic, "Nooooo, I do not love this girl." He then said, "Look Bill, you are so young and have a whole life ahead of you. There are so many girls out there and you need to get to know many more girls before you decide which one you really love. But if you want this letter and the photographs back, they are yours to keep. No one has the right to take them away from you."

I could not believe my ears! Still, my response to this was a violent

No with a good deal of headshaking. He then asked if he should tear them up, since he certainly did not want to see the photographs or read the letter. With my permission, he tore them up in front of me and threw the pieces into a rubbish bin nearby. Then he said, "Come on Bill, let's go back and talk to Mum and Dad."

My step was already lighter and I literally skipped along with him, back to the parlor. I remember feeling elated, even overjoyed and my view of my brother changed forever. He had gone from being a tyrant to being my hero and savior. Mind you, I was not sure what he was going to say in front of my parents; but I was prepared for anything after he had been so gentle and understanding with me.

When we got back to the parlor, Mum was waiting expectantly— to see me shamed, head bowed in contrition. Dad was, in fact, smiling as if he expected what was to come. Tony made small talk for a while and then, as if on cue, Fr. Banon excused himself.

After he had left, Tony addressed our parents and said he understood their concern perfectly well but that there were other things to consider in my favor as well. He repeated what I had told him about the distractions at home and that he thought it may be beneficial if I were to be enrolled in a boarding school for a year's trial to start with, just to see if it helped me with my studies.

In the garden, I was convinced he would oppose my request to go to a boarding school and here he was, supporting me. Moreover, before Mum could bring up the subject about the letter and photographs, Tony said that he and I had "mutually" decided to dispose of them and that they now had no cause for any further concern. He did not say whether he had read the letter or not and Mum must have had second thoughts about asking him if he had. The way he put it, he left me and Mum respectively with our dignity intact. I have to say that scored very high in my book. All through the encounter, he kept his composure never once showing any sign of taking either one side or the other.

My parents did send me to St. Mary's High School as a boarder. I remembered my silent pledge to Tony and thereafter not only took to my studies but excelled on the sports field as well. That's something Tony was always in awe of. Whenever we met, he would smile broadly and remind me of my sporting exploits and point out that he himself was clumsy and flatfooted!

After that encounter with Tony, I was convinced that a miracle had occurred in my life. I had expected to encounter a strict, rigid Tony, applying the rules, putting me in my place, and lecturing me. Instead I discovered a completely changed man. His attitude encouraged me to strive to be a much better student and person.

While writing this book, I discussed this incident with one of my correspondents who has become a friend over the years since that first biography. I was so touched to receive this from her:

> Tony loved you and accepted you right where you were, trusting that you did not need fixing. How awesome for you to be loved by your brother in such a way as to allow you to be who you are and not needing to change one jot or tittle about yourself . . . like the way God loves us. . . .

Following this incident, I discovered that Tony accepted me for what I was—a young brother lost in his own world. He would have remembered his own childhood, attending catechism classes coupled with his school studies. He took to these like a duck to water; but he realized that not everyone was cast in the same mold. He applied this understanding to me, his younger brother, as well. He did not expect me to emulate his academic and spiritual behavior in any way. Throughout his life, I don't believe Tony ever forced people to listen to and blindly follow what he taught. He said what he had to say and left people to take their own course of action.

This encounter with Tony and my parents encouraged me to speak more freely on any subject with Tony, without fear of rebuttal or disapproval. I began to take comfort in the fact that Tony never expected anything from me except that I attempt to do my best in whatever I undertook.

In those days, it was only the Jesuits who were ordained after three years of theology and they completed their fourth year as priests. (Today they do not enjoy this privilege anymore.) Tony was ordained on the twenty-fourth of March 1961. I served at his First Mass at St. Peter's Church, Bandra where he was ordained. There were a number of Tony's Indian and Spanish companions who were ordained along with him. I recall our parents organizing a big function to celebrate the event and inviting a number of friends and relatives, including those Spanish newly-ordained who did not have their families to celebrate the event with them. Tony only made a brief appearance at the function, after which he excused himself and left.

He returned to Pune to complete his fourth year of Theology. In the next year—1962—he went for his "Tertianship." One might ask what is the Tertianship and why is it called so? Once again my correspondents helped me out:

> "Tertianship" is like a Novitiate again. It is compulsory before the Jesuit is allowed to take his Last Vows. It is usually a period of eight months or so during which he does a Long Retreat again and has other specialised pastoral and relevant studies.

On February 2, 1965, Tony took his Last Vows, including the Fourth Vow, which made him "fully Professed."

Two years prior to that he was sent to the USA where he got a master's in Pastoral Counseling from Loyola University, Chicago. This was probably the foundation of his reasoning to merge spirituality with psychological counseling. But the time was not yet ripe for him to venture in this direction. Instead, when he returned to India, he was sent to Rome in 1964 to do a postgraduate degree in Spiritual Theology at the Pontifical Gregorian University. I have heard that Tony wanted to learn more about Clinical Psychology but instead, in Rome, he found that he was learning more about spirituality. In fact he returned from Rome without completing his studies. He was then sent to the Catholic Ashram in Nashik.

There he completed his studies in Marathi in 1966 and was ready for his first pastoral appointment as a Jesuit priest.

CHAPTER SIX

MISSION IMPOSSIBLE AND THE SPANISH CONNECTION

IN TONY'S TIME, AS now, when the Jesuits spoke of a "mission station" in India they were generally talking of remote areas where the people were poor, marginalized, often exploited, and oppressed. Working in a mission station involved hardship, living away from the comforts of the large city, dealing with people who were struggling to fulfill their basic needs; a people who had the mindset that it was their fate to be poor and downtrodden—always. It meant bringing these people hope for the future besides merely bringing about social uplift. This was not an easy task.

The Spanish Jesuits came to work in the Mumbai Province of the Jesuits when the German Jesuits working there were interned or repatriated during the First World War. For the Spaniards who came to India the word "missions" would have conjured up images of faraway lands filled with masses of people who did not know Christ, needing to be "saved."

One Spaniard who was to feature largely in Tony's life for a time was Fr. Vincent Ferrer SJ. Biographies of Ferrer mention that when a mere teenager he fought in the Spanish Civil War and the war's carnage inspired him to fight every form of human suffering—which was what moved him to join the Jesuits and come to India as a missionary.

A Spanish Jesuit who was junior to Ferrer at the time told me there were reports that when Ferrer first came to the Manmad mission he would enter every village with a crucifix in hand, proclaiming the Good News. This could be a fanciful story that seems unlikely given that the man was a war veteran. Or it could be true. What is well-known, however, is that Ferrer soon realized the plight of those poor people in the Manmad area. They were *Dalits* belonging to what was largely spoken of in those days as the "lower castes."

Ferrer, along with a couple of Spanish Jesuits, began to throw himself into developmental work helping the farmers build wells and percolation tanks so that water from the monsoons would percolate down into the water table instead of simply flowing away wasted. The international charitable organization *MISEREOR* got into the act and began helping out with Food-for-Work Schemes.

The stage was now set for the kind of drama for which not all the players were ready. On to this stage came Tony in 1966, enter left. This was the ardent Jesuit who had this strong desire to work in the missions probably ever since that retreat that he often mentioned later. In that retreat the Retreat Master had told them that the ideal of every Jesuit should be to serve in the missions. Having just spent a year mastering Marathi in Nashik he must have been raring to go.

This desire on the part of the younger set is explained by a Jesuit who was familiar with that era:

> At that time, many Jesuits were being trained (or opted) for the Jesuit schools and colleges in Bombay. Accordingly, there was much talk among the younger Jesuits about the fact that living in this city, in school and college communities, was "comfortable." Hence, the sentiment (and talk) arose about "giving up" the comforts of city life and opting for the missions, where life was far more arduous. In this connection, I had heard that Tony on his return from abroad, opted for the missions, and was posted there. His stint in the districts provided little or no scope for the expertise gained from his native abilities (speaking) and M.A. in Counselling (insights), and so he was often out for talks and counselling. However, the perspectives that he gained there in the district were invaluable in balancing city-based mores against more "down-to-earth" initiatives.

What he heard about Tony opting for the missions is true. According to one of his colleagues, Tony had gone to his Provincial to request him to send him to the mission areas. Unfortunately for him, the Provincial beat him to the punch and asked Tony to go to Manmad even before Tony could ask! Apparently he always felt "cheated" out of the opportunity to ask instead of being sent. Tony went to Manmad as Superior of the mission which was arguably a great responsibility for one so young and inexperienced in mission life.

It would have been a strenuous but not unduly difficult task had there been no Ferrer connection. By now Ferrer was going his somewhat brash way oblivious to the rumblings in certain quarters, rumblings that were not missed by the new young Superior who was Indian and sensitive to Indian sentiment and the local situation. Very soon, all hell was to break loose.

Ferrer established a large "model" farm in the area, fertile, with good water supply, thanks to the new wells he had built. He employed local labor and started a co-operative for local farmers, aiding them to become self-sufficient.

Apparently Tony could sense the storm brewing and was advising diplomacy and caution which fell on deaf ears. From what I gather from some who were close to the action at the time it appears that while Ferrer did great development work he had no time for those who had objections—well-founded or otherwise—to his undiplomatic way of going about things. With *MISEREOR*'s backing Ferrer had all the money and machinery he needed for his work. This made it very hard for Tony to control Ferrer and his Spanish companions and one Jesuit says, "Even the Provincial could not control him. Ferrer was a Provincial unto himself."

The young and raw Tony must have found it very challenging to not only deal with a very delicate situation but to also control and counsel strong-minded men who were determined in their own sincere way to help the local population, with no regard for whom they were upsetting in the process.

In 1967, Tony was transferred from Manmad to Shirpur within

the same mission and continued as Superior of the mission. In addition he was also appointed to the Province Consult. As Superior, he had to supervise the finances of the mission, continue with the religious duties first put in place by the founding Jesuits, and set targets and aims for the entire district. As a Consultor he would be required to attend the occasional Province Consult in Bombay. These meetings are held to discuss major decisions about policy or personnel. A Consult is held once every quarter unless circumstances require an emergency meeting.

In writing this book I have had information and stories coming in from the rarest of quarters. I truly appreciate the generosity and sincerity with which people have shared their memories of Tony. How true it is that an act of kindness is never forgotten. The following story comes from a nun who was one of the pioneers who started her Congregation's Shirpur mission.

Her story is from the mid 1960s and she remembers it after all these years:

> We had just established a primary school at Dhule. We were now looking to reach out to other places. One day our Superior in Dhule sent me with another Sister to see what we could do in Shirpur. We met the Jesuit Superior there. He seemed to be a man of few words. He did not explain anything to us. The next thing we knew was we had to live in a godown (warehouse) which doubled as a dispensary! This was a strange and helpless situation for us. Strange for obvious reasons. Helpless because we did not know what to do. If we returned to Dhule what would happen to the girls in our care? So we were stuck with the situation.
>
> After a month of this difficult situation Fr. Tony deMello came there as the new Superior. What a refreshing change. He would visit us every day and ask if there was anything we needed. He insisted that we have our meals with the Fathers. He would regale us with humorous stories and jokes at table. He would tease us Sisters a lot! For the first time we saw the new Indian Mass with all of us sitting cross-legged on the floor.

Then our Superiors came to visit us. Fr. deMello called us with our Provincial and her assistant for a meeting. He explained what was needed in the new mission which was a predominantly tribal area: the education of girls, need for a dispensary and healing ministry, socio-pastoral work among women and so on. The next day a truckload of necessary provisions arrived. The opening of our new mission at Shirpur was confirmed. Work began on a new building. The foundation for a hospital was laid. We weathered many storms and upheavals after that. Today Shirpur is a thriving mission station and the hospital is catering to the local people. Whenever I think of those early days of the mission I always remember Fr. deMello for his kindness to us. He was such a saving grace.

An average day in Tony's life at this time would have been to leave early in the morning for a remote village, cater to the spiritual needs of the people, celebrate Mass for the Catholics of the area, have a meeting with the catechists, instruct them and others in the village, and meet Jesuits and associates doing developmental or other work in the area. If time permitted he would go to another village or return late at night to Shirpur. In a few days it would be another village. His day would also involve looking after the smooth running of any schools that came under his watch, co-ordinating efforts of various members of his team, and so on.

His work would often require him to spend many hours driving, often at night and according to a friend of Tony's, he took to smoking cigarettes to "stay awake while driving through the night."[1]

All of this would have been a cakewalk for Tony. This is the kind of hard but fulfilling life he had envisaged—bringing hope to the downtrodden, denying self to reach out to others, all for the greater glory of God. What Tony could not have foreseen was a phenomenon called Ferrer. Ferrer continued acting more or less as a power

---

[1] Later when he went into his "Gandhian" phase he gave up this habit and never took it up again.

unto himself, going his tactless albeit well-meaning way, with no regard for authority either Jesuit or governmental.

The Ferrer controversy raged on. Ferrer challenged anyone who came in his way and this included Tony. This does not take away from the fact that Ferrer meant well. He had a great vision for the poor about whom he was passionate. He was not going to allow any person or thing to come in the way of fulfilling his dream of a better life for his beloved Dalits. Going through the proper channels would have entailed a lot of unnecessary delay and Ferrer was eager to proceed without interference.

It was rumored or suspected at the time that the real instigators of the Ferrer controversy were the money lenders and politicians who felt threatened by the fact that the Dalits were becoming self-dependent and might soon be demanding their rights. While this may well be true it is not easily verifiable today. What is known for sure is that Ferrer was accused of helping these people in the name of development while actually following a hidden agenda of converting everyone to Christianity. He was labeled a "subversive" and soon some elements started a "Ferrer Quit India" campaign. Accusations flew back and forth and the entire area reached a boiling point with Ferrer's farmers starting a counter-protest in favor of him. The fact that foreign monies were coming into India was another factor. This moved the government of Maharashtra to start an inquiry into the matter and the upshot of it was that Ferrer was deported from India in 1969.[2]

Tony's time in Manmad and Shirpur was truly an ordeal. It was his first venture into the "real" world. Till then, he had led the rela-

---

[2] By then Tony was long gone from the arena. Later, through the intervention of the then-Prime Minister Indira Gandhi, Ferrer was permitted to come back to India but not Maharashtra. He did return to India, after he had left the Society and got married, and settled in Andhra Pradesh where he vindicated himself by doing yeoman work in community development. He died just a couple of years ago at the ripe old age of ninety-two and is survived by his wife and sons who continue his good work in the region.

tively sheltered and protected life of a student. Now he was thrown into the harsh reality of Jesuit work and in the middle of a highly controversial and tumultuous situation. It called for all of his diplomatic skills, his administrative acumen, and his determination to ensure that controversy did not engulf the entire Jesuit community.

These years in Manmad and Shirpur must have also been a time for serious reflection for the young Tony about what he truly wanted to do with his life as a Jesuit. On the one hand, there was the option of continuing to work in the missions. On the other hand, he must have felt a strong calling to dedicate his life to assisting people spiritually and psychologically. His recent studies in Rome and Chicago in both spirituality and psychology (and their inherent links) had obviously been initiated due to his strong and natural inclination to these areas. Inevitably, he must have felt strongly drawn to this vocation.

One of the responsibilities that Tony undertook here was to act as counselor to many priests and young scholastics. An ex-Jesuit who was sent to Tony when the former encountered a few personal and vocational problems writes:

I joined the Jesuits at the tender age of sixteen—not the wisest decision in retrospect. Four years into Jesuit training and I found myself struggling with all sorts of internal demons, some typical for a young man of my age, others a consequence of a difficult family background.

I had first met Tony when he was a Regent in my school. Now Tony crossed my life's path again when he was the Superior at Shirpur. By then he had gained a reputation for being not just a deeply spiritual person, but a wise and effective counsellor. I was sent to see him and welcomed the opportunity, remembering the warm and engaging teacher I had encountered in my eighth grade in school. Tony ran true to form. Despite his numerous responsibilities, he set aside all and sat me down for a full-fledged day-long therapy session. I still distinctly remember how he systematically and skilfully helped me work through my issues, as we sat together on the terrace. By evening, the scales were falling off my eyes. Questions were being clarified. Actions that I needed to work on were becoming more obvious. Tony had started me on a healing journey, which while long and difficult, was to be life changing.

For the next two years, Tony always welcomed me, wherever he was, however busy, for ongoing therapy sessions that helped me along that journey. He was the most perceptive, skilled and supportive counsellor I have come across. Even today, some forty years later, I remain grateful to him for making his time and his phenomenal array of intellectual and counselling skills available to help me on my life's journey.

I believe that Manmad/Shirpur became Tony's crossroads. There was his apparent failure to control the Ferrer maelstrom. It must have set him thinking. But what came to the fore was his talent for spiritual guidance and counseling. A lot of Jesuits were sent to or streamed to him on their own at regular intervals for guidance and counseling. It was perhaps logical that the next step in his Jesuit journey was the move to Vinayalaya, the Jesuit novitiate. Appointed in 1968, it would be here, as Rector that Tony would dedicate his time and talent to the challenging task of guiding the young while further researching his fields of expertise and refining his skill at spiritual guidance and counseling.

Much was to transpire here that would make him turn his steps on to pioneering paths and seek new horizons.

Chapter Seven

RECTOR OF RULES

IN 1968, TWENTY-ONE years after he entered the Novitiate as a raw lad Tony took over as Rector of this very institute. The Novitiate was called *Vinayalaya*, which is made up of two Sanskrit words: *vinaya*—literally "leading out," also "discipline, education" and *aalaya*—"home." Perhaps *Home of Discipline* would be the most appropriate English translation of the term. It was a meaningful name for a place where men began their initiation into the life of the "contemplatives in action" that Ignatius wanted his men to be.

It may not seem important at this stage but after my research of these years I just wonder whether Tony's interpretation of *Vinayalaya* was *House of Pioneering Thinking* as in "leading out." Certainly the way he handled his position as Rector of this large institution seems to have been innovative and unusual and bears this out.

Vinayalaya (every Jesuit I have spoken to calls it "Vinay") housed the Novitiate, the Juniorate, and the language school for Marathi, known as the *Marathi Ghar* (*ghar* is Marathi for "house"). Since each of these institutions had their own directors one could ask what Tony's role was. Tony was overall-in-charge, as all Rectors are, in every Jesuit institution. In addition there were others who would come directly under Tony—the staff of the three institutions, older Jesuits who were retired and living there, and sundry others. All major decisions—should one of the novices be given the unhappy news that he should leave?—would be in consultation with the Rector. All disciplinary matters were attended to by the Rector and all permissions—from going to a movie to going on a home visit to going to another city or town on official work—were given by him.

The Rector is like the head of a household. He is responsible for everything. The buck stops with him—at least in House matters.

Already when Tony was at Manmad/Shirpur, Vinay was his stop-over House when he was passing through Mumbai or when he attended Consults. At such times he was usually asked to address the budding Jesuits. So he was already a familiar figure to the novices and Juniors and others. I have reports from some of them that they were awaiting his arrival as Rector with bated breath.

One of these said when interviewed:

> The first time I saw Tony was when he was passing through on his way back from somewhere abroad where he had gone to give a retreat in 1967. And most of us were listening to him with our tongues hanging out. He came across as quite different from anyone we had encountered before in our training. We were all spellbound.

From the questionnaires I sent out, the interviews conducted, and the information that has poured in about the Vinay years, what emerges is that after a fiery time in the mission field at Manmad/Shirpur, it was at Vinay that Tony began to find his niche and his true calling. Here was a large House that represented the foundation of a Jesuit's training. If nothing else it was a House of Rules. Tony was to begin implementing the rules in ways that were off the beaten track. Rather than an enforcer, Tony was a persuader.

What made him so effective, loved, and popular during the Vinay years? This was the question I asked many of those who knew him during this period.

First of all, Tony came across as an extremely understanding person. Perhaps this was the result of his training in America in Carl Rogers' Person-Centered Therapy which emphasizes understanding, unconditional positive regard, acceptance, and empathy. People have written to say that he seemed to understand their situation or position so well that this alone would make them feel as if half their burden was gone.

I can relate to this one having had more than one experience of this sort with him over the years. My encounter with him in DeNobili with my parents is testimony to this.

Secondly, Tony had a great sense of humor. He was an entertainer par excellence and could keep his hearers enthralled with stories, jokes, quick wit, and repartee. It was a joy to be in his company. One friend of his told me that he could write a whole book called *Jokes and Amusing Stories I Heard from Tony deMello.*

Most of the younger ones were in awe of him since his "rising star status" had preceded him before they had even met him. Apparently his position as Rector did not make him a stuffed shirt, holding on to his dignity and going about with a worried look on his face that showed the world what a burden of responsibility he was carrying. Tony broke the stereotype of "Rector." He had this great capacity to build rapport with whomever he was dealing with because he was able to get to their level. The younger ones from the *Marathi Ghar,* for instance, were thrilled to have a Rector who would play volleyball with them.

One of them says:

> He would laugh his booming laugh and tease us when we lost a point and he was great fun to be with. He was one among us and yet there was no doubting that he was the Rector and there was always mutual respect and no over-familiarity.

Another one tells of returning from some remote village in a rickety pick-up along with some of his companions and Tony. To while away the miles they started singing group songs and then one of them summoned the courage to ask the "Guru" to sing a song fully expecting he would demur:

> because gurus singing in a pick-up or anywhere for that matter are not a common sight. For us, he was the admired font and focus of wisdom, not an incarnation of Mick Jagger! Imagine our

shock and awe and delight when he started singing, "I'm forever blowing bubbles . . . pretty bubbles in the air . . . " (and quite well too!). I mention this because what has remained with me is the humanness of the moment more than anything else.

Those post-Vatican II years were transition years when the Society was moving from the "old" Society to new measures, new discipline, and a new look at everything. In the old Society there was no doubt that the Rector was "up there" while the subjects were "down here." Along with this remarkable ability that Tony had to build rapport was an equally remarkable ability to treat even the youngest member of the House as an equal.

The same scholastic who asked Tony to sing a song in the rickety truck adds:

> Any Rector who would tell an awe-stricken, tremulous nineteen-year-old who says to him, "I have heard so much about you, Father!" to "Call me Tony" is sure to earn more than respect from everyone.

And another scholastic from that period adds:

> Tony was the first Superior to treat me as an equal, to make me realize that I am responsible for my future and that I should not hide behind permissions. He made me feel like a *person* and he made me feel I was a *good* person.

Another factor that contributed to Tony's effectiveness as a Rector was his spirituality. It must be remembered that this is the man who had selected Fr. Calveras as a mentor when in Spain. Later when he was studying Theology he attended a Course in the Spiritual Exercises.

A Spanish Jesuit colleague of Tony's reports:

> With Tony I attended a Course on the Spiritual Exercises in Pune. All of us tried to present the different parts of the Retreat in modern language and terms. Tony surprised us by going

through all the possible meditations—even the Meditation on Hell and on the Application of the Senses. It was pure Calveras and very traditional!

It may come as a surprise to some to find Tony labeled as traditional. This would not be the case for long. What followed after that course were changing times. Vatican II was over in 1965. The winds of change were soon blowing in the Catholic Church with gale force. Major changes were taking place and the repercussions were being felt all over the world. For example, the pre-Vatican II concept of *Tu es sacerdos in aeternum* (You are a priest forever) was now gone and priests—young and old—and even Bishops were leaving the priesthood at an alarming rate. As is the case with all liberation movements, there is a tendency at first to go to the other extreme before counter forces and better adjustments kick in and balance is restored.

One speculates that Tony, being a thinking sort of priest as is evident, must have realized that changing times called for new thinking. I think that while getting his master's in Counseling at Loyola University, Chicago, Tony began to see the value of psychology as a useful ingredient in spirituality.

Even though Tony was in the boondocks in the three years prior to coming to Vinay he was not "lost" there. He was moving out, giving Ignatian retreats—even one abroad—and had established himself as a counselor and spiritual guide by the time he came to Vinay. Tony's preaching was exceptional and his treatment of the Spiritual Exercises was to gradually become less "traditional."

Here is a short description of how he conducted the retreat at Vinay in June 1971:

In the Ignatian retreat there is a meditation on the birth of Our Lord. Tony made it like Christmas. He organized a choir made up of a whole lot of non-retreatants from the House which went around the corridors singing "Christus Natus Est" at 11.30 in the night to wake us up for the midnight meditation on the birth of

Our Lord. Who can forget an experience like that; and a retreat like that?

It takes a special kind of thinking and self-confidence to be able to take bold steps and dare to be different. That Tony *thought* differently was evident. The novice who reported that they all had their "tongues hanging out" when Tony spoke to them was not the only one who saw this "difference."

An ex-Jesuit who was a Marathi student when Tony was appointed to Vinay says:

> Tony was a master charmer, possessed of an acute intellect that saw three steps ahead, with the words and elecutory ability to go along with it and verbalise what few others could, in ways only his quicksilver mind could devise. Also, his lightning, jackdaw mind and silver tongue enabled him to see, too, too clearly, that Mother Church could never, would never, accede to the conclusions he was grasped by. These he came to, not only through his vast and extensive reading but also through his openness to a variety of experienced contexts.

A language student of three years later says:

> Tony had an utterly different way of thinking and putting things. It was totally fascinating. I heard somewhere that someone claimed that he had been mesmerised by Tony. I hope he meant it figuratively and not literally because while Tony could be very convincing when he spoke he would equally convincingly—and constantly—tell us to challenge in our mind anything that was out of the ordinary and never to accept it blindly. Young as we were, this is what we did. I recall how in later years he and I would argue about or disagree on various issues. In fact he once said to me at a Gestalt Therapy[1] group session that he admired the fact that I never hesitated to stand up to him and challenge

---

[1] Gestalt Therapy was developed by Dr. Fritz Perls, who believed that a person could become whole by living in the present.

him—both in public and personally—on some of the things he said though we were such close friends.

Yet another quality that contributed to Tony's success as a Rector was his personal life and example. He lived a very simple life and his personal possessions were only what were essential.

The first change that Tony made when he came to Vinay was a personal one: he changed the Rector's room which was a large, spacious one.

A young Jesuit was involved here. He writes:

In 1969 I took my First Vows. Tony had already taken me under his wing and entrusted me to move his belongings from the Rector's office to a tiny, pokey room, which used to be our Socius' room. In fact, I was a Junior at that time and the Minister of the House was angry because Tony gave me the keys to his room. Normally it should have been kept with the Minister. Tony asked me to move his room while he was away at his retreat.

In fact when he came to Vinay Tony was into what the same Jesuit who moved his room calls "his Gandhian policy." Tony used to speak of living a simple life. In those days he was much impressed by Mahatma Gandhi as a son of the soil who had made such an enormous and palpable impact on the world. Like Gandhi, Tony used to fast regularly, sometimes overdoing it.

Inspired by Tony's eloquent speeches on Gandhi, a number of Jesuit scholastics decided to take this to the next level and began giving up their Western garb for simple Indian garb. They gave up their shoes for rough sandals. The life of this venture is best described in the words of the same Jesuit who used the term "Gandhian policy":

When he became the Rector here in 1968 Tony started the Gandhian policy. Of course, though I loved Tony and he was my friend I was also a rebel. And all these guys? They were all giving up their nice clothes and were wearing kurtas and lenga and so on.[2] A friend of mine and I went and took those new clothes and defiantly started wearing them. Then when it came time for them to go to De Nobili for Philosophy there were long queues of these same people to stitch new [Western] clothes and I asked Tony, "What happened to all that Gandhian policy, Tony? Now they are all standing in a queue to stitch new clothes. What happened to your Gandhian policy?"

Tony himself was in a constant state of flux. He was always experimenting with new ways of doing something and with different prayer methods. He kept what worked for him and discarded what didn't. Some he adopted. Others he adapted. He was always dynamic, never static. There were a few people who remarked that they found it hard to keep pace with Tony. They sometimes found it confusing that he was saying one thing one day and the complete opposite the next. Tony often quoted Gandhi on this topic. He would say that Gandhi's followers would often complain to him that they could not keep up with his changes—one week he would be doing one thing and the next something quite another. Gandhi would reply that he did not expect his followers to do whatever he was doing. He was still experimenting and he wished his followers to do likewise. It was typical of Tony that he did not even respond to this young Jesuit who baited him. He just let it pass.

And now for the last and, from what emerges from my research, perhaps the most important ingredient of Tony's success as a Rector—his inimitable approach to discipline. In the old Society the Rector ruled with an iron hand—not necessarily by choice but as a duty. The rules were strict and strictly adhered to. The rules in themselves were good for promoting self-discipline but were also self-defeating. They implemented discipline which is necessary in any establishment but they did not bring out the more human side

---

[2] Kurta is a loose Indian-style shirt. Lenga is what the British came to call pyjamas. It is generally white in color.

of those who hoped to serve in the Society as "soldiers of Christ." If followed strictly by the book, a Jesuit could assume for example, that as long as he followed and obeyed the rules, he need not think further. Tony set about introducing some changes which delighted and surprised the House members. His attitude would not have pleased everyone. In fact, I am informed his changes irritated some of the older members of the House. Most of the older Jesuits living there were retired or infirm and would see out their days at Vinay. I smile when I think of what some of them might have been thinking: "What does he think he is doing, changing what has been in place for centuries? If those rules were good enough for us, they are good enough for these young upstarts."

The way Tony managed the House was something that was unique. The ex-Jesuit who was a Marathi student in 1968 has this to say:

> I first became acquainted with Tony when he was appointed Rector of Vinay. I distinctly recall telling a friend, that the then-newly-appointed "Provincial opened the windows; Tony, the doors" referring to the openness that the Provincial exuded in brief meetings with everyone and the ranging freedoms that Tony instituted with his ways and talks and sermons. After the stifling "control" of the earlier years, Tony breezed through the hallowed corridors of Vinay, his charm and incisive experience sweeping out much that was cramped and crabbidy, and opening out to us then-young students the freedom to "discover ourselves."

One matter that a Rector has to handle with great sensitivity is the matter of permissions. You are walking a tightrope here. If you grant permissions too easily people will take advantage of you. If you don't you get labeled as a tyrant. Tony's out-of-the-box solution was to give permission—with a twist. Here is an instance of how Tony handled this delicate matter.

An ex-Jesuit who was a language student in 1971 tells me:

Tony was like a breath of fresh air. We never felt constrained by him. On the contrary he left us "free." Let me explain that with the help of an incident. In the Society you need to get permission for things—if you want to go out or go on a home visit and so on. Permissions can become an inordinate shelter. So long as you have the permission you can feel justified in doing things that might not otherwise be OK. There is a relevant—but obviously apocryphal—story of a Jesuit and a Salesian (or a Capuchin or a Franciscan—it does not matter; this is about the Jesuit) who wanted to smoke so they went to ask for permission from their respective Superiors. The Salesian said, "May I smoke while praying?" The Jesuit said, "May I pray while smoking?" Guess who got permission?

My companion liked to go to the movies. There was nothing wrong with that. Tony did not think so either so Tony gave him the permission very easily. The following week my companion went to Tony for permission to see a movie again. This is when Tony told him something that remained with me for the rest of my life and it was something that I later used when I was in a position of authority as also with my children.

Tony told him, "Look, you are old enough in the Society to know what you are doing and where you are going. If you believe that it is the right thing for you to go to a movie again this week, then I leave it to you. Again, if you feel it is OK to go to a movie every week or with whatever frequency you choose it is entirely up to you. All I request is that you inform me where you are going so that I know where you are and can back you." I was not present at this meeting (I wish!) but that is, in essence, what Tony told all of us at a general meeting without naming names. Of course the companion, red-faced, had already told us of the incident. And er . . . no, he did not go to that movie.

I believe what he says next sums up Tony as Rector rather neatly and succinctly in just one sentence: "Tony never had to enforce anything; we *wanted* to do it."

This was neither the iron hand nor the iron hand in the velvet glove. This was a gentle, guiding hand.

Having established what went to make up Tony's overwhelming success as a Rector I must now draw the attention of the reader to certain happenings at Vinay that would have repercussions on Tony's personal future and eventually on the future of the Catholic Church both in India and abroad.

One of the tasks assigned to Tony while at Vinay was to go on a regular basis to De Nobili College, Pune as a Spiritual Guide for the philosophers.

One of my correspondents confirms this:

In 1967-68, I was then a junior and Tony came as superior (of Vinay) in March or April 1968. That's when I first came to know him though only for a couple of months. For the next four or five months I came to know Tony more closely through his interaction with us but more so through certain friends. That continued even after I left for philosophy at De Nobili, as Tony came to Poona (from mid-1970 onwards), I think once a month, maybe more often.

Putting together what I have gathered from the Jesuits and ex-Jesuits I interviewed, I postulate the following:

From the problems that these scholastics were facing Tony must have come to see a pattern. Looking into his own formation Tony must have realized that these patterns were different from the ones existing when he was a scholastic. Would what worked for pre-Vatican II Jesuits still work now that there were not just changes but upheavals in the Church? What had to be done so that these young men were to continue as true soldiers of Ignatius' army? He must have begun to realize that there needed to be changes at the *formation* level. Now, what is at the foundation of the formation of a Jesuit? The Spiritual Exercises. Could the Spiritual Exercises be added to and adapted for happenings in the post-Vatican II Church and Society of Jesus?

The "anti-Gandhian policy" Jesuit declares this starkly,

> While Tony was the Rector at Vinay he was already visiting De
> Nobili as the Spiritual Father and that is the time he said that
> we need to change the way we train our spiritual directors for
> our scholastics and planned to start the Sadhana Course. After
> going to De Nobili as a visiting Spiritual Father, he must have
> conceived the concept of Sadhana.

There was one Anand Nayak who was a Theology student at
JDV and residing at De Nobili at the time. Later he left the Society
and became a Professor at the University of Fribourg in Switzerland.
He wrote a book on Tony and corresponded with me before his un-
timely and tragic demise. In his book he puts it more sophisticatedly:

> A few days after arriving there at Vinay, Tony conducted the
> eight-day Ignatian Retreat that every Jesuit makes every year.
>
> Tony came to us at De Nobili not so much to convince us of
> his missionary life, as to satisfy our thirst for psychology applied
> to spiritual life . . . The first Sadhana group was being birthed
> there.[3]

He speaks of the birthing of Sadhana symbolically, of course, because Sadhana had not yet been started at that point.

A stray but interesting event took place at Vinay that was to lead
to a different set of changes in the Catholic Church in India. In the
academic year 1971-72 Tony used to meet the language students
once a week to conduct Intercessory Prayer meetings.

One of those language students writes:

> One day one of us prayed aloud for God to give us all "the gift
> of tongues." Tony later said that he was stunned by that prayer
> and asked the scholastic what made him make that prayer.
> The latter said he just felt like making it. Tony then revealed
> that he had opened his Bible at random at that point and got

---

[3] *Anthony deMello: His Life and His Spirituality*, pp. 24, 26.

a passage precisely about the gift of tongues! Two or three days later by a strange coincidence there was a phone call to Tony which happened to be a wrong number or something but the gist of it was that it was a call from or concerning an Indian who was involved with the "Catholic Pentecostals" in America and had returned to live in India. Tony got their number and then sent a language student who was senior to the others along with a member of the language school staff to meet this man and his wife. That meeting led to many more meetings and soon all of us—including Tony—received the Baptism of the Holy Spirit and were speaking in tongues. The Charismatic Renewal Movement in India was born. That language student who went to the first meeting went on to take the movement to great heights and become for a time the leader of the Movement in Rome.

The Catholic Pentecostal movement as it was then called had begun at Duquesne University, Pittsburgh, in 1967 and really came to fame when it reached Ann Arbor, Michigan. It was initially looked upon with suspicion within the Catholic Church, as it smacked of the Pentecostalism of the Pentecostal churches. So it was a bold and arguably controversial step for Tony to encourage this. However he saw that the Biblical foundations of the movement were strong and he went ahead. History proved him right and the Movement was accepted by and in the Catholic Church.

When I contacted the Jesuit priest who took the movement to great heights in India and the world he was unable to remember the details of that story but he did write the following:

Tony gave me the (incorrect!) address [of a couple] in Feb 1972. [A language school staff member] and I managed to locate them somewhere in Juhu, and the first meeting started in Vinay, with a nun from Snehasadan, Tony, [the staff member] and I (maybe others whom I can't remember) making up the group. [Tony] gave me that address because I was going through a crisis of faith, and had been helped by the novel he had given me to read (*The Cross and the Switchblade*), after reading which, in my personal prayer I was "baptized in the Spirit" or had my "Abba experience." A few days later I was "prayed over" by that couple and Tony helped me to "pray in tongues." This was the beginning of the Catholic Charismatic Renewal in India. But Tony was not involved for long. He slowly became more and more psychological in his ministry.

As it turned out the language students who were the core group of this Movement also went to De Nobili that year to study Philosophy while Tony was preparing to start Sadhana there. They spread the Movement to De Nobili College and Pune.

One of my correspondents writes of this period:

The Charismatic fervor had just hit Mumbai and Tony brought it with him to Poona [Pune]. I can still distinctly recall the charismatic sessions, and new-found fervor of some. Tony soon "distanced" himself from this.

Perhaps this was because he wanted to integrate psychology with spirituality and formation.

A third set of events took place at Vinay that was to affect Tony personally and eventually his teachings.

I am given to understand that Tony was gradually shifting in his counseling from Person-Centered Therapy to Gestalt Therapy. What I get from people who were around him then was that he would often mention Fritz Perls, the founder of Gestalt Therapy and read his books. One place that Tony found he could try out his new ideas was the language school at Vinay in 1971-72. With the same students with whom he conducted intercessory prayer meetings, he also conducted some group dynamics sessions. These lasted three days and were an eye-opener for the participants and, as Tony revealed later, a great learning experience for him. What was stressed in these sessions was total honesty and self-disclosure—not in the sense of revealing intimate details about oneself but disclosing how one was thinking and feeling and reacting to the ongoing situation. There was much ill-feeling that was vented. Old scores which were hidden and suppressed were now revealed, revisited, and dealt with. All round it turned out to be a great experience for the participants though there were reservations about it from some. It was during these sessions that one innocent statement by one of the young participants had a colossal impact on Tony.

The participants were all sharing their answer to the question, "Whom do you love most in the world?" There was not much variety to the answers. It was either one or other parent or, in some cases, the grandparent. But one young scholastic said, "Tony, I was thinking about this. Till now I would have thought it was my father but now I am quite sure it is *you*!" This then-young man told me that Tony made no comment about this but later told him how knocked out he was by that response. Tony told him that in all his life no one had ever told him that they loved him the most in this world and that he felt tremendously moved by that. To which the young man said, "Oh you know but it's *really* true. I *do* love you the most in the world."

Said this friend to me lately, "Looking back I now realize I had no idea of the full impact of my telling him the first time. I went and repeated it to assure him that I *really* meant it. It must have totally floored him. I should have at least waited till he found a chair to sit on before letting him have it with both barrels like that."

This was the start of what Tony called "my first deep relationship." It was strange that two persons so unequal in age, seniority, knowledge, ability, and thinking should strike up such a deep and lasting friendship. To avoid any misconstruction let it be stated for the record from corresponding with this man, who is now also a close friend of mine, that this was a non-physical relationship, as all Tony's relationships were—a deep friendship where two people came to understand what it is to truly love.

It must be recalled that these were still the days when the Common Rules discouraged the "particular friendships" that I spoke of in the chapter on Tony's Novitiate experiences. But by now everything was being looked at again. This deep relationship that Tony formed was to make him more human, more understanding of people and would affect his approach to formation, spirituality, and psychology and an integration of the three.

I choose to end this chapter with a personal testimony from this same young man, now not so young. I believe it sums up, confirms, or completes what I have tried to convey in this chapter:

I met Tony for the first time when he was the Rector of Vinay. It was his last year there—this was in May 1971—and he would move the following year to De Nobili College where he would set up the nascent Sadhana course.

I had just finished a year of Juniorate and some of us were assigned to go to Mumbai for a year of Marathi studies. We had a companion who was in a delirious ferment about this and he would constantly say, "In Bombay we will meet Tony deMello!" It was like the name was in capital letters. I did not even know who this Tony deMello was but I was quite prepared to dislike him, sight unseen! I do not know how this guy got to know of Tony but he was certainly making him out to be a celebrity and it was irritating. "This Tony deMello is a man, right?" I would ask this companion. "So why are you making him out to be some sort of demigod? Less of it!"

I arrived at Vinay with no particular expectations except to do my best to master Marathi. The first night we saw the demigod at dinner. I told my companion that he looked pretty ordinary to me—no halo, no aura, nothing. Then we were told that Tony wanted to meet each one of us separately. When I entered his room, I was struck by how tiny it was—and so very plain. I thought this man was quite simple for someone who was the Rector of such a big House.

I had to admit that at first hand there was something warm and definitely fascinating about Tony. In fact the demigod was definitely very human as I was to find later. Nothing special happened at that first interview. Tony just asked me questions to put me at ease and to get to know me a little better.

A few days after arriving there at Vinay, Tony conducted the eight-day Ignatian Retreat that every Jesuit makes every year. What a difference! Wow. I recall his sermon where he spoke of the parable of the Prodigal Son. He spoke of it as the parable of the Prodigal Father and we all looked at each other with understanding, thinking Tony had made a mistake. But he told us that he did mean Prodigal Father. "Prodigal," he said, "means spendthrift. The Father was prodigal with his love—he wastes it on us even though we do not deserve it. That is how loving the Father is." Ooh! I was beginning to see why my companion spoke of Tony as if he were a demigod.

Tony would often tell us that in India people do not believe you are a person of God if you cannot claim that you have personally experienced God. Whenever Tony preached a sermon or gave a talk I would be in no doubt that this man was very close to God—that he had indeed experienced him.

There was definitely something different about Tony. He would come and join us when we were playing volleyball. The Rector playing with us! Nice.

I said earlier that he was very human. He was also compassionate. This incident involves the "demigod" guy who claimed one day that he was terribly ill. He would not say what exactly was wrong with him; he just kept groaning. I—and a good many of my companions—were convinced the man was just faking it. We used to call this AGB—attention getting behavior. Tony came down to see him, asked him what was wrong, and made no comment. He went out to the garage, got out the House van, and himself drove the man to the hospital. We were touched. Tony could have asked the Infirmarian or anyone from the House to do it but he drove him to the hospital himself.

When I told him later that I suspected the guy was just faking it to get attention he told me, "If his illness is real he is probably suffering a lot. And if he is faking it, it means he is suffering even more if he has to fake something like this." He did not reprimand me for thinking the way I did. He just showed me how to be understanding and good without reading me a lecture.

Tony was always so very understanding and gentle. Even when I went to him with some petty problem that was bothering me he would never make light of it or belittle me. I would always feel that he understood me extremely well and that he accepted me unconditionally. Somehow everybody felt that they were his special friend and they were—because Tony could always see something special in people and he had a way of letting them know that.

The best thing about that year in Vinayalaya was that we would be going to De Nobili for our Philosophy studies at the end of it—and Tony would be coming with us. And in the bandwagon that followed Tony around, I who had objected to his being made a demigod, became the driver. Yes, "Fools who came to scoff, remained to pray." Indeed!

Left: Caridade Castellino,
Feb. 8, 1872–April 30, 1929.

Below: Mum and Dad wedding,
September 27, 1930.

Left: Grandma Leonildes with Tony, Merlyn (who died months later) and Grace, circa 1935. *Right:* Tony's prayers for a brother answered, circa 1945.

Above: Tony's (center) last day at home, July 1, 1947, with Dad, Marina, Me, Mum and Grace.

Left: Tony and I,
First Holy Communion,
circa 1950.

Below: At the docks in
Mumbai, Tony
heading to Spain for
Philosophy, June 1952.

Above: Philosophy in Spain, 1953.
(left to right) Jesus Moragues, Gandia, Spain; J. M. Feliu, Mumbai; Francisco Dardichón, Cochabamba, Bolivia; Tony; Laate Fr. Lluis Lamolla; Herbie Alphonso, Mumbai; Late Luis Espinal; Juan Boix, Spain; John Misquitta, Mumbai.

Left: Fr. Vincent Banon and Tony, circa 1953.

Left: Mum and Dad's 25th Wedding Anniversary, September 27, 1955. *Standing:* Grace, Tony, Marina. *Seated:* Dad and Mum with me in front.

Below: At the 25th Wedding Anniversary, with Fr. Solare SJ, Parish Priest, St. Peter's, Bandra, described as "this holy man" by Tony.

Above: Tony ordained by Valerian Cardinal Gracias, March 24, 1961. Tony is kneeling 3rd from top.

Left: With Dad and Mum after the Ordination.

Celebrating his First Mass, March 25, 1961.

Above: Mass on Mum
and Dad's Golden
Wedding Anniversary,
September 27, 1980.

Right: At the Lonavala
Lake that he loved,
1986.

Tony the musician,
1984 and 1985.

In the garden at
Sadhana, Lonavala,
circa 1985.

Chapter Eight

Sadhana—Birth and (R)Evolution

To dream the impossible dream
To fight the unbeatable foe
To bear with unbearable sorrow
To run where the brave dare not go.
— "The Impossible Dream" FROM *The Man of La Mancha*

T HE DIFFERENCE BETWEEN THE great and the commonplace
person is the difference in the quality of their dream and the
strength of their passion to fulfill it. Everyone has a dream but
the great are those who passionately desire to fulfill it. They just
do not give up.

In the Spiritual Exercises, St. Ignatius tells the retreatants to ask
themselves three questions: *"What have I done for Christ? What am I
doing for Christ? What will I do for Christ?"*

Every Jesuit would be asking himself these questions at his
eight-day retreat every year. These questions serve a dual purpose:
they fire him up and fill him with a sense of purpose; and they help
him to clarify his dream. Without a doubt, Tony must have had
dreams of doing great things for Christ; but during his tenure as
Rector of Vinay, I suggest, these dreams were beginning to form
into something more than just dreams. Nebulous at first but becoming increasingly clear with the passing of the years in Vinay
was a vision of a new kind of Society—a Society responsive to a
changing world.

One can get an idea of the events that must have led up to this vision from the Jesuit Miguel Lafont's website:

By the time he ended his term as Rector [of Vinay] he had attained considerable competence as a spiritual director, and since in the initial stages of development he tended to stress the Spiritual Exercises of St. Ignatius, he actively set about directing month-long Ignatian retreats. These retreats were not merely for Jesuit scholastics but also for priests, and hence many Jesuits participated in them and benefited greatly from his guidance. These month-long retreats continued for a considerable period of time. The influence he exerted on the younger members of the Society of Jesus was great, and consequently it did not take long for him to attain the ranks of a proficient spiritual director. During 1974-75 he was chosen to attend the 32nd General Congregation[1] of the Jesuits in Rome as a delegate of the Bombay Province, and here too he conducted daily prayer sessions for some of the participants and served as spiritual director, all of which activities enhanced his reputation even more.[2]

From reading what a Jesuit who later did the Sadhana course writes one gets an idea of the awesomeness of Tony both as a teacher as well as a retreat master and why he was recognized all over the Indian Assistancy for his Ignatian retreats. Mind you, this is the same Jesuit mentioned in the chapter on Regency who got off on the wrong foot with Tony during his English classes:

I was at St Mary's, Kurseong for Theology. Of all the four years there, which I enjoyed tremendously, the most impactful was the second one and that because of Tony. (In 1967) the Rector managed to get Tony to give a week's course in Counselling to be followed by an eight day annual Retreat. That week was my first

---

[1] The General Congregation is an assembly of Jesuit representatives from around the world. It is the highest authority of the Society of Jesus.

[2] *Sophia*, #1.

introduction to psychology and psychotherapy; before that I had nothing but disdain for these two disciplines: they didn't seem to have anything to offer the spiritual elite. I am still embarrassed by what I then presumed out of gross ignorance. Tony not only lectured brilliantly but also put us through a hands-on experience of counseling, especially through the non-directive method of Carl Rogers, and it is from him that I first heard of Carkuff and Fritz Perls and Eric Berne. Thereafter I had the greatest respect for Psychology and psychological matters. Even more enlightening was the eight-day retreat that followed. It was for the first time that I experienced the positive influences of the Ignatian Spiritual Exercises. What had to be undergone before through sheer endurance, because of its ascetical implications as brought out by former interpreters and retreat preachers through slogans about indifference and detachment and agere contra, the "Principle and Foundation" at the start of the First Week of the Exercises suddenly became the bedrock of spirituality and so it is for me till this date. And Tony's expositions of the process and dynamics of the four weeks of the Exercises had the whole Theologate spellbound, and during the Retreat I even had a couple of "spiritual talks" with him about certain clarifications that I needed. Those days ended for me with a great sense of liberation.

Anand Nayak gives his take on what took place when Tony used to go to De Nobili College from Vinay:

Tony came to us at De Nobili not so much to convince us of his missionary life, as to satisfy our thirst for psychology applied to spiritual life. All of us had plans then to become spiritual psychologists. Contact with him began with an annual retreat of eight days. We noticed that he was a preacher unlike others we were used to. He seemed to preach spirituality in a newer, fresher way, making it a joyful experience in comparison to our old spiritual fathers, whose counsels and exhortations were highly soporific. What he taught was not new. He would bring us back to what he termed fundamentals of spiritual life. For example he spoke with unction of mortification and of fasting as wonderful means of awakening the spirit from within. There was also a lot of applied psychology. He had begun to seriously apply Transactional Analysis and Gestalt (Therapy) to the problems of spiritual life. We formed for the first time "workshops" on the subject of group therapies and group counselling. The pursuit of such a spirituality inspired much confidence and hope for the future. We formed around him a small team of young Jesuits interested in spirituality and in the application of psychological principles to spirituality, group dynamics and counselling.[3]

From this one gets the unmistakable impression that Tony was already experimenting with certain procedures. Evidently, he was building toward something new, something different, some sort of integration.

The question may be asked as to why Tony was so keen on bringing in something new or different. I remember, when growing up, I was led to believe that when a priest preached we were to consider it sacrosanct. We had to accept his word without question. In boarding school some of us could clearly see that priests had their faults; they were human. Unfortunately, we were not allowed to question or dispute the issue. Thereafter, I privately developed a healthy attitude of questioning, in my mind, the preaching to which we were subjected.

Tony recognized the humanness of all priests and nuns. He realized that before they instructed and trained their charges they themselves had to come to terms with their own weaknesses and shortcomings. It was important to train the trainer first, before he or she could, in turn, train others.

From his experience of giving Retreats Tony had come to understand the kind of problems that Religious were facing. Having been surrounded in Vinay by novices and juniors and on his regular visits

---

[1] *Anthony deMello: His Life and His Spirituality,* pp. 24, 26.

to De Nobili by philosophers—the three initial stages of formation of a Jesuit—Tony then formed a plan to bring in changes in the formation of the Jesuit on an experimental basis. This he proposed to bring about by training the trainer—training those who were in the business of formation: Novice Masters, Professors, Superiors, and so on.

The trainees would be Jesuits from all over India. De Nobili College which was one of the "Common Houses" was selected as the ideal venue for the new venture. After all De Nobili was already housing Jesuit philosophy and theology students who came from any or every Jesuit province in India. Since the trainees would also serve as counselors to the students at De Nobili as part of their practicum it was hoped that there would be a domino effect. Whatever took place here had the potential to affect the Society all over India.

In 1972 Tony lived at De Nobili and was in the process of setting up the center along with Fr. Ignacio Errazquin the resident psychologist at De Nobili. He continued to give Long Retreats as well as the eight-day version both in India and abroad: Japan, Hong Kong, Singapore, Malaysia, Philippines, and Australia. By now Tony was a well known exponent of the Spiritual Exercises and it was mainly to set up the institute for spirituality that he was sent to De Nobili College. Even the General knew of Tony in this regard. While the institute would be formally inaugurated in the following year as the Center for Pastoral Counselling and Spirituality it came to be known to the world as Sadhana.

However Sadhana nearly died stillborn!

In 1972, certain matters were already in the pipeline—and Tony was aware of them—that would seriously jeopardize the fledgling project.

The Provincial of Mumbai Province at that point was Fr. John Macia SJ whose term was due to end in 1973. The Province was seeking to appoint a new Provincial. Tony's name came up. According to the Jesuits and ex-Jesuits I interviewed Tony's name was *bound* to come up for this post.

The job of Provincial which carries with it tremendous responsibility and administrative work is not one which a Jesuit generally looks forward to—and certainly not one to which he aspires. In fact, *aspiring* to a post like this makes for automatic disqualification from the post. Tony not only did not aspire to this post but also feared it because it would have delayed if not destroyed the achievement of his vision of a new Society and, as shall be seen later, a new world.

Tony's "Gandhian policy" friend was privy to some details about this as he had access to some of Tony's letters after he died:

> Tony was to be the provincial in 1973. I know this from a letter from Fr. Nubiola his Novice master. Tony had written to him and Fr. Nubiola replied saying, "Tony, you have been my novice and now you are asking me whether you should take this step? I take your judgment to be the right judgment. If you think you are going to do good by doing Sadhana then say no to the General but if you think you can do something good as the Provincial then [go ahead]."

But it was not as simple as that. Tony's name was already in the *Terna*—the list of three names that is submitted to the General for final selection. Tony would have known that his name was in the Terna and it must have been like waiting for the Sword of Damocles to fall. There was also the very slim chance that he would not be selected; there were, after all, two others in the list. That year, 1972, Fr. General came to India and, in fact, spent a night at De Nobili, much to the delight of the Philosophers, Theologians, and Staff there. An interesting sidelight is that Tony's room was selected for the General to sleep in, so Tony vacated his room to accommodate him. He must have been sorely tempted to meet the General and state his case but apparently that is not how things work in the Society. Procedure has to be followed. Prior to coming to Pune or perhaps after that, Fr. General went to Kolkata where he had a formal meeting with all the Jesuit Provincials from India. It is the latter who expressed the strong wish that Tony be made available to the whole Indian Assistancy to give his retreats and seminars. The General conceded. The rest is history. Tony must have felt like a free bird after this. He could now get on with his plan to fulfill his vision.

We know that Tony was giving retreats during the academic year 1972-73. What else did he do specifically toward preparing for the first Sadhana course that was to start in the following academic year?

Tony's interest in and fascination with Gestalt Therapy continued. In Gestalt Therapy Tony saw a quicker way of dealing with problems than with Person-Centered Therapy which he valued but considered a trifle slow. Gestalt had the advantage of using group therapy to great avail. He had already been experimenting with this. By now he was using mostly Gestalt Therapy in his personal counseling. He saw it as quick, clean, honest, and lasting.

Gestalt Therapy belongs to the Humanistic/Existential school and stresses the here-and-now. Perls claimed that being in the present moment was a healthy way to live. The similarity between this and Buddhist forms of meditation was not lost on Tony. Having heard of S. N. Goenka who was a master of Vipassana, a form of meditation that came out of Myanmar, Tony invited him in October 1972 to give a ten-day Vipassana Course at St. Mary's Villa, Khandala. A lot of Philosophers from De Nobili College also attended and a few remaining places were given to lay persons.

In May of 1973 Tony offered a special course to the Philosophers of De Nobili College on a first-come, first-served basis at "Ecstasy" (XTC—Xavier Training College), Desur which was the Novitiate of the then-Goa-Pune Province. This was a great opportunity for the junior Jesuits to experience some of what would be done at the soon-to-be inaugurated Sadhana Course. One presumes that for Tony this was another opportunity to try out his ideas. During these twenty days, the Philosophers were divided into two groups according to their Provinces with the (larger number of) Goa-Pune Scholastics forming one under Tony and the Gujarat and Mumbai Scholastics forming the other under Dick McHugh. Both facilitators conducted Gestalt Therapy group sessions in the mornings, each with his own group. In the afternoons there were common sessions in which Tony gave them theory classes on Gestalt Therapy. Tony would devote the latter part of this session to receiving reports about and discussing any difficulties that the scholastics had had with their Vipassana meditation. In the evenings there were talks on the Spiritual Exercises of St. Ignatius.

At this point it is apt to note two matters of significance that took place at Ecstasy that would deeply impact Tony's life and his preparation of the Sadhana Course.

The first concerns the time he was at Ecstasy prior to the beginning of the Ecstasy Course. He was giving a Long Retreat at this time. He wrote a letter to one of his Jesuit friends in April 1973:

> I have been reading two fantastic books: *The Betrayal of the Body* [Alexander Lowen] and *Summerhill*. When you come here I will share with you the books and the notes I have taken from them. I'd like to discuss some of the stuff with you. It is quite revolutionary and it really puts into words what I have been feeling in my guts for quite a while. The second book deals with the education of children. Written by a fellow called [A. S.] Neill. He believes that learning is of very secondary importance, chiefly academic learning, in the upbringing of a child. Infinitely more important is play, lots of play and formation of the *feelings* of the child and, above all, complete freedom to do what he chooses and what interests him [*emphasis Tony's*]. I think the bloke definitely has a point, even, perhaps, the whole point. . . . I am actively proselytising for these theories inasmuch as they are applicable to the formation of Ours [*= Jesuits*].

The same friend adds the other matter of significance that took place at Ecstasy:

> I have never forgotten how in those evening sessions he would expound on contemplation in general, the Spiritual Exercises in particular and the importance of enlightenment. He said until we could "see" we had not arrived. He would mention how the

mystics of the Church who had reached the highest stage of contemplation had reached enlightenment. He said that mystics from different parts of the world and from different religions all seemed to say the same things when they reached enlightenment and he compared what Teresa of Avila and John of the Cross were saying to what non-Christian enlightened persons were saying. He also said that, alas, you could be in the Society for years and yet never reach enlightenment.

He and I used to go out for walks in the evening after tea—he, because he loved walking and I, because I loved him—and one day he told me of an experience he had had that morning. He said he was looking out of his window and he saw some trees— just the same trees that he would see every morning. But that morning it was different. He said he noticed the different shades of green and then, he said, "Quite suddenly I saw! I understood"! With all those talks he had been giving us about enlightenment I immediately understood what he meant but, needless to say, I did not experience that kind of enlightenment myself. Since that day, however, like a perfect dope I often look at trees and hope one day to see what Tony saw. Sometimes when I see a tree I remember the accuracy of that little verse, "I think that I shall never see / A poem lovely as a tree." But that's about it. No enlightenment.

These two matters of significance give one an idea of what would be in store for the first group of Sadhana-ites. One also gets an understanding of what moved Tony, what made him tick, what led him to say and initiate the kind of things he did.

The Ecstasy Course, as it came to be called, was a huge learning experience for the Scholastics—something that brought about major changes in a short period of time. For Tony the significant learning must have been that the judicious combination of group therapy, spirituality, and contemplation was a powerful mix that would serve him well in the new academic year when he would begin Sadhana.

Sadhana was officially inaugurated in June, 1973. Sadhana is Sanskrit for "practice" or "means." What is *sadhana* the means to?

In India *sadhana* is seen as a means to something higher, to the divine. Tony meant it as a means to God, to a better life, to a life that counts.

Tony told one of his friends how he envisioned the Course. This friend wrote to me:

> The main segment of the Course would be the one on spirituality, specifically the Spiritual Exercises and Jesuit spirituality. Tony saw spirituality and psychology as intimately tied up with each other. He saw Gestalt Therapy with its stress on taking responsibility for one's life and actions, its emphasis on getting in touch with one's self through becoming aware of one's feelings and its advocacy of total honesty with oneself and others as the perfect foil to spirituality. Accordingly, besides the main segment on Ignatian spirituality he decided to have one segment of the course devoted to group therapy and also another segment devoted to prayer methods and spirituality in general. In addition Tony and Errazquin would be available to the participants for individual counselling. Changes in the schedules as well as additions to the Staff would be made already in the next year. This first year of Sadhana was going to be tremendously important and its success was crucial. You could say the whole Assistancy would be watching.

I was extremely fortunate to get in touch with one of the participants from this first Sadhana group. From this Jesuit who is an established retreat director and counselor today, I got some much-awaited information. This was the first Sadhana, ten months long and he gives an inside look at it:

> We were all Jesuits in the Course—no women yet. The classes were shared by Errazquin and Tony. Dick [McHugh] was a student with us then. We had group counselling—mostly Gestalt [Therapy], theory classes on counselling, classes on psychological precepts and principles and inputs on spirituality and the Spiritual Exercises. Besides Tony and Errazquin there

were visiting staff members who came and gave us occasional seminars or workshops.

At De Nobili we had a readymade resource for our practicals. We were appointed as counsellors to the students there. In October of that year (1973), I guess since I had already done a Vipassana course in the previous year at Chennai, I was put in charge of arranging for a course in Vipassana by S. N. Goenka at St. Mary's Villa, Khandala. This was attended by the Sadhanaites and some others.

He adds one very interesting point:

In those days the emphasis was mostly on spirituality. Tony was known as a Long Retreat Director and he told us that he had discovered that the retreatants had huge personality problems and they needed counselling. This is why he decided to integrate spirituality and counselling.

Tony was like a rolling stone and his ideas kept changing. He believed then that we were too stuck up as a result of our formation and suggested that we needed to form deep relationships with others in order to have a healthy personality. He also emphasised that one needed to have a feminine aspect in one's life and advocated deep relationships also with women. I would not agree with him here and I guess he was not too enamoured of me!

He was not the only one who resisted some of Tony's ideas. There were others in the course who genuinely and honestly could not agree with Tony. There was much healthy discussion and sometimes heated arguments. From this, one gets the idea that Sadhana was certainly "different." It was questioning old ideas and provoking thought and much soul-searching.

Gestalt Therapy being from the Humanistic/Existential school dwelt on the "here-and-now" and honesty with one's feelings. Other participants, both male and female, have told me that the Gestalt Therapy sessions led to much ill-feeling in the group initially. The participants—all Jesuits in the first year—did not take kindly to being told exactly how they were perceived by their fellows. These were men who were quite senior in the Society. They were holding important and responsible positions as Superiors, Novice Masters, Retreat Directors, and Spiritual Guides and Professors. Initially they were all awestruck and shell-shocked by his new approach!

At different points of the Course there was questioning of existing or long-established rules and procedures. The idea was not to throw out the old but to see it in a new light. In fact, Tony at this point was conservative in many ways, personally believing in mortification and fasting as seen above.

A participant of Sadhana later on mentions this method of questioning old values, also known as the Socratic Method which forces one to reconsider the values one imbibes without questioning:

> On one occasion during the Maxi-Sadhana, Tony came out with some strong statements about Superiors. Naturally we were up in arms and asked him how he could say such things. Tony asked us to consider the fact that Superiors were cruel without being aware of it. It set us thinking.

A dear friend of Tony's—a Spanish Jesuit who did the Midi-Sadhana later on—expresses this as only these learned men of Christ can:

> Tony broke barriers. . . . With him it was like the Sabbath was made for humans, not humans for the Sabbath. He was not an iconoclast but a man who made you aware of the values which you are frightened to discover and even more frightened to live accordingly. We are frightened to open our eyes to the real values, for example, freedom. Passive obedience is a relative value. *Real* obedience is difficult but challenging and is a source of growth.

The reactions and responses of the participants of this innovative first Sadhana Course were overwhelmingly positive. The same respondent quoted above who disagreed with some of Tony's ideas tells of the effect of the entire Sadhana Course on him:

> What I got from Sadhana and then later with Fr. Rebello influenced my ministry and way of being; it is something I carried for the rest of my life.

Good reports had reached the ears of the authorities as well. One would have thought that Sadhana would surely get the go ahead.
It did.

In the second year of Sadhana already there were some changes in the emphasis on the various segments as well as one major shift: women were accepted to the Course. Tony's Spanish friend gives what he considers the rationale for this:

> I remember that women (all of them religious Sisters) were present in all the courses I participated in when Sadhana was in Lonavla. I suppose that what was behind the fact of women being admitted to his courses was, first, that they too deserve it and need courses like those offered by Tony, and second, the way women participated showed that it was something absolutely natural. It even added to the matter-of-fact aspect of the course. Life is made of men and women living together, and priests and religious sisters are part of human society.

According to a participant in the third Sadhana group:

> The First Sadhana Group, all male, [in their] final evaluations of it highly recommended the incorporation of women in future groups. It must have required some politicking to have the okay from higher authorities. I know two of the Sisters who were in the Second Group: 1974-75; they seem to have been much disappointed that for more than a couple of months Tony was out of the Sadhana programme because of his required attendance at the General Congregation in Rome.

Tony was very open to suggestions and the first Sadhana group were the pilot group, so their opinions and ideas were much valued and many of them were taken on board. Accordingly the schedules and segments were adjusted and changed. Already with the admission of women to the Course Sadhana was becoming broader in scope, going beyond the needs of only the Society of Jesus.

Even as I am finalizing this chapter more information has come in, this time from a Jesuit, now eighty years old, who was in the second group of Sadhana:

> We were the first group of Sadhana that admitted women—six of them. We had a full ten month course and there was no Long Retreat or any retreat for us then. Our "grouse" against Tony in this course was that he was absent for more than two months because he had to attend the 32nd General Congregation. Hardly his fault. He made up for this upon his return by holding us spellbound while he spoke to us for two full hours and gave us a complete account of the General Congregation. He had a fabulous memory and he spoke without any notes giving us important information as well as interesting sidelights interspersed with humor and riveting tales. He left us with such a fulfilled feeling—as if we were present there ourselves.
>
> In some ways I found it good that Tony was not there. Tony was brilliant but he was also all over the place. One had to be smart to catch the right things from him. While Tony was away Errazquin who was a psychiatrist took over and he gave us some beautiful stuff that was organized and worthwhile. Also Herbie Alphonso SJ [*a world-renowned expert on the Spiritual Exercises*] gave us fifteen days on the Spiritual Exercises. I still use what I learnt from him when I give the Long Retreat.

The Jesuit who got off to a bad start when Tony was teaching him English in his Novitiate now features again as he writes about the scheduling and other aspects. He was in the third Sadhana group. His opening words tell us that he has not lost his verve or boldness:

> Knowing well that I can be charged with chauvinism, I nonetheless confidently hazard the opinion that this third group of Sadhana

('75-'76) was the best ever. The Group jelled well despite the diversity of background, and everybody was serious and open and ready for total self-investment. Mutuality and readiness to serve came easily. And the teaching and inputs were solid, comprehensive, and totally absorbing. Besides the mainstay, Tony, the others on the Staff were Ignatius Errazquin, Dick McHugh, Philip Terrasa and Joe Aizpun, and there were others from abroad and from the JDV campus that gave short courses that were geared to our needs.

I kept a daily and detailed diary and it tells me that there were daily three sessions, often exceeding the time limits: 10:15-11:15 am taken up by Tony, 11:30 am-12:30 pm by Errazquin, and 5:30-7:00 pm by others (on various relevant topics like family therapy, Indian Spirituality, Moral theology), but sometimes even by Tony or Errazquin. The bulk of the time was taken up with personal counseling, with everybody in the Group present at the sessions, conducted either by the teaching Staff (chiefly Tony and Errazquin) or by one of the Group itself, the interactions being supervised. The trust within the Group led to very intimate facts being revealed and rather than respect being lost it was only increased within the Group. . . .

For over two months, we had Tony expounding to us on the Spiritual Exercises, the talks recorded on a dictaphone, then meticulously transcribed through a typewriter, and carbon copies given to each one of us. This was followed, just before the Christmas break, by an eight day Retreat in the Khandala Prayer House, each one directing and being directed by another. Tony was a credible guru because like Gandhi-ji, he had his own "experiments with truth," and that meant going through the Dark Nights and suffering fools gladly; whatever he spoke about had the backing of intellectual vigour and personal experience. All through the year, to balance high seriousness, we had a lot of fun. We had birthday parties, and Tony's on September 4 was done in high style, and any reason was good enough to celebrate within or without DNC [De Nobili College]—the Jesus & Mary Convent at 5 Boat Club Road was always a good host, especially for the Christmas Party with Christmas Pudding and all the other trimmings—and we went for picnics and even had a four-day tour of Ajanta and Ellora.[4] In whatever we did together, there was always at least tacit support from Tony.

This group of Sadhana is also significant for another reason. Those talks on the Spiritual Exercises that were transcribed and given to each participant were shown years later by this same Jesuit to a Jesuit in the USA who saw a book in it. Three American Jesuits worked at re-transcribing and editing it and this led to a new book by Tony being published in 2009, twenty-two years after his death—*Seek God Everywhere*. But that is another story.

You now have an idea of what the Sadhana Course was like. Further changes would take place every year because Tony was constantly experimenting and learning new things and moving on.

One of the changes that came about as the Sadhana years went by is very interesting. Tony realized that priests and Religious had come to develop certain mindsets. As one participant puts it, "Some of us had thinking that amounted to 'mindtraps.'" As long as they were trapped in this thinking there were few ways out of the kind of problems they were facing. I am told that Tony introduced something that was not new. But it was uncommon to use it in group therapy. My correspondents tell me the way Tony conducted it was innovative and powerful.

Since I am not familiar with therapy or counseling I will let one of my correspondents describe what took place:

Playing Devil's Advocate in a group therapy session has the

---

[4] Ajanta and Ellora are a set of caves that depict beautiful Buddhist art and sculpture. They date back to anywhere between the seventh to fourth centruies BCE. They lie in Maharashtra in Aurangabad District, about 375 km from Mumbai.

advantage of being a deceptively light exercise. This means that it has far-reaching effects which are reached in a fun way. It gave us the freedom to speak freely without necessarily hurting anyone.

Tony had developed a way of indicating to the group that he was about to play Devil's Advocate. He would begin with the formula words, "I am a. . . ." "I am a 32-year-old late vocation named Desmond (or Juniper or some other fictitious name) and I find the training in the Novitiate very childish." Or, "I am a battered child. . . . " Or, "I am Sr. Anastasia of the Angels over Bethlehem and I find the nuns in my convent very narrow-minded. Nobody understands me. . . . "

Tony would then elaborate on his "problem" and invite anyone to counsel him. The problems that Tony selected were not as "simple" or straightforward as the ones given in the example. Tony would cleverly select some truly complicated cases. It was spellbinding to see how the "case" would unfold.

Anyone who chose to be the counsellor was getting into the "hot seat" (or hot water!) because Tony would make it extremely difficult for him/her. He would present more and more counters and excuses to any argument or advice being offered. By the time the counsellor(s) finished with "Sr. Anastasia" "her" situation had become even worse. And the counsellor would be reduced to a state of confusion! It would seem there was no way out. Sometimes one or other of us would break through and achieve the purpose of the exercise. That would give us a tremendous feeling of achievement. In most instances we would fail though.

Then Tony would step in and get into the "hot seat." When he did this any one of us participants could become "Sr. Anastasia." But Tony would counsel "her" beautifully because he would get to the heart of the matter and show "her" where she was wrong in her underlying beliefs, mindsets and paradigms. Generally all of us too were trapped in the same kind of thinking as the "client." This is why we would find it so difficult to counsel Tony when he was playing the client.

The idea was to re-examine our thinking and values. There are several such mind traps: believing it is my duty to play Rescuer, believing I cannot survive if I do not have the approval of people, believing that I am indispensable—that if I am not around to do a job no one will be able to do it quite like me, believing that people should only follow *my* way. . . . Tony was bringing about paradigm shifts that were liberating.

I am told this method was well accepted as a form of awakening. A number of these participants have written about their experiences in these sessions and in Sadhana. I have chosen to quote one in particular. This sums it up pretty well:

> Tony DeMello was a Master Counsellor and Teacher. He did not counsel or teach in the stereotyped manner people expect. He was a man on a mission and he was fired with the lines from the Gospel he often quoted, "I have come to give life and to give it more abundantly."
>
> His sense of humor and understanding of human nature because of his extraordinary spirit and charism made every session important for us. The role-playing sessions were examples of this. One important lesson I learned was that judgements and critiques are more often than not subjective. Many, many people are richer because of him because he helped them discover the riches within.

It is important to distinguish between the Devil's Advocate exercise and the Empty Chair Therapy that took place during the Gestalt Therapy session. The latter also had a kind of role-play. The former was always used for *fictitious* cases where Tony played the person with the "problem." One of the Jesuit participants of Sadhana clarifies:

> [In the Empty Chair Therapy sessions] no one could ever say that Tony played devil's advocate and made the case more and more difficult. If Tony did play an advocate, it was to ferret out the

truth, from the client's own experience and through the client's own efforts. Surely, Tony had the talent that could be the envy of the best of trial lawyers, to have the witness in court, against his client, all tangled up in his own words, yet never did he misuse it in any of his many counselling sessions at which I was present. When I was in Sadhana, Tony was well beyond the need to draw attention to himself by the exercise of any punditry and by put-downs of clients if he was not making headway with them. Not once did I notice any client humiliated by him or browbeaten to accept his judgments or principles. I don't think Tony himself ever veered, during his career in Sadhana, from what he constantly dinned into us: that no one is helped unless one is made to learn and do what comes out from the unbiased self-awareness of one's own experience.

In carrying [Empty Chair Therapy] out successfully, a lot of psychological principles and ethics are involved. Tony made abundant use of it simply because of the good results it provided, the ones that mattered most to him, the ones that made him to be more gratefully honoured and remembered for than the benefits from his spirituality and friendship and, scholastic genius—that through challenging those who came to him to face unflinchingly and with equanimity whatever was going on in their psyche, to accept that all psychological problems were of one's own making, and to acknowledge that it was totally unfair, and ludicrous even, to blame them on others. Tony's great merit was that, by radically avoiding [in Empty Chair Therapy] any gimmickry that was sometimes practiced by lesser hands, he led persons to the only genuine sanity and maturity possible by being fully responsible for their own lives.

Earlier we saw the meaning of the word Sadhana. Now for some clarifications about the way the term Sadhana is used and should be understood in common parlance when speaking about Tony. Already in this chapter you will have come across the expressions Maxi-Sadhana, Mini-Sadhana, etc. What was the difference? When Tony went to other places to give his seminars were those all "Sadhana retreats"? There is a certain amount of confusion about this.

Let me start with Tony's first book which was published in 1978. It did not help that Tony chose to name this book *Sadhana*. This most valuable book on prayer and meditation containing forty-seven "Christian Exercises in Eastern Form" has seen twenty-two editions and been translated into over forty languages. After the book was published Tony was recognized as one of the great spiritual guides of his time. In fact as I write, I am told that it is still a best seller. *Sadhana*, the book is not to be confused with Sadhana, the Course.

What is Mini-, Midi-, and Maxi-Sadhana? Although these were started later, in 1979, I will explain it here. I myself had much difficulty with the various terms which is perhaps why I wish to make these clarifications. I got my information from my respondents as well as from Fr. Miguel Lafont's excellent website with his kind permission, freely given, for which I am deeply grateful.

Sadhana was very a successful program but only twelve persons were admitted to the course. There was a general clamor for more persons to be admitted or at least for more people to be reached. By 1979 Sadhana had moved to Lonavala so Tony et al. introduced two more programs besides the main one. They were also accommodating Religious from other Congregations and Orders.

Mini-Sadhana was a month-long course.

Here some sections involved an experience of prayer, such as the prayer of Benedict, the Jesus Prayer, St. Ignatius's contemplation to obtain love, and so on, and here I myself encountered Tony's inspiring guidance. Apart from Christian prayers, oriental forms of prayer such as the Vipassana meditation were also included, and I personally found this to be a good example of Christian prayer with oriental influence. Viewed from a psychological perspective it was as though he enabled us to penetrate the realm of our unconscious, and by the use of games and exercises freed us from the control of past wounds.[5]

Midi-Sadhana was a ten-week course.

Here the participants consisted mainly of spiritual directors of Priests and Religious, those in charge of religious formation, novice masters and Provincials of religious congregations. The participants totalled 24 men and women, and the course aimed at the overall development of the person. It was a place to experience and know oneself, and results showed that the participants on gaining experience were able to help others. The course began with community building, followed by three weeks of Group Therapy, Neuro Linguistic Programs, Focusing, and other training sessions. Besides this the participants were led through five days of Progoff's "Intensive Journal," where reflecting back on their past they experienced the stillness in their hearts as well as their feelings and inner movements. By these means they attained among others an awareness of their unconscious leanings and release from the influence of past wounds, and their relationship to others showed a marked enrichment.[6]

Tony's Spanish friend who was his Philosophy companion at San Cugat, Spain adds two sentences which tell one what could happen at such a course:

I did the Midi Sadhana with Tony (with a follow-up later). He made me aware of what I really wanted: enlightenment.

Maxi-Sadhana was the regular six-month course (though Tony mentions it as a five-month course in one of his letters):

Here the male and female participants together did not exceed twelve persons, and to be accepted into the Maxi-Sadhana it was necessary that the Midi-Sadhana course be completed. During

---

[5] *Sophia*, #4
[6] *Sophia*, #4.

the first month the members reviewed the methods used in the Midi-Sadhana, and received training in the more effective use of these techniques. While the Maxi-Sadhana course was in progress the new Midi-Sadhana would begin, and so as part of their training the Maxi-Sadhana members would guide and direct the members of the Midi-Sadhana. They would for instance employ techniques of Neuro Linguistic Programs and so on in their guidance. The purpose here was to build up further the experiences they underwent during their Midi-Sadhana, and prepare them for their future role as guides.[7]

During these years till his death Tony was also going out of Sadhana Institute to other places in India or abroad to give what came to be called seminars rather than retreats. These are called "Sadhana Seminars" by some, basically associating Tony with the institute Sadhana. These are not to be confused with *Sadhana* the book though it is quite likely he conducted a few meditations similar to those found in the book. Today these seminars are called "deMello Retreats" or by some purists with a leaning toward accuracy, "de Mello-type Retreats."

Sadhana was shifted to new premises at Lonavala in 1979. Was this move solely for the convenience of having one's own premises, designed for the special needs of Sadhana? Or were there other reasons?

Tony told a few of his friends that Sadhana began to face objections from some quarters right from the first year. This is not surprising considering that it was started a mere eleven years after Vatican II. Right at the outset Tony had brought in innovations that were bound to disturb. He had brought in Vipassana meditation albeit in "Christianized" form. He had brought Gestalt Therapy in particular and psychological principles and precepts in general into the purview of spirituality. By the second year, almost as if to add

---

[7] *Sophia*, #4.

fuel to this fire, Tony began admitting women to the course! This, in itself, was not a major objection though it was a bit unusual.

The objections seemed to be more against the new kind of values that Tony seemed to be promoting, chiefly his advocacy of freedom without license. His encouragement of deep relationships with both men and women was seen by some as an attempt to denigrate the vow of chastity and an encouragement to the young to be irresponsible in this regard. This was definitely not what Tony meant but this was how it was being interpreted by the objectors.

The Jesuit from the first Sadhana group quoted above said in his interview:

> Tony was not quite aware of his own influence. If he told someone that he did not think he had a vocation, for instance, he was only giving an opinion but the other person would take it as a missive to leave the Society. I remember, I intervened in one such case and the man stayed on eventually but it was incidents like this that increased the friction between Tony and me.

According to my respondents, many of these objections were not unreasonable. All agree that Tony was ahead of his time but some believe that Tony could have been more diplomatic and a bit less hasty in making his innovations. The Church was still in the process of recovering from some of the body blows it had received since Vatican II. How far would this liberation movement go? Where would it end? What were the limits?

One of the objections to Sadhana was that some very promising Jesuits with a brilliant future ahead of them eventually left the Society and the priesthood as well, after doing the Sadhana Course. Nayak, who was a brilliant professor at JDV, was one such. There were others. Whether their leaving could be attributable to Sadhana or not is debatable. What is indisputable is that some of those who went to Sadhana—and they were quite senior in age and position—did leave. Some Jesuits saw Sadhana as an institution that was leading to a new chapter in decadence in the Church. Somebody had to draw the line.

One of my respondents, a Sister, said something to me here that I consider to be of some relevance:

> Tony never compromised his views. Had he compromised, he would have been very famous many years ago. If he had said some of the things which the Church was saying at that time, he might have gone very high—maybe even become the General. But he was never interested in fame. He was more interested in "man fully human, fully alive" as [the Jesuit Pierre Teilhard de] Chardin said. And, in fact, Chardin also was in trouble.

The Sister was definitely right about one thing: Tony was never one to back down when he believed that he was right. And he was not afraid to rock the boat. His purpose was not to make people fall off but to let the ballast settle in optimally so as to make the boat more stable. He let the results of Sadhana speak for themselves and answer the objectors. And there was no doubt the results were wholesome. This did not mean that the objections subsided.

When I first heard of these objections I had just relocated to Australia from France. I did not hear of these objections from Tony but from others. In those years I was too involved with my family and my struggle to start life anew in a strange country to concern myself with what Tony was doing or experiencing. At any rate correspondence between us was limited to snail mail in those days and we hardly spoke on the phone. However, my initial reaction to stories of the objections to Tony's Sadhana was to automatically defend my brother in my mind and attribute the "detractions" to jealousy.

After corresponding with, interviewing, and having personal and telephone conversations with so many Jesuits and ex-Jesuits and others in this regard I now realize that not all the objectors were moved by clerical jealousy—though this could have been motivating a few. The objectors, by and large, had genuine misgivings about Sadhana and they were as sincere in their concern for the Church as Tony was.

One of Tony's friends reports:

Tony told me that he was not upset by the objectors because if he were in their place he might have had objections too; only the way he would have gone about it would have been different. He took these objections as a challenge for him to clarify his own thinking, to communicate it more accurately and to make adjustments where necessary. Of course, very few confronted Tony face-to-face as he could be quite a formidable opponent in any debate.

A Jesuit who is an ex-Sadhana-ite from the early years threw some light on why Tony could have been misunderstood. He also gave me some information that I have not been able to get confirmed from anyone else but I shall divulge this anyway:

Tony's strategy was to say shocking things so that you will do your own thinking. But some Sisters used to take these things literally. For example one day [during the Sadhana course] Tony and a Sister were having quite a hot discussion in which she said that something [that she was supporting or defending] was in the Bible. Tony said, "Throw away that Bible." Most of us understood in what sense Tony meant this. However the Sister reported to her superiors that Tony was advocating that we give up the Bible!

Tony would challenge values that people seemed to accept without questioning. He would also tell a lot of sex jokes, some of which were quite outrageous. One day we Sadhana-ites cornered him. We told him that we were all formators and he owed it to us to let us know what his personal views were on matters of sex and chastity. Would you believe it? He gave us such a traditional exposé and showed us how conservative he was in his personal life. He also made clear that by deep relationships he meant friendship and not sex.

A couple of years later in response to some complaints a Two-Man Committee looked into Tony's views. They ruled that Tony and his teachings were okay but they asked him to be a little careful about his clientele. They recommended that the Sisters he accepted to the course have a fairly good grounding in Theology and have good knowledge of English, so as to avoid misunderstandings. I may add it was, in fact, often through his "dirty jokes"—and he had many!—that he communicated many of his insights. Somehow, his jokes never sounded "dirty" when he told them.

Despite this, the rumblings continued and there were indications that there were orchestrated moves in place to at least get Sadhana off the premises of a House of Formation like De Nobili College. By now Tony was beginning to tire of the objections and criticism.

In a letter to a friend in 1977 he wrote:

The trouble regarding Sadhana continues. There's a certain amount of hostility towards us from some quarters in the community and I am becoming more and more convinced that we have to get out of DNC and as soon as we can possibly manage it we shall pull out. I am convinced DNC stands to lose. Others think differently. Too bad for the House and especially for the scholastics! Bertie Phillips has written to offer us a whole wing of Vinayalaya which, to me, would be like having Sadhana jump from the frying pan into the fire.

This letter is significant also in that it shows that his superiors at least—Bertie Phillips was the Provincial of Mumbai Province then—believed in Tony and what he was achieving. Tony had previously told some friends that he was contemplating moving into St. Stanislaus Villa, Lonavala which had fallen into disuse. He figured that if they could have a new building there, things would be fine. By also starting the Mini- and Midi-Sadhana he would have people available to Maxi-Sadhana-ites for the latter's practicum.

And so it came to pass that on October 1, 1978 Sadhana made the big shift to St. Stanislaus Villa, Lonavala. By 1979 it was operational. It would be some years before they got that much-desired building and the going was a bit rough. But at last they were in a place of their own. I do believe their joy would have been not unlike that of an Indian daughter-in-law who, after years of living in a joint family, finally gets to live in a house of her own with only her husband and children. The house might be small and the luxuries few but no pesky mother-in-law or busybody sister-in-law to contend with anymore.

One would have thought that once Sadhana had shifted to Lonavala the rash of objections would diminish. It did not.

In a letter dated January 26, 1983, Tony wrote to his friend about the work he was doing with the Provincials of India and in this context he mentioned something of significance:

> There was an enormous amount of controversy connected with Sadhana. We eventually had Sadhana evaluated officially and professionally. The report ran into nearly 200 pages and the result is that we have gone up in everyone's estimation—especially in the estimation of the people in Rome.

That last line is of tremendous importance. The Evaluation turned out to be a good move after all. Since it was professionally evaluated and found to be good it pushed Tony higher up the totem pole, perhaps to the chagrin of some. More importantly, Sadhana could now forge ahead without distraction in the sure knowledge that it had been officially commended. Forge ahead is exactly what it did, continuing in force till Tony's death, after which the Institute still lives on.

Soon there would be a new building. One of Tony's close Jesuit friends feels grateful that Tony lived in the new building, however briefly:

> The foundation for the new building (of Sadhana) was laid on March 25, 1985. Tony lived in the new building till May 30, 1987. On May 30 he left by the Deccan Queen for Mumbai and went to his sister Grace's house from where he was to leave for the airport for America. . . .

That Sadhana was an entirely new approach to formation and religious life has already been seen. How was this new approach perceived and received by the recipients? What exactly *did* Sadhana do for them? What did it achieve in their lives?

I spoke to a number of Sadhana-ites, both men and women. I asked them a few questions in regard to their experience of Sadhana and their personal interactions with Tony. They openly and honestly shared their innermost feelings with me. Their accounts opened my eyes to the nature of my brother, about whom I knew so little. They are all so fortunate to have had him not only as a spiritual director, counselor, and friend, but in many ways as the brother and mentor I so sadly missed out on throughout my own life. I am grateful to them for their contribution and their willingness to permit me to share their thoughts and experiences with others who read this book. I am devoting the final section of this chapter to a few select responses in no particular order or chronology.

Fr. Miguel Lafont SJ who traveled three times from Japan to attend a midi- and a maxi-Sadhana writes on his website:

In the Maxi-Sadhana, what stimulated me the most was to listen to the talks of Tony and discuss their subject matter with him, and in fact on my completion of the course what remained ingrained in my memory was the content of his talks. These talks, the content of which had to do with oriental spirituality and inner liberation are dispersed among the topics dealt with in his books, and in getting to know Tony thus I was afforded a glimpse (of) his charisma. Under his guidance we realized that in all matters of importance it was essential that we take our own decisions, in an ambience of freedom. He led the members towards a realization of their innermost inclinations and to a grasp of the feelings lying within them, of whose existence they were unaware. Since he himself was alert to the feelings of others he never pressured another if he felt that the person was as yet inwardly unprepared, but once he was convinced that the participant was ready, he subjected him or her to the full force of his guidance and direction.[8]

A very good example of the "full force" of Tony's guidance comes from Anand Nayak. He had just spent three years doing his doctorate in France and had returned to India feeling the need to refresh his spiritual resolve. He had already experienced Tony as a spiritual director and approached him once again for guidance:

> I asked him (Tony) if I could do the Spiritual Exercises under his guidance. "No," came the answer. "I have given up giving the Exercises. You see, Anand, the problem with the Jesuits is that the Exercises do change their life. But only for three months. Then they go back to their old rut. I have now created Sadhana. It is very effective and will change you to the depths of your being, making you a new man." He then offered me a chance to join a Sadhana, which would start the following week. I gladly took it up and went through an intensive work with him for three weeks. He was right—it changed my whole outlook in life. I began to see that I did not have a religious, Jesuit vocation. I was merely holding on to it as an ideal in life, but was not really called to live a life of poverty, chastity and obedience as the Jesuits understood it. I felt God was calling me to something else—a more simple and joyous life with and in the world; above all, a life of liberty and freedom. This discovery filled my heart with a gush of joy. Within a few days, I decided to leave the Company of Jesuits without regret or pain. I have however, not left them in my heart. I was and still am perfectly thankful to Tony.[9]

From an interview with a Sister who did the maxi-Sadhana in 1978 I came to understand how Tony functioned in Sadhana. I find her narrative particularly moving:

---

[8] *Sophia*, #4.
[9] *Anthony deMello: His Life and His Spirituality*, p. 35.

I did the maxi-Sadhana under Tony's guidance and the experience was unbelievable. I had never experienced anything like it before or since. He was attempting to take away our ideas of false devotion and piety, breaking down barriers we had held on to for years. Tony liked to shock you—just like Christ used to. When you're shocked you sit up and take notice. We needed to be shocked. Tony would get us to question our beliefs and ideals and to open ourselves to free thinking. It was such a wonderful experience. During one of the sessions, Tony said to me, "You are such a wonderful person and yet I cannot seem to get close to you." During one of the group therapy sessions I broke down. I was completely broken. That's when I saw a totally different side of Tony. He was so very gentle with me, so understanding and comforting.

After Sadhana I became a freer woman and, in ways, a rebel within my Congregation. In fact later Tony told me to tone down a bit.

The entire team at Sadhana used to co-ordinate very well. But Tony was the heart of the Course.

He was not interested in religion for religion's sake. He wanted us to go beyond religion and the sacraments. He changed my views forever.

Tony's Spanish Jesuit friend who did a midi-Sadhana with him got a special privilege:

Later he had a "Special Sadhana" for ten Novice Masters of India. Not being a Novice Master I was the only exception, but Tony asked me to be there. We had eight hours of therapy a day. In the beginning no one had problems. In one week we all were immersed in problems, our insecurities and fears! Tony always had time for others. His attitude was one of a loving confrontation. He would be figuratively holding your hand while confronting you with some hard truths. He would often say to me, "You are contradicting yourself" but he would never abandon me.

The Jesuit from the second Sadhana group says:

Tony was an extraordinary person—a person you could love or hate, but not ignore. When I look back, I realize that I have been much enriched by my contact with him in many ways. I was especially impressed by Tony's insights. They were fantastic and would always give us a new kind of direction after he had explained them.

To locate participants from the early Sadhana Courses that happened over thirty years ago was a very difficult and intimidating task for me. After months of contacting a friend and then the friend of the friend of the friend (like "the soup of the soup of the duck") I would sometimes despair of finding anyone. And then some unexpected person would turn up without my trying at all. Imagine my joy when I managed to get in touch with a Sister who was in this second Sadhana group; the first group to admit women. When contacted she said, tongue-in-cheek, that she was told that "Sadhana had not done me any good." She was referring to Tony! It appears Tony used to tease her a lot.

She writes:

When I joined the course I was very shy. The first week was torture for me and I felt terribly out of place. I told the other Sisters (we were six Sisters) that I had to meet Tony and deal with this. They told me this would be a long procedure and that I would first have to make an appointment and so on. So I met him that day and told him I wanted to talk to him about a problem. He said, "OK, come let's talk about it just now." Huh? They told me I would need an appointment and so on. I was not even prepared! Somehow I explained to him about my fears, my low self esteem and so on. He appreciated me so much. From that day on I changed. Later he would publicly tell the group what he liked in me. I do not know that I was special in any way but somehow Tony believed in me. No one had ever done that with me before. He—and the group—began to see aspects of me that I was unable to see in myself. Sadhana was such a major experience for me.

I include comments here from a Spanish Sister who knew Tony for years before he died. She has this to say:

Many years after I first met Tony, I met him again when I attended the maxi-Sadhana. I was captivated by his personality. I found him very changed in attitude and way of thinking. He had some magnetic force. I became a good friend of his; I used to call him my guru and my friend.

During those days of Sadhana at De Nobili College, I discovered him as a wonderful person very intelligent, initiative, great! And he was a mystic. He helped us to be free, loving, caring, more daring, more detached, more selfless, and also helped us to go deeper in our experience of God. How many people changed their life in contact with him, and became "all for others." He talked about awareness, to live the present here and now in fullness and joy. Often he repeated, "Be awake. Be aware."

The Jesuit from the third Sadhana Group quoted earlier speaks of his experience:

Very often the end experience of the [group therapy] sessions bordered on the mystical, despite the full range of even negative emotions fully expressed. . . . It must be admitted that we began Sadhana as a mature Group but we ended it much more mature, besides much more competent in therapy skills and in spiritual direction. For my own Jesuit Tertianship needs, I could not have had a better package; there was enough free time for me to read on things connected with the Society, especially the Constitution.

I managed to track down a Sister from the third Sadhana Group who is now in the USA. She was delighted to give her response to Sadhana:

Sadhana has had a profound impact on my life. This is not only in terms of lasting friendships with other participants but also and more especially in terms of what I learned. To this day, I find myself quoting Tony e.g. he used to say, "It doesn't matter whether you are in or out of religious life, what matters is that you are following God's call." Tony was a listener; he listened with his heart not with his head. His many stories always had a strong and powerful message and were relevant to the topic that the group was discussing.

These are but a few of the people whom my brother came into contact with in Sadhana. He changed their lives. He has continued to change the lives of others through the legacy of the several books he has written and the conferences he recorded. His humanity, humility, and down-to-earth approach to life in general was much appreciated and absorbed by people who, in turn, passed on his teaching of waking up and dropping the "I." Reading or listening to their words I ponder on the brother I rarely met and hardly knew and reflect on the great changes he wrought in people. In researching and writing this biography I have come to understand Tony so much better. And this has inspired me too to begin my personal journey into myself, to discover who I am and what my life is about. And my gratitude for this is due, in no small part, to these wonderful, wonderful people who have generously and unreservedly shared these intimate details of their lives with me.

PART II

THE SINGER AND HIS SONG

CHAPTER NINE

MOVING ON: HE CHOPS WOOD.
HE DRAWS WATER FROM THE WELL[1]

"Before enlightenment; chop wood, carry water. After enlightenment; chop wood, carry water."

—ZEN PROVERB

"SADHANA WAS TONY AND Tony was Sadhana." That is how one of my respondents summed things up about Tony and Sadhana. With Tony's Institute as well as his first book being called *Sadhana*, there may be a tendency to think that Sadhana was Tony's only passion. In fact many of my respondents have indicated that Sadhana was Tony. That may have been true but I very much doubt whether it could be said that Tony was Sadhana. There was so much more to Tony than only Sadhana.

In this chapter I wish to demonstrate the sheer volume and variety of the work that Tony did outside of and besides Sadhana, the Institute. Also I wish to show the changes he underwent over the years—not so much the personal changes but the changes in his approach, his teachings, his spirituality, and his life view.

We have seen that as a young priest who had returned from the United States and Rome, Tony had already begun to make his mark as a retreat preacher even though he was in a remote mission station. In fact one of my ex-Jesuit respondents says:

---

[1] See *The Song of the Bird,* p. 18.

I had heard that Tony, on his return from abroad, opted for the missions and was posted there. However, I also heard the criticism that he was often out of the districts, mostly in Bombay.

Whether it was "often" may or may not be an exaggeration but Tony did go out to give retreats—especially the Long Retreat. Already in 1967 Tony went abroad to give a Long Retreat. As far as is known, between 1967 and 1976 he went to give retreats or seminars in Singapore, Philippines, Hong Kong, and Japan. In this context I want to mention a relevant incident concerning Tony's "first book."

It is now common knowledge that the Jesuit promotional series *Ah! These Jesuits!* was actually Tony's first book. But during his life time this was only rumored and never known for a fact. This is why *Sadhana—A Way to God* is taken to be Tony's first book. However there is a little-known story that is an interesting sidelight here.

Tony had given some talks or a seminar in Hong Kong or possibly Singapore somewhere between 1972 and 1975. A few months after this seminar Tony got the news that he was the author of a book! Apparently the Congregation of the nuns to whom he gave that seminar put his talks in book form and published it. Tony was disappointed that they had not consulted him, not because he wanted any copyright on it but because he could have at least edited it. He told a friend: "They transcribed it exactly as I spoke; they even put the 'ums' and 'uhhhs' that I use when I speak!"

That book has not been heard of again. For all one knows it is still making the rounds within that Congregation or elsewhere. If it is, then it is entirely possible that the nuns from that Congregation (whose identity is known to me!) will come forward and make it known to the world—if they see fit. If that happens it would be interesting to see how Tony had changed from those early years to what I will call the "Awareness Era" toward the end of his life.

But already in this early period of his ministry Tony was changing. The same ex-Jesuit who writes of Tony in the missions, continues:

It was in 1967-68 that I first heard about some of Tony's views, not from him, but from someone I was very friendly with. Tony had spoken with him about matters he [Tony] was mulling over. Already, at that time, his ideas were nothing short of "revolutionary." I distinctively recall that, on hearing them, I reacted by saying that the Church would never, could never, accept such views (having to do with the *growing* awareness of Jesus, as he grew up, of his "mission").

To get an idea of how Tony's ideas were changing there is no better source than the man himself. In a letter dated April 8, 1973 he writes in his inimitable style of serious topics couched in humor to one of his friends. This was just before the start of the Ecstasy Course and he was giving a Long Retreat at Ecstasy:

> The novices are after my blood to give them talks on, of all things, Poverty, Chastity and Obedience. I told their Socius [Novice Master's assistant] these subjects don't appeal to me. He said, "Then talk to them about what appeals to you." Tony: "Well, what appeals most to me now is a theory on nudism." Socius: Speechless!
>
> Oh yes and there are the homilies. I gave a nice one this morning on the Greeks who come to Philip (or is it Andrew?) and say, "We want to see Jesus." Topic: Is it possible to see Jesus in this life? "Yes, Lord, it is the one thing I want more than anything in all this world—and I know it is possible." I even gave a talk to the St. Paul's community (Belgaum) when I stopped over there on the second evening. The old Minister there is quite a revolutionary at heart and asked me to talk after supper. I went on and on and on till 10:15 p.m., sharing with them my notions on love and the expression of feelings and the danger of some of our rules etc. etc. much to the delight of the scholastics and the obvious discomfiture of some of the older (old in heart) persons in the community.

As usual one notices Tony's good-natured—sometimes atrocious

—teasing. But notice through all the banter the deep desire to see Jesus, the knowledge that he has seen Jesus, and the desire to help others see him.

Once Tony had tasted the success of the Ecstasy Course in the summer of 1973, he had the microcosm of the Sadhana course. And once Sadhana got underway and found its feet Tony gradually began giving fewer retreats. Of the several invitations he received to give retreats abroad he passed on some to other Jesuits who were good at giving retreats.

In the opinion of one of my ex-Jesuit respondents:

Tony gave up "guiding" people on 30-day retreats and moved to "counselling" sessions—he saw that the "fruit" of the Spiritual Exercises could not be savoured in full because people were locked up in psychological problems and insecurities and were at emotional dead-ends. At that stage, they needed counselling (more than spirituality) to free them from these blocks (as evidenced by the testimony of so many) so that they could then more deeply drink of the waters of the Ignatian vision.

When he did give retreats he introduced new features in them. This becomes clear from a description given by a Sister who was perhaps the woman whom Tony loved the most. She made a retreat under Tony just before her first profession.

She wrote to me:

Making a retreat with him was an experience of coming close to nature and God and to other human beings with joy and laughter and with lots of love. For me, the characteristic of this retreat was guiding me to get in touch with myself, to understand myself so that I could then relate to others with an open, clear mind. I learnt to recognise my strengths and weaknesses but without feeling elation for the former or guilt for the latter. He coupled spiritual exercises with counselling. Once again, I noticed the technique he used was so very different from what I had experienced before, doing a retreat with other retreat directors. His retreats were not all Scripture; they involved a lot of personal therapy in that I learnt to examine myself in depth without self-hatred or fear. When he did involve Scripture, it was such a joyous experience. For example he would describe a scene from the Bible, say the Nativity, and ask me not to just meditate on the scene but to actually imagine myself at the scene. He would ask me to picture myself as part of the scene and to then describe what I had experienced. I will always remember those experiences. They always left me feeling elated, refreshed and happy.

The last part of this quote—the nativity scene—is exactly the meditation as given by Ignatius in his Exercises. But one can also see the innovations made by Tony where he brought in the idea of therapy and self-discovery without fear or comment.

Without a doubt, however, the most significant change that came into Tony's teachings was the introduction of Vipassana meditation. Tony saw this as a form of contemplation as he explained at the Ecstasy Course. He had found this method of attaining awareness of the present moment to be tremendously efficacious. He gives a very detailed explanation of how this form of meditation is actually contemplation in the tradition of Teresa of Avila and John of the Cross in *Sadhana—A Way to God* (p. 24ff).

Continually experimenting with or discovering new ways of praying, Tony gradually added to his repertoire. He began to give prayer seminars where he taught people how to pray. By the end of September 1977 he was due to go to Indonesia to give a prayer seminar for Jesuits. However, in a letter to one of his friends he writes:

I should have received your letter on the 14th. But I got it half an hour ago. I was supposed to have gone to Indonesia but, at the last minute, failed to get a visa and had to cancel the trip. Deep down I was quite relieved. I now have two whole weeks on my hands with absolutely nothing to do except unwind. (October 5, 1977)

Though that trip got cancelled it is one of the indicators that

Tony was becoming as well known for his prayer seminars as for his retreats. These prayer seminars eventually became *Sadhana—A Way to God* in 1978 which still remains a classic in its genre. The fact that the inside page has the legend, *Christian Meditations in Eastern Form*, is an indication of the path Tony was taking. In meditation after meditation in this book Tony begins with the Vipassana method of awareness of breath or bodily sensations which has the effect of calming a person, quietening them, and leaving them receptive to God and matters spiritual.

The prayer seminars were something that Tony continued giving almost up to his death. In fact just three days before he left on what turned out to be his last flight, Tony completed giving a prayer seminar at JDV, Pune and it was attended by a large number of laypersons including Grace, our sister, and her friends.

A Jesuit who attended this particular seminar mentions its structure and gives his comments on Tony:

> It was his usual six-day prayer seminar. The structure of these seminars was unique.[2] Tony would speak for six hours a day without notes. It was impressive the way he could hold the hall in rapt attention for six hours interspersing his inputs with stories, humor, and practical exercises. What was amusing was that when he had finished a talk sometimes he would not leave the hall by the exit. Instead he would just walk out of the French windows near the podium and disappear.

As expected the prayer seminars contained Eastern meditations and practices.

Closely related to his prayer seminars were something called "Spiritual Workshops" or what Tony himself called "Spirituality Courses." The young Sister quoted earlier on Tony's new kind of retreat writes about these spiritual workshops:

> [Tony] conducted spiritual workshops which I attended. I will

---

[2] See Appendix, *Topics of Tony's Last Prayer Seminar at JDV, Pune.*

always cherish the experience of those exercises. The workshops I attended before I made a proper retreat under his direction were experiences like none I had ever experienced. It was like being in another world, another dimension, in a world of angels. . . . There were the workshops which we novices attended during 1976 and 1978. His main aim was to show us who we were and accept ourselves as we were; to be happy with ourselves and be confident. He had a way of making us see what we had never known about ourselves. He would correct my shortfalls with so much love and tenderness and in a non-threatening manner and that made me change without any pain.

What is amazing is how he found the time for all this activity. In addition to running the Sadhana Course he was also accepting people for individual counseling. He would often be awake well into the night and whenever he was asked by a friend how he managed this he would just laugh it off. This friend was impressed by the fact that Tony always put in an hour of prayer before going to bed, however late and always woke up, Jesuit style, at 5:30 am. This was in the years 1972-1975. I am told in the later years he used to keep more regular hours.

It was the individual counseling that Tony found particularly wearing. However, in a letter written from Ecstasy to a friend he indicates this and also adds something curious:

Life here continues to be on the dull side. It is proving to be a good rest and I'm glad there aren't those interminable interviews. On the other hand I sometimes catch myself wishing there were some people to interview. I suppose the blessed thing has got into my blood. (April, 13, 1973)

One sees this strong desire, almost a need, to reach out to others. Generally Tony got the "most desperate" cases, the ones where the client had tried "everything and more" and so they were difficult.

One of his friends reports to me that Tony was almost magical:

Before entering his room I would have this terribly overwhelming problem. As soon as I entered his room I would feel a calmness and two minutes after Tony had heard me out he would say just a few words to me or ask me a question that made me see my so-called problem in a totally different perspective. The whole thing took what seemed like seven minutes. And with my problem out of the way we would then be free to just chat away as friends. Many will bear me out on this magical quality about Tony.

What all my respondents have told me—even the ones critical of him—is that Tony always seemed to find the time for everybody who asked. He did slip up on this once in a partially amusing incident which will be related later in this chapter. It is mind-boggling to think of how he also found the time to do all that reading and then the writing. It may have helped that he was brilliant and had a keen intellect but nonetheless his output was humungous.

Let me give an idea of the kind of activities he was involved in besides running the Sadhana Course. This information is garnered only from the few surviving letters of Tony to one or two friends. (One difficulty I have had regarding letters from Tony is that most of his friends had picked up his idea of detachment and had destroyed his letters to them. So they are only left with their memories. One particular set of letters was forgotten in a desk drawer and was discovered when this friend was contending with termites that had attacked his desk drawer!) From this point on, unless otherwise indicated, all Tony's letters that are quoted are written to one or other of these two then-scholastics who were among his close friends.

By 1973 Tony was in high places. He was at a Colloquium in Old Goa. Tony writes:

There is absolutely no time to write letters these days because I am kept so busy with the Provincials and Fr. General. . . . There is so much to say about the Colloquium here that I would rather say nothing at all. I'll tell you heaps and heaps of stuff when I come to Poona. . . . Yours in Christ Our Lord, Tony. (Old Goa, 7 January 1973)

In 1975 Tony was at GC 32. Apparently Tony was conducting prayer sessions here as well. He writes the following in a letter to a friend:

Wow! My Prayer sessions in English and Spanish continue to be well attended and appreciated. And I keep getting more and more invitations: the latest are from Spanish Provincials and the South American Provincials to conduct seminars for their Novice Masters. (January 15, 1975)

Then Tony made a speech in the Hall at the 32nd General Congregation on January 28, 1975. He mentioned this in a news bulletin he used to write to a friend who in turn would put it up on the notice board at De Nobili College for all to read.

The next day he wrote to another friend:

In the news bulletin, I tell of my speech in the Hall yesterday. I received an overwhelming response to it. What I said was so very simple, and yet all sorts of people are coming up to me (pretty famous and talented people) to say things like it was the best speech of the day, it had moved them deeply, personally etc., etc. I was also pleasantly surprised to see how often people in the Hall quoted me in the speeches that were made afterwards. I think I'm going to lie pretty low for some days now and not stand out too much . . . just to make sure that they do not get it into their heads to keep me for some job here in Rome. I am always ready to do what the Lord wants of course . . . but I don't want to push myself into anything.

A little later in the same letter, Tony mentions an unusual event:

You know, the other day I received a letter from Br. Guerola SJ telling me, quite mysteriously, to prepare myself to be used by God as the instrument of his Holy Spirit to help the General Congregation and I was wondering how on earth this could be so because I had more or less made up my mind not to speak in the Hall unless it was something absolutely necessary. Then, one

thing led to another and I made this speech . . . and from what
people are telling me it could have a decisive influence on the
approach the Congregation takes. I wonder if this is what God
wanted through that "message" of holy Br. Guerola. Anyway my
attitude is one of the joyfulness of a child who sees the Lord
doing so many wonderful things through him and at the same
time claps his hands with joy. How very, very good and wonderful
the Lord is, really. He is just spoiling me with his love.

The following year Tony and Sadhana went truly international
according to Fr. Lafont:

In March 1976 Tony conducted a week's Sadhana retreat for 40
Jesuits of the Japan province at the Retreat House at Kamishakujii,
and with this began the history of Sadhana in Japan.[3]

In fact Lafont is responsible for building a Sadhana legacy in
Japan.[4]

By 1977, even though he had cut down on giving retreats Tony
was still involved in giving courses on the Spiritual Exercises—his
first love. Of course, he had added his own twists and interpretations
to them.

He writes to a friend:

Do you know I went to Delhi to give them a week's course on
the Spiritual Exercises at Vidyajyoti [Jesuit Theologate]? When
I got there it turned out that Herbie [Alphonso] had just given
them a course on the Spiritual Exercises, so they told me to
talk on whatever I wanted—which is what I was going to do
anyway, except that I would have kept referring to the Spiritual
Exercises whereas now I did not even feel bound to do that and
I talked to them about all sorts of things—some of them pretty
revolutionary: about prayer and the spiritual life and God. . . . etc.
etc. etc. As I was talking things began to fall more into place for

[3] *Sophia*, #4.
[4] *See* John Wataru *and* sadhana.jesuits.

me and I began to realize what a great distance I had travelled in these past few years. (September 12, 1977)

In the same letter Tony continues, "Then on my return (from Indonesia), I will conduct a mini-Sadhana for our Provincials at Lonavala. I have twelve or thirteen of them already."

So Tony, as indicated earlier, was continuing to reach out to and influence the upper echelons of the Society in India. But his influence was not limited to India. If he had already reached out to the Jesuits of the world in 1975 at GC 32 and to the Jesuits in Japan in the next year, by the end of this one (1977) he landed on foreign soil again. He indicates this in a letter along with an event of personal significance to him and his family:

I go to Hong Kong for my Christmas holidays—a five day seminar to SJ's. (And) I shall spend Christmas Day at home for the first time in exactly 30 years! They are all quite thrilled about it. (December 12, 1977)

What kind of seminar he was to give in Hong Kong is not indicated but from reading his various letters I can conclude that this was probably a prayer seminar.

By 1983 Tony was going even higher in the estimation of the Society:

I got to Goa on January 5 and rushed to Baga where the Jesuit Provincials were meeting. I've now become a kind of Councillor-in-General for the Jesuit Provincials. We gave them a course in July lasting ten days—a kind of Sadhana course. They liked it so much that they asked me to come to their meeting in Baga. This time I gave them four days. Now they want me to come to all their meetings. I am a little hesitant about accepting the invitation. . . . From this detail you can see that my star is on the rise. (January 26, 1983)

In 1983 Tony was attending GC 33 in Rome where he was officially conducting the prayer services. He wrote a letter where he gives his itinerary which serves as a good summary of the kind of work he was doing in addition to Sadhana. By now America was added to the equation. Tony had become a kind of reverse missionary—a native of the old missions now going back to Europe and the West to give God to them. Tony had become a bit of a jetsetter as well:

> I arrived here in the first week of September and will probably be here for another week or so. Then, if possible, I shall hop over to the States for a couple of days (business—as I'll explain to you later) and return to Bombay on the 31st of this month. Back in Lonavla by the 1st of November to begin what we call the maxi Sadhana—five month course. Then I go off to Poona for a ten-day Spirituality Course starting on November 4. Wish you could be present for that—it is for theologians on the Campus. Will probably create something of a revolution. Then I shall be back in Lonavla for eight days. Next, off to New York again to give two one-day retreats . . . and back to Bombay where from December 4-9, I shall give a course to the diocesan clergy on "Fostering Creative Thinking In The Church"—those guys did not know what they were asking for when they invited me to speak on the above mentioned topic! And finally, on December 10 back to dear old Lonavla where I expect to be till the 31st of March of next year. . . .
>
> Have you ever seen that book of mine "The Song of the Bird" by the way? If you haven't, write and let me know and I shall get my publisher to send you a copy. It is being read and enjoyed by lots of the men at the General Congregation who make all kinds of flattering comments on it. It has become a best seller in Spain—it has already gone into the third edition there in eight months' time—and in the States Seabury Press has bought the rights to publish it and they assure me that they will make a best-seller out of it there too. . . .
>
> I was quite elated when I heard from the Indian publishers that Herder in Germany and Desclee in France have asked for rights to publish it in their countries.

I have made good use of my stay here in Rome (quite dull from every other point of view—except for the election of our new General) by putting the final touches on the manuscript of my next book "Spiritual Exercises" [Wellsprings *came out in April 1984*]. This one is more pious. But quite deep. In the opinion of George Soares who, incidentally, is also here with me, this book is the best thing I have written so far. I'll send you a copy of this one too. Only it won't be out till some time in December the earliest.

I have become pretty famous in the States thanks to a fairly innocuous TV interview I gave on a Church-sponsored programme. The programme went on the air in New York State and the response they got to it was so favorable that I am being asked to prepare six half-hour programmes on Oriental Prayer. Total cost of programmes: about one hundred fifty thousand dollars. I am supposed to raise half of that sum and the Catholic Bishops of America will chip in with the other half. When we meet I shall give you a detailed (and extremely amusing) account of how things are done in the States whereby I give in my half of the stipulated sum without actually giving it. Can you imagine me having seventy five thousand dollars for TV programmes? Anyway the prospects are very good not so much for my becoming famous (I don't give a damn to that) but for collecting a fair amount of money for my Sadhana building by way of royalties on those programmes. That is why I shall be going to the States for a couple of days later this month. (October 17, 1983)

It was at one of the New York week-end retreats mentioned by Tony in this letter from Rome that a lady from the USA first encountered Tony. She would then attend every one of his talks in America. She became one of my correspondents.

In one letter she wrote to me:

I first met your brother when I was given a brochure about his retreats and workshops in Syracuse, NY. I immediately checked into that and I met Tony at that weekend retreat in about 1983. I then went to two full week retreats the following two years. I was registered for a retreat at Fordham University in June, 1987 here in NY but he died. . . .

Before I move on, a brief word about *Wellsprings*. Tony's out-of-the-box thinking led him to write this very unique book of spiritual exercises that was the result of years of experience of prayer and contact with God. *Wellsprings* is an amazing book of spiritual exercises. Just as the founder of his Order St. Ignatius had written a book of spiritual exercises so now did Tony. I do not profess to know much about these things but my respondents, Jesuit, ex-Jesuit and non-Jesuit assure me that this is an unusual book in that it consists, quite literally, only of a series of spiritual exercises and meditations, without any explanations, inputs, or commentary between the exercises. As with many of Tony's books, one does not read it as one reads a novel. One does the exercises prescribed. And this is the beginning of a wonderful journey into the realm of spirituality, God, enlightenment, and the mystery of life.

After the October 1983 letter there are only two more letters to Tony's friend that have survived either his attempts at "detachment" or the attacks of termites. In the last letter but one, Tony writes:

I will not be passing through London on my way to the States in May. I shall be abroad for nearly three months this time, mostly because I will have to spend two or three weeks working on some television programmes in the States and because I shall be visiting Latin America for the first time in my life. I am certainly looking forward to that. I shall be back here in Lonavla only in October. (April 6, 1984)

Tony does not specify which country in Latin America but it is nice to see he is actually excited about visiting a new country.

From another respondent I know that he had started giving week-end discourses at JDV, Pune around this time. These discourses were mostly attended by Religious. These discourses were in addition to the usual Prayer Seminar that had become a fixture there. The Prayer Seminars were open to lay persons as well.

In the last surviving letter to this friend written in 1984 Tony mentions the load of work he has:

> I should never have been able to write this letter to you if everybody hadn't gone away for the Christmas holidays. I decided to stay back and tackle my Christmas correspondence. This gives me two full days to be by myself. Otherwise I hardly have any time to breathe in. In addition to the sessions that I am giving here (at Sadhana) I am working at a new script for a fresh series of television programme that I plan to make in the States next summer. Also on the manuscript of yet another book. (December 24, 1984)

I have been unable to find out the topic of the television programs Tony gave in the States in 1985. I can only hazard a guess that these were the *Awareness* conferences which were later put in book form and brought out on DVDs (1990). That he was in the States in 1986 is known because of the two sets of DVDs that came out—*Rediscovery of Life* and *A Way to God for Today*.

It is interesting to note that all my respondents tell me about the number of letters Tony used to write if not to them then to people they knew. While one may marvel at the volume of Tony's work and the extent of his reach one may also admire how he found the time to write all those letters to such a vast array of people. He lived at a time when email had not yet become common usage in India and he did not even own a word processor to write his books. In fact his manuscripts were either typed or (the earlier ones) written in his beautiful handwriting in a plain exercise book. Most of his letters were written by hand and later he had his trusty portable typewriter.

Alas, sometimes in his eagerness to serve Tony did make mistakes. The Jesuit quoted above on Tony's last Prayer Seminar told me that Tony was his spiritual guide for sixteen years. When he was talking to Tony in the course of that last Prayer Seminar he mentioned that he would like to have a talk with Tony. Tony graciously invited him to Lonavala for lunch on May 28, 1987, the day following the end of the seminar after which they could have their talk. What both he and Tony had not anticipated was that my sister Grace and some friends who had attended the seminar would decide to visit Tony on the same day. What followed was a comi-tragedy. I got this story both from this Jesuit—call him Jesuit 1—as well as another Jesuit (Jesuit 2) who was with Tony during this incident.

Let Jesuit 2 tell his side of the story first:

> Since Tony's sister, her husband and friends were all there they told Tony and me that they would like to take us out for lunch. So we set out. As we did so we saw (Jesuit 1) entering the Sadhana complex. Tony was aghast and told me he had clean forgotten he had invited him over for lunch that day and asked if we could take him to lunch as well. I told him there was no place in our vehicle. So Tony just ducked behind one of the others while I spoke a few words of greeting to Jesuit 1 who did not say much.

When I first heard this part of the story I thought Tony's feeling must have been similar to that of Nasruddin who came home one night and told his wife he had invited his friends over for dinner. When she told him there wasn't any he went and hid under the bed and told his wife to tell his friends that he was not at home. But I digress. This story is not funny from here on.

Here is why Jesuit 1 did not say much:

> As I turned into the gate I saw this vehicle and I noticed Tony in it. When he saw me he ducked behind one of the others. I was nonplussed and hurt. To make matters worse (Jesuit 2) had this wry grin on his face that made me feel they were all laughing at me. I went into the Villa and met the Minister of the House. I told him how Tony had let me down and the fact that they were all laughing at me. I was very angry and upset about this. He tried to calm me down and gave me lunch. Later in the evening I met Tony and spoke to him over a cup of tea. Tony realized that

I was very upset and asked me to spend the evening at Sadhana Institute. But I had an appointment with a lady at St. Mary's Villa, Khandala. So I could not stay. The next thing I heard was that Tony had died! I was very, very sad about this. Later I reconciled the matter within me. Tony was not my Spiritual Guide for nothing.

There must have been other instances like this one where Tony could not quite accommodate people and must have inadvertently disappointed them. I particularly like one sentence from one of my respondents, a Sister who was a close friend of Tony's: ". . . at the same time [Tony was] a person who had his vulnerabilities and insecurities." It is a relief to know that Tony was but human and had his failings. It brings hope to us lesser mortals.

My Jesuit and other respondents have helped me trace the course of changes that Tony underwent in his teachings. They have pointed out that toward the end of his life he had come full circle—with a difference. In the beginning of his ministry Tony was fully and almost solely into spirituality with the Ignatian Spiritual Exercises as his guideposts. His *Rooted in God* is an excellent example of what some people call the "old" or traditional Tony. When Sadhana, the Institute was started, one could see the effect and influence of psychology—Gestalt Therapy in the initial years and also Neuro-Linguistic Programming in the later years. It was during the early Sadhana years that he was himself experiencing the joys of deep relationships and an experience of how being in such relationships can bring one closer to God.

A Jesuit who was part of the first Sadhana group says:

A month before Tony died he had a reunion of ex-Sadhana-ites at Lonavala for ten days. It was a kind of refresher course. I was stunned to see how Tony's ideas had changed again. I even remarked to a companion, "The way he is changing we might see him walking up and down reciting the rosary!" He also clarified some of his earlier statements when asked. He said that he had never ever encouraged sex: "What I have always said is that we require intimate relationships; these kinds of friendships are not sexual."

Tony was definitely working toward reaching the divine by getting in touch with the human—with ourselves—through awareness.

Sadhana, the book, was a blend of Eastern Spirituality, Western Spirituality, and psychology. But as the years passed psychology and psychotherapy began to take a back seat in his books and prayer seminars and conferences. Increasingly it was coming round to spirituality alone again. Listen to *Rediscovery of Life* and *A Way to God for Today* and you find Tony is back to only spirituality. But this is a different kind of spirituality, what my respondents call a new school of spirituality with its blend of East and West and infused with humanness. With Awareness Tony brought enlightenment and the attainment of the peace that comes from understanding—matters that were only within the grasp of "specialists" before—within the reach of the non-specialist or lay person. With *Awareness*, Tony's quest to find a simpler, more powerful way was over.

One of my respondents told me,

> You read or listen to Awareness and change will come. You do not have to do anything complicated or go for an elaborate course on what to do, when and how. Just have awareness. And change and understanding will surely come—in a flash for some, in a lengthy, slow way for others—but come it will. Awareness is simplicity itself. . . . In a sense, his work on this earth was done.

In this respect, of the hundreds of responses I have received since I posted the short biography of Tony on the Net in 2000, the one that stands out the most for me is the testimony of a man from Serbia who read *Awareness* when he was very young:

> I am from Novi Sad, which is a small city (300,000 inhabitants or so) in Serbia, Europe. I am 34, and I discovered Anthony's book *Awareness* as a pretty young child. I was maybe fourteen or

fifteen, and it struck me immediately. Later it really helped me big deal staying sane when we were bombed back in 1999; it was a great help knowing how to look at things, and how to act more and react less, as Anthony would say. So, as were many other people, I was really blessed to find his words, and I was double blessed to find them at a young age.

If *Awareness* could enable a young man to undergo bombing with equanimity it is a demonstration of the power of Tony's teaching.

In the previous chapter I gave a few select responses to Sadhana. In this one I present a few responses to his retreats, prayer seminars, spirituality courses, and the like. These were given mostly to non-Jesuit Religious though Jesuits were not excluded. It may explain why many of my respondents are Sisters.

The Sister who wrote the following was a dear friend of Tony's:

I attended Tony's retreats from 1980 onwards, with annual retreats right up to 1986. From these retreats, I learnt to live in the present moment (awareness). [I learnt to see] relationships as a way to the divine, inner discipline, search for my own truth. I learnt to experience God in the midst of lived reality. I became aware of the unconditional love of God, to go beyond man-made rules and regulations. I learnt not to get stuck with anything, to search for my own truth and be open to move on, focusing on the Center. I learnt to be life-giving and to nurture life, and to practice detachment. According to Tony "spirituality is to learn to unlearn"; it is not "to gain something new, but to drop something" and transform oneself. He used to say that the cause of all misery is "Self." When you drop the self there is no more suffering. He also taught me how to disassociate myself from my role as provincial. This helped me not be very upset when things happened contrary to my expectations.

The Jesuit who had the unfortunate missed luncheon appointment with Tony writes of that last Prayer Seminar given by Tony:

The Prayer Seminar made me more practical in my approach to prayer and life. It made me realize that I need to be a good human being first before I can be a good Religious. It taught me the value of silence, emotional freedom and how one needs to be truly free to pray and communicate with God.

A Jesuit who has progressed to great heights in the Society acknowledges:

I made my Long Retreat with Tony in 1969 at St Xavier's, Khandala. Tony was then the new guru of the Spiritual Exercises. That was a turning point in my life as it brought a taste for prayer I had not experienced since my novitiate.

An ex-Jesuit who was a close friend of Tony's writes about how the programs he attended served him in good stead for life:

I attended 3 Summer All-Jesuit "Growth Labs" conducted by Tony in Stanislaus Villa in Lonavala. Those months, and living and loving Tony were mega moments of growth. As Tony himself would say to me, "Join the Human Race." . . . I did, thanks to him. Developing my "Feeling" world and growing empathic was a direct effect of "The Tony Impact."

A Jesuit who is now in a senior post in the Society as well as an author attended a Gestalt Seminar and a three-day workshop both conducted by Tony in the 1970s.

He wrote to me of his experience:

There was a sense of hope of being able to break out of issues where I had felt trapped before. There was a sense of adventure in dealing with these issues as I felt I was in competent hands. Most of all these programmes brought about major changes in me.

Tony came at a time when there were so many constrictions on behavior which were accepted at the time as part of our forma-tion. Tony broke out of this rigid understanding of Jesuit lifestyle. He wanted to bring in the freedom and sheer joy of religious life.

He succeeded!

A Spanish Sister living in India writes:

I did a retreat with him. What he always wanted from us is to be ourselves, to be aware, to live the present moment fully, to be free and stand on our own feet and to lead us to have an experience of God.

A Jesuit friend of Tony's, a counselor and author in his own right, has this to say:

I have attended one prayer seminar and made a number of retreats under his guidance. His insights were an integration of psychology and spirituality from an eastern perspective. He enjoyed shocking people and through that to question their view of the world and other aspects of life. He tried to build your self-esteem and came across as a very positive and supportive person. He created an atmosphere which made it easy to share with him everything. He could connect with people at the heart level and could be very affectionate.

Another Sister responds:

I saw Tony for the last time in 1986 in Poona where he was giving a week-end workshop at the Papal seminary to over three hundred people. I noticed a change in him then. He had become somewhat quieter and spoke about unconditional love and change. He said he was beginning to see a relationship as much deeper than before and from a different platform. He talked about being detached from possessions, the absence of clinging not only to worldly possessions but also in relationships and love of others. He was talking about freedom of the spirit.

A Sister once came to Tony unannounced and asked him if he could give her an individual retreat. Tony took an hour out every day to guide her in this retreat. According to her he did her this favor only because she was the sister of one of his friends.

She has always appreciated that favor and prized the learnings from that retreat:

> Tony deMello touched my life in a very powerful way through that retreat and a prayer seminar he conducted for us.
>
> The retreat of 1975 had been unique as Tony gave me the prayer exercises he later wrote in the book "Sadhana." These exercises brought me to a deep intimacy with Jesus which gave me a positive and joyful perspective in life. It helped me withstand the storms of life.
>
> I attended Tony's Prayer Seminar in 1984, the time when I was doing research in Palynology. I was anxious, wondering whether I would successfully finish in time. His seminar showed me the wonders of AWARENESS and the simplicity of living in the present moment. It made me enjoy my work and complete it, ready for the next assignment. All my life after that has been a success story of enjoying God's presence in all that I do, of never carrying hurts, of living in inner freedom.

A Jesuit from the USA who wrote to thank me for my e-biography of Tony says:

> I am just a Jesuit who attended his workshops when he was in the US in 1986. I travelled from St Louis where I first heard him speak to Indianapolis where he was giving a weekend retreat. He changed my life and I continue to reflect on his writings. How blessed we have been. I hope you are well and continue to be influenced by Tony's spirit.

I find the account by an American lady, quoted below, particularly interesting and most touching. Remember, this woman was never a religious sister. She was going through a very difficult phase in her life at the time she first encountered Tony and to this day says she is grateful to him. I first heard from her quite a few years ago, when she wrote to thank me for the first short biography. We have corresponded ever since and she has been constantly encouraging me and urging me to write this story about Tony.

In my opinion, she sums it all up very nicely and I believe it is fitting to end this chapter with her words:

> I was absolutely mesmerized by Tony from the moment he began to talk. I felt "at home" on a very deep level. I loved the depth of his spirituality, his keen intelligence and how he flowed. Once in a while Tony used to say to us, "You will no longer be the dancer but the danced" and that was Tony; he was "danced" by God. No wonder he enthralled us. I have absolutely no doubt of that. And the dance was incredible to watch. He flowed from one story to another with ease and most naturally. I was like a sponge before him, soaking in all I could. Having had difficulties with the Church in the past, I felt that I had finally found what I was looking for. I did not understand some of the things he said, because he spoke in stories and symbols but I asked questions and he answered them very honestly and directly. In this sense, he was very true to himself and to me (us). I knew that he knew! I sensed that he spoke the truth even when I did not fully understand exactly. He exuded truth and joy and answered questions on a very deep level. He got to the core of things. He was the most amazing teacher I ever had and I loved him immediately and ever since. Time only confirmed my impression of him. He was, I knew, a mystic.

Tailpiece:

I thought of this one as I was driving in my car and I was contemplating the end of this chapter. One of my favorite songs began playing on my music system. I wonder how many of my readers know Paul Anka. Paul Anka composed a song which was made famous by Frank Sinatra. Later, Paul Anka sang the song as well.

As Paul Anka's voice singing "My Way" filled my car I began to reflect on the words: *I planned each charted course / Each careful step along the byway / But more, much more than this / I did it my way.* And

I began thinking how aptly every word in that song applied to my brother and how appropriately this song described him. The Eastern Catholic Mystic from India, preaching Christ to Catholics and others in the West, as well as to people from all walks of life, doing it All, standing Tall, and doing it *his* way.

Chapter Ten

Inspiration and Controversy: "Very Well, Very Well"[1]

"**W** HO INSPIRED TONY?"
This is the question I have often been asked by various correspondents responding to my e-biography of Tony.

I myself never personally discussed with him the matter of where he obtained his inspiration. As far as I knew, Tony was an enlightened soul who knew how to deliver his message of self-awareness with unmatched skill, holding his audiences and readers spellbound. He delivered eight hour talks without notes interspersed with stories and jokes to fit the theme of his messages, thus enlightening as well as lightening the hearts of his audiences and readers. I had always left it at that.

I have mentioned that since beginning this book, I have met, spoken to, and corresponded with many people who personally knew Tony and who all have views about him. From discussing this with them I have come to certain conclusions in this regard.

In the first place Tony was definitely a person in contact with God. He certainly was not unique in this. There have been thousands

---

[1] Referring to the story of the village girl who became an unwed mother and claimed the father to be the Zen Master. The villagers denounced the Master as a hypocrite and told him to keep the baby. All the Master said was, "Very well. Very well." After a year the girl confessed that she had lied and that the father was the boy next door. The villagers apologized to the Master and took the baby back. And all the Master said was, "Very well. Very well." *The Song of the Bird,* p. 107.

before him—and thousands after him—who also were in contact with God.

What makes a person stand out from others? Without a doubt it is the power of their dream and the intensity of their passion to fulfill it. Tony had a great vision which he wanted to fulfill. I contend that, to an extent, this vision was fulfilled by the time he died. In fact, it continues to be fulfilled twenty five years after his death. Besides living on in the hearts of people, Tony lives on in his books. He does not fail to surprise even today. It is an astounding fact that he has more books "written" by him posthumously than when he was alive.

I have not been able to contact anyone in whom Tony confided his dream as, let us say, a young man about to enter the Society. There are enough people who knew of his later dreams. However, I do have a source for his early dreams and inspirations. The promotional series he wrote gives us an idea of how he got his vocation and what his early inspirations were.

A "Fr. Richard" had given him some books about the Jesuits while he was making up his mind whether to join them or some other Order. The following lines from the booklets take on huge significance:

> I returned the books within a week and asked for more. The large-heartedness of the Ignatian ideal had been irresistible. . . . And I began to say within my heart those words which Ignatius used to repeat to himself after his conversion. St. So-and-so did such great things for God and for others. What shall I do? Why can't I become a great saint too? The thought made me feel generous and gave me deep inner joy.[2]

The story of Ignatius of Loyola and his conversion from a vain man of the world to a humble, fiercely loyal, and outstanding soldier of Christ is a story that is not only well-known but also one that inspired countless men to join the ranks of the Society of Jesus. It cer-

---

[2] *Ah! These Jesuits! Going My Way*, pp. 64-65.

tainly inspired Tony as well. The seed was sown here. The idea was to do great things for Christ. This, no doubt, is what Tony wanted to do—just like every other Jesuit.

But Tony wanted *magis*. Magis (Latin for *more*) is an Ignatian trademark, also contained in that great Ignatian motto *Ad maiorem Dei gloriam*—all for the *greater* glory of God.

I wrote to one of Tony's close friends and asked him if he knew from whom Tony gained his inspiration. His reply is most appropriate and I transcribe it here because I am quite convinced that this man knew Tony very well, had lived with him, and worked out what Tony was about. His words are brilliant and hopefully will answer all those people who have asked me countless times, "Who, do you think, inspired Tony?"

This friend replies:

I do not think it is correct to ask *who* inspired Tony if what is meant by the question is which human being inspired him. I do not think any human inspired him. The answer is obvious. GOD inspired Tony. He was always marching to the beat of a different drum.

However, one may ask: From *where* did he get his ideas? This is an entirely different question. I think there were many different sources. I see it like this. He did not get "inspiration" from any source. He had an idea or a hypothesis and then he looked for or found material that supported his hypothesis. In my opinion he was always looking for ways that would draw people to God and make God accessible to people. Everything he found was first tested by him in his own experience. Then he would tell it to others and tell them not to accept anything that he said, blindly, but to experience it for themselves. In this sense Tony was a lot like Carl Rogers. Carl Rogers says, "Experience is, for me, the highest authority. The touchstone of validity is my own experience. No other person's ideas, and none of my own ideas, are as authoritative as my experience" (*On Becoming a Person*, Houghton, 1961, pp. 23-24).

This is also why Tony was constantly making small and big changes in his ideas, always adjusting them according to his changing experience.

It is not as if he had not found God. He had. But he was moving towards discovering a way to find God that was simple and easy to follow. He wanted many to have this experience. So he kept looking. Vipassana, Bertrand Russell, A. S. Neill, Mahatma Gandhi, Carl Rogers, Frederick Perls, J. Krishnamurthy—all these and more were studied by him. His brilliance was that he integrated this plethora and variety of ideas and still kept them compatible with the teachings of the Church.

(In fact, Tony had recommended that *I* read Krishnamurthy many years ago but his advice fell on deaf ears until recently.)

Whilst I was happy to receive this contribution from Tony's friend, I was not quite satisfied. I have read several articles and a couple of books which make mention of Tony being preoccupied with the teachings of the Buddhist sage Aachan Cha as well as those of Sri S.N. Goenka. Some of my correspondents also asked me if Tony had studied with Aachan Cha. So I wrote to Tony's friend again and asked him how much influence the teachings of these men would have had on Tony's inspiration.

Here is his reply:

Tony attended a Vipassana retreat at Khandala in 1972 (October or thereabouts) along with several Jesuits (including me) from De Nobili College and elsewhere. The retreat was conducted by Shri S. N. Goenka and as far as I know Tony had organized the retreat. To my knowledge Tony did attend at least one more Vipassana retreat along with the first Sadhana group in October of the following year. This may have been for the benefit of the Sadhana-ites. For Tony, the one retreat was enough, I think, because already in the summer of 1973 he was expounding on Vipassana like an old pro.

I myself attended the one Vipassana retreat. I never attended another one and still practise what I learned then. Vipassana promotes the Buddhist concept of constant awareness in the here-and-now. The here-and-now is a concept also promoted by or found in the existential philosophies and therapies e.g. Frederick Perls' Gestalt Therapy. Because it is a Buddhist concept it does not mean that Perls became a Buddhist. By the same token if Tony liked the idea of constant awareness it does not make him a Buddhist.

When I attended a Gestalt Seminar conducted by Tony at Ecstasy, Desur in the summer of 1973, he explained to us that enlightenment was common to many different "religions" and that the experience of enlightenment seemed to be the same for people of all persuasions. This was just before he had started the Sadhana Course. So his ideas along these lines were at the developmental stage then.

Another ex-Jesuit who knew Tony more from a distance and is a keenly analytical person has this to say of Tony's developing ideas:

His Tertianship (and Jesuit background) and Spain experience locked him into the religious (Christian) perspective, but his psychology studies (and US experience) opened him out to new experiences, un-gainsay-able, as also his experiments with Zen and Goenka, and the years of study in an Indian context, where attitudes and thinking are not so strait-jacketed as in the West in certain matters.

Life in the Society of Jesus offers every opportunity to its members to meet God especially through the Spiritual Exercises starting with the Long Retreat already in the first year of the Novitiate. What becomes clear about Tony is that he was looking for other ways that would be simpler and easier to follow so that more people could meet God. This one theme remains at the heart of everything he did—whether he specifically mentioned the word "God" or not.

Significant people and philosophies that Tony drew from were

Fritz Perls, A. S. Neill, and the concept of Constant Awareness or Mindfulness. Awareness was to become his abiding theme toward the end of his life.

Tony's sources are patent in his books which feature stories: *The Song of the Bird, The Prayer of the Frog,* and so on. There one sees that he has drawn stories from Sufi mystics, Zen Masters, Hindu mystics, and the lovable Nasruddin, among others. Tony was Eastern enough to realize the value of a story. He explains in those books why he prefers to tell stories—"because a story will worm its way into your heart and break down barriers to the Divine."[3]

But Tony was not just a compiler of stories. He could also write a regular article and achieve the same effect as a story. This is because he was someone who knew what he was talking about; he was someone who lived what he preached; *he was someone who had seen God.*

There is a little-known article of Tony's; little-known because it came out in a very scholarly theological journal and will have been read by only theologians and "specialists." The average layperson will not have had access to this fine article which appeared in 1982 in an international theological journal called *Concilium.* I am extremely thankful to Mr. Wilfred Felix, the President of *Concilium,* and his Board of Directors but for whose kind permission this article might have been lost to the world at large.

I quote a few of the opening paragraphs of this article by Tony. From reading these you will see that no one but God inspired Tony:

> Why is God invisible? He is not. Your vision is blurred so you fail to see Him. The screen in the movie theatre becomes invisible when a film is projected on it; so, though you ceaselessly look at the screen, you fail to see it—you are too caught up in the movie. . . .
>
> In one's quest for God, then, one must realize that there is nothing to search for or to attain. How can you search for what

---

[3] See *The Prayer of the Frog,* Vol. II, pp. xxi.

is right before your eyes? How can you attain what you already possess? What is called for here is not *effort* but *recognition*.

The disciples at Emmaus had the Risen Lord right before them, but their eyes had to be opened. The Scribes and the Pharisees excelled in effort and failed in recognition. And mankind on the Last Day will exclaim: "You were with us, and we failed to see you!" The quest for God then is the attempt to see.

A man sees a woman every day and she seems no different from other women until one day he falls in love with her. Then his eyes are opened and he is amazed that he could have been contemplating this adorable goddess for years and failed to see her. Stop searching, stop travelling, and you will arrive. There is nowhere to go! Be still and see what is before your eyes. The faster you travel and the more effort you invest in travelling, the more likely you are to go astray. People ask WHERE they will find God. The answer is HERE. WHEN they will find Him. The answer is NOW. HOW they will find Him. The answer is BE SILENT AND LOOK. (An Eastern tale tells of an ocean fish that sets out in search of the ocean; it finds no trace of the ocean wherever it turns, only water!)[4]

Like an artist who can turn out a portrait with a few deft strokes, Tony uses a few choice similes and examples to bring out the ease—and difficulty!—with which one can find God. The difficulty, of course, is of our own making. This is not just a person who happens to be clever with words. This is a person who has experienced what he is talking about. Anyone who reads these few quoted paragraphs would want to read more.[5] Even if the readers of this article are atheists or agnostics they are gripped by the sheer authority of the words and know that in reading them they are very close to an awakening. Tony's words can stir.

---

[4] *Concilium* 159 (9/1982), *Learning to Pray*, pp. 77-81, published by T. & T. Clark.

[5] This is why the entire article has been available, courtesy *Concilium*, in Appendix III, *An Eastern Christian Speaks of Prayer*, p. 250.

At the time of his death, and also after it, Tony became well-established as a preacher, teacher, writer, guide, or guru, if you will. There are a lot of gurus, however, who fall into the category of "Physician heal thyself." While such gurus have an unusual ability to use a good turn of phrase or exceptional communication skills they are sadly lacking in practicing what they preach.

Did Tony fall in this category? This is well worth exploring.

Tony was first and foremost a Jesuit and a priest. To the end of his life he remained faithful to the Society and faithful to his vows. Everything he did, he did for God. He was always concerned for the Society especially its younger members and made sure they too had an opportunity to benefit from his work. That is why he would have programs every summer for the scholastics: Gestalt Therapy, Growth Workshops, and spirituality courses. He was a delegate at GC 32 and GC 33. In fact he was the official leader of the prayers at the latter.

The Spanish Jesuit who was Tony's close friend already at San Cugat, Spain says of him:

> He was for me a First Class Jesuit. He was in a sense the elite of the Society. He was selected to conduct the prayer at the 33rd General Congregation of the Jesuits. They would never appoint a man for this who was not doctrinally sound. . . .

I know from one of his friends about his faithfulness to prayer before bed—however late that was. The same friend, as well as others, mentions that Tony often said in his sermons to them that the day one gave up personal prayer was the beginning of the end of one's vocation. Prayer for him was paramount.

Tony, at one point in his life, seemed to have had some difficulty with praying as has been mentioned. Once Fr. Calveras sorted that out for him he never looked back. And he also was remarkably facile at teaching people to pray.

In the Introduction to *Sadhana—A Way to God* he writes:

> I have found it relatively easy to help people to pray. I do not attribute this merely to some personal charism I have. I attribute

it to some very simple theories that I follow in my own prayer life and in guiding others in the matter of prayer. One theory is that prayer is an exercise that brings fulfilment and satisfaction and it is perfectly legitimate to seek these from prayer. Another is that prayer is to be made less with the head than with the heart. In fact, the sooner it gets away from the head and from thinking the more enjoyable and more profitable it is likely to become. Most priests and religious equate prayer with thinking. That is their downfall.

Tony loved to pray. It was in order to help people pray that Tony used to have those Prayer Seminars of his. Toward the end of his life he was giving these to lay persons as well and—as he told me on the night before he died—he was seeking to reach bigger and wider audiences in India on his return.

Tony was intensely loyal to the Society. He dedicated *Wellsprings—A Book of Spiritual Exercises*: "To the Jesuit order that I feel so proud and so unworthy to belong to."

Not only was he a great Jesuit, he helped other Jesuits to become great Jesuits as well.

A companion of Tony's reminisces:

When I began my theology in DNC Pune in 1961, Tony's room was exactly opposite mine, and he was in his final year of theology, already an ordained priest. I don't think I had much interaction with him all that year; we were practically strangers to each other. Then in 1971 I made my thirty-day retreat under Tony at XTC Desur, together with thirty-nine other Jesuits. It was an extraordinary experience where I learned firsthand the powerful dynamics of the Spiritual Exercises of St Ignatius. Tony was a master director! How he managed to direct forty fully-fledged Jesuits, all at the same time, is a wonder. After that retreat, I felt I now really knew St Ignatius and the Society and the Spiritual Exercises. Finally it was Sadhana 1974-75 in DNC Pune. Of those ten months, Tony was away in Rome for more than two months for GC 32. It was not from Tony's "lectures" (he rarely lectured) but from his frequent flashes of insight that I gained so much—not only for my own personal growth but also as preparation for the Novice Master's work I was going to take up.

The late Prof. Anand Nayak says of Tony: "His permanent and unconditional loyalty to his Order, the Society of Jesus, was, in fact, a concrete expression of his loyalty to the Roman Catholic Church."[6]

In fact it is to the Catholic Church that Tony dedicates *The Song of the Bird:*

> This book has been written for people of every persuasion, religious and non-religious. I cannot, however, hide from my readers the fact that I am a priest of the Catholic Church. I have wandered freely in mystical traditions that are not Christian. . . . It is to my Church, however, that I keep returning, for she is my spiritual home; and while I am acutely, sometimes embarrassingly, conscious of her limitations and narrowness, I also know that it is she who has formed me and made me what I am today. So it is to her that I gratefully dedicate this book.

I know from several sources about his lifelong devotion to Our Lady. I have already mentioned that one of the first things he did as the Rector of Vinay in 1968 was to shift to a smaller, cramped room. At that time the only specific instructions he gave to the young Jesuit who was entrusted with the job of shifting his things were, in the latter's words:

> The only personal belonging of his that he instructed me to take care of was a statue of Our Lady which he had. He wanted me to find a nice stand for it and make sure there was enough room on the stand to place the lamp which he lit in her honour every night.

---

[6] *Anthony deMello: His life and His Spirituality*, p. 88.

A Sister who was very close to Tony—one of the (it now emerges, quite a few!) recipients of one of Tony's last letters writes:

> Tony used to talk plenty about your parents, especially about your mother. He told us he inherited his devotion to Our Lady from her.

Of course I was too young when Tony left home to know whether Mum specifically gave this devotion to Tony but I came to know of it later from "family talk." Tony learned from Mum his devotion to Our Lady, the Blessed Virgin Mary. It was Mum who taught him that his life would be filled with joy, were he to put his faith and trust in Our Lady, and he proclaims this in that fiftieth birthday Mass tape which I listened to recently. He carried this devotion with him throughout his life.

In the previous chapter I made reference to a Jesuit who expressed surprise at how Tony's ideas had changed when they met him at the Sadhana Refresher Course in 1987. He had told his colleague that he would not be surprised if they were to see Tony walking up and down rosary in hand. The amusing fact is Tony did used to recite his rosary as described! It happened once that the Sisters at a convent where he was staying tried to trap him on that. They told him that he was always making fun of their devotions so how come he was reciting the rosary? Tony's reply was typical. "That is none of your business," he said, amid peals of delighted laughter. "I say what I want to say with conviction and I leave you free to recite whatever you want if you wish. But there is a difference between my rosary and your automated recitals." That may sound a trifle conceited but remember it was said in a light-hearted context.

Sadhana—A Way to God is dedicated unabashedly to the Blessed Virgin Mary—a fact noted even by the Explanatory Note of the Notification against his books. It is worth quoting this dedication here:

I dedicate this book to the Blessed Virgin Mary who has always been for me a model of contemplation. . . .

In Tony's book *Rooted in God*, the first five prayer services are dedicated to Mary the mother of Jesus.

In connection with his devotion to Our Lady, I was fortunate to receive from a close friend of Tony's a letter written by Tony himself describing a mystical experience he had in November 1975!

I quote this in full because it is worth noting it in Tony's own words:

I got a tremendous experience of Christ when I was in Khandala, during the retreat. It would not be possible for me to describe it adequately in this letter. One morning, I went to the top of the hill and sat down there after saying *a brief prayer to Our Lady* [emphasis mine]. After a while of sitting on top of that hill and looking at the lovely scene below, I sensed the presence of Jesus near me and He was telling me (of all things) how lovable I was. When I got up to come down the hill, I sensed a great loveliness everywhere and especially within myself. I felt a great love for Him and a great closeness to Him. Then I suddenly developed a thirst for prayer (greater than what I had experienced in the past) and a great thirst for spiritual reading; a sort of desire to get in touch with the Life inside me because I sensed that when I am in touch with that Life I begin to live truly and until I get there all the rest of life is pretty superficial. With this came a great desire to give this Life to others. One day I suddenly began to feel a great softness and tenderness for everyone. Then I sensed this being said inside me; "Till now you have been loving people with your heart. From now onwards I shall show you what it means to love people with my Heart." And I sensed as if the bottom of my heart had opened up to let currents of love from underneath to pass through it. And I felt very, very happy. I'm just longing for this experience to come as often as possible. All of this is too inadequate a description.

It is imperative to note that this experience unlike the other mystical experience that Tony had at Ecstasy in 1973 is of tremendous consequence in the context of this chapter.

Tony's personal life was always exemplary. Even the Notification that I will speak about presently does not make a single negative statement about his prayer and spiritual life or about his life as a priest.

A Sister who did the Maxi-Sadhana says of Tony:

> He always advocated deep relationships and so on and one often got the impression he was advocating a lot of freedom in relationships. But this was not true. And he himself was not that way. He was very strict about these things and his relationships. By his life he taught us a lot.

Tony had several "deep relationships" with both men and women. I have had the privilege of meeting or corresponding with some of these persons. It is they who knew a lot more of my brother than I— and this was only natural. I am indebted to these lovely persons for sharing with me Tony's personal spirituality and lights. The Sister who received one of the letters written by Tony on the day before he died was especially close to Tony. Apparently he would speak quite freely to her about his personal understanding of things and where he was going in his understanding of God and life.

We are privileged to read about Tony in her words:

> From the very beginning I felt that Tony was a deeply spiritual person and my view of him never changed. . . . There was also the dimension of a searcher and mystic in him and that reinforced my feeling about him as a spiritual person, who is very human and fully alive. . . .
>
> I last met him towards the end of 1986. He was already being gripped with new insights, non-attachments, becoming free, yet loved his close friends with more intensity, without any attachments. . . . He was talking about something that gripped him, some insights which he alone could follow. He was talking about something beyond, about another world, which I found difficult to understand. During one of our walks in the woods in Lonavala while we were discussing about love and freedom he spoke about

his insights and longings. He wanted us to understand his journey, his transformation. Suddenly he stopped and looked at me and said, "How I wish, I could show you what I am seeing and experiencing." I told him that I could not understand what he was saying. He was very patient and said, "Someday I will be able to explain this to you; may be better, you will have to come to it yourself." It was painful for him, I knew, to accept that I did not see what he saw, but he let me be free.

It is hard to describe all the thoughts and feelings that flooded through in those days. Sometimes I felt so inspired during the sessions that I rapidly took notes of the things he said soon after the session was over. For instance, he said, "I almost had the sensation that someone else is talking through me. And mysteriously I have never felt so detached and so happy and so gentle and loving in all my life."

He later wrote to me something about Sadhana: "Every time I go to the building I think: we prepare things and look forward with so much eagerness. But each time we prepare a house and decorate it with such loving care, it is our tomb really that we are decorating, because we are birds of passage."

Tony seemed to be moving into a place much deeper than the one before; to a world of freedom and detachment. . . . He was on a transforming journey all through—a journey towards Truth, towards Life in its fullness and towards God. Nothing could stop him from following what he found as truth.

Previously, I neither had an idea of this side to Tony nor an interest in it. Whenever he and I met we always interacted lovingly and happily. I used to tell him jokes I had heard for his collection of jokes and he in turn would tell me a few that he had heard. Our meetings were filled with laughter and mirth. He only but briefly discussed his professional path with me and I was content to simply revel in his company, our time together being always limited.

After hearing from the people who loved him and whom he

loved so well I was much moved—both by their sharing and by the fact that my brother was such a deep person. I do not profess to understand much of this myself, but it is clear even to one unschooled in these affairs that Tony was intensely spiritual. He was into something other-worldly and different and it resonates in me as something that is definitely good.

I often think back to the time that Tony died and my feelings about it both then and now. Time has worn the edge off the sense of injustice I felt at the time that a man who was doing so much good should be taken away in his prime. Tony had just got going as a truly international personality with the potential to make a huge difference not just in his Society but in the world.

I always consoled myself, however, with the thought that even though he had passed on he was still living in his books. Consequently, imagine my shock when one day I came to know of the *Notification Concerning the Writings of Father Anthony deMello* adopted by the Congregation for the Doctrine of the Faith (CDF), signed by the then-Prefect Joseph Cardinal Ratzinger and approved by the Sovereign Pontiff John Paul II on June 24, 1998.[7] I myself got the news when a correspondent who had read my e-biography of Tony wrote and asked me what opinion I had regarding the Notification. My first reaction was, "*What* notification?" I was not up to speed with the goings on in the Catholic Church or in any other religious organization, for that matter. Therefore, after I read it I was completely floored. To say I was gobsmacked would be an understatement. I felt totally ambushed. I could not understand it at all.

My correspondents who had read my first biography of Tony seemed to ask the same question in one voice: Why did the Church issue the Notification against Tony's teachings? I was at a loss as to how to answer that. Why did the Church wait till eleven years after Tony died to issue this Notification?

---

[7] See Appendix II: *Notification Concerning the Writings of Father Anthony deMello, SJ*, p. 239.

This is the question I put to all my new-found friends and re-spondents—Jesuit and otherwise—when I first began to entertain the thought of writing this extended biography of Tony. Over the months I have come to understand a fair amount of how things op-erate in the Catholic Church.

When a book concerning religious or Church matters is written by a Catholic priest or Religious, the faithful have a way of know-ing whether it is suitable for reading. Such a book would have the *Imprimatur* ("let it be printed") of a Bishop of the Catholic Church. When a Jesuit or Religious writes such a book, the Provincial of the Order or Congregation is vested with the authority to give an *Im-primi Potest* ("Can be printed") in which case an Imprimatur is not considered necessary.

Sadhana, The Song of the Bird, Wellsprings, One Minute Wisdom, One Minute Nonsense, The Prayer of the Frog I & II, Contact with God, and *Call to Love*—the nine books published by Gujarat Sahitya Prakash, Anand all have the Imprimatur of a Bishop and some have the Imprimi Potest of the concerned Provincial in addition.

From Nayak who made a spirited defense of Tony I came to un-derstand that the CDF for its purposes had also taken into con-sideration two works which were purportedly written by Tony but actually were not. The first was an article in Spanish called *La Il-luminación es la Espiritualidad* that came out in the magazine, *Vida Nueva* and was attributed to Tony.

After much investigation Nayak found that it consisted of an article of about forty pages, composed of notes and commentaries taken down during talks and conferences:

The author, given as "Anthony deMello," brings in a lot of ideas *full* of fantasies and ruminations from different fields. My student and friend, Luis Rodrigues, gave me an understanding of the whole story: La Iluminación was probably the work of Maria Paz Marino. Vida Nueva apparently published it without mentioning her name but attributing it to Anthony deMello. It was only later, when people discovered its abominable contents, that the true author reworked it and published it under her own name in another edition, which is very different from the first with totally different contents.[8]

The other book was *Walking on Water*, apparently a translation of a work written in Portuguese in Brazil, namely *Caminhar sobre as águas: Quebre o ídolo* which in turn was based on retreats given by Tony in America. I can only think that the phrase, "lost in translation" would apply here quite literally. While I am not sure in which South American country Tony gave his seminar, it would most definitely not have been Brazil. Tony did not speak Portuguese in spite of having come from Goa, a Portuguese colony. Both our parents spoke the language but not Tony.

The Society of Jesus issued a warning in March of 1997 about these falsely attributed works, a year before the appearance of the Roman Notification. The Roman Congregation makes a small note of acknowledgement of this letter in the French edition of the Notification. There is no mention of it made in the English edition.[9]

I have mentioned, in the previous chapter, a book that was published in Tony's name circa 1975. At that time Tony was upset that he had not been given the chance to edit it. To have had books published from notes and commentaries and then attributed to Tony was, in my opinion, grossly unfair and highly unethical on the part of unscrupulous elements who seemed more keen on cashing in on a name that sells.

After reading the Notification and Explanatory Note several times, it seems to me that Tony could have been read out of context. Virtually any work, read out of context, can be misunderstood.

Six of the nine books by Tony published by Gujarat Sahitya Prakash were done so after Tony died. They were garnered from

---

[8] *Anthony deMello: His Life and His Spirituality*, p. 86.
[9] *Anthony deMello: His Life and His Spirituality*, p. 87.

talks and conferences that he gave mainly to Jesuits and Religious—audiences who understood the background against which Tony was speaking. I contend if Tony were alive he would have edited the books so as make certain clarifications for a wider audience.

Secondly, the thrust of the objections by the CDF to what Tony wrote or taught seems to be more about what Tony did *not* assert clearly or unmistakably. For example, the Explanatory Note says: *Who or what is God and what are men in this "dance"? And again: "If you wish to see God, look attentively at creation. Don't reject it; don't reflect on it. Just look at it" (The Song of the Bird, 27). It is not at all clear how Christ's mediation for knowledge of the Father enters into such a description [Underlining mine].* Again it can be contended that had this been pointed out to Tony when alive he would have made such assertions as were necessary.

Thirdly, many of my respondents assert that to their knowledge no one has left the Church as a result of reading or hearing Tony. On the contrary Catholics have got a better understanding of the Church and religion. They insisted that, in reality, many people have left the Church and started hate campaigns against the Church after reading the Bible! I have quite a few letters from people from all over the world telling me how much they have been helped by Tony and/or his books and talks. I also have messages from people who say they had left the Church before they heard or read Tony and that they were inclined to come back to the Church after hearing him.

I sometimes wonder whether the CDF simply failed to understand Tony. I am only a layperson and do not have much of an idea of these things. So I tend to think it was just a case of misunderstanding; that if the CDF had actually attended Tony's seminars they would not have misunderstood him. Maybe I am just naïve.

Again I avow I am no expert on these matters and so would let matters rest here. I only wish to register my intense sadness that this was done to a man who considered the Church as "my spiritual home"; a man who was unable to defend himself from the grave. Let the record show that at least while he was alive he had acted totally in accordance with the rules. All the books published in his lifetime had the Imprimatur and in some cases also the Imprimi Potest.

On the other hand I acknowledge that the Church is an institution and as such was acting in good faith to clarify its stand. I am certain that were Tony alive he would have defended his statements or explained them adequately. If he were genuinely at fault he would have acknowledged as much and retracted his statements. He was bound by the special Jesuit Fourth Vow of Obedience to the Pope.

Was the Notification a "ban" on Tony's books? The Notification proper concludes:

> With the present Notification, in order to protect the good of the Christian faithful, this Congregation declares that the above-mentioned positions are incompatible with the Catholic faith and can cause grave harm.

The Explanatory Note concludes:

> For this reason, those responsible for safeguarding the doctrine of the faith have been obliged to illustrate the dangers in the texts written by Father Anthony deMello or attributed to him, and to warn the faithful about them.

These two texts would make it seem as if the CDF is merely issuing a notice to be careful. In practice it amounted to a ban—at least as far as Catholic publishers and bookshops were concerned.

Gujarat Sahitya Prakash naturally could not continue printing new editions of Tony's books and they disappeared from the shelves of Catholic bookshops overnight until the controversy was cleared.

What this led to was precisely what the Church did not want. It is common knowledge that as soon as a book or movie is banned more people want at it. Tony's books were no exception. They continued to be available commercially. Even if pirated editions were being made there was, for a time, confusion as to who would—or could—protest about it.

One of my many correspondents told me that according to Canon Law the Church may not put sanctions on an author who is dead as they would be unable to defend themselves. I have no idea if this is true and I have not troubled myself to investigate whether there is, in fact, such a clause. My reason for not concerning myself with it is because it would be merely an academic exercise.

The fact of the matter is that the Church has shown that it is not the cold, unmovable, unbending, dogmatic body it is made out to be. Perhaps realizing that Tony is not alive to defend himself and also perhaps acknowledging that his books are doing a lot of good all over the world, the Church retracted the "ban" and permitted Tony's books to be printed along with a Caution that reads:

The books of Father Anthony deMello were written in a multi-religious context to help the followers of other religions, agnostics and atheists in their spiritual search, and they were not intended by the author as manuals of instruction of the Catholic faithful in Christian doctrine or dogma.

I think the Church is making her own stand quite clear and has the right to do so. Weighing matters objectively and putting aside personal feelings and blood relationships I have to admit that this is not an unreasonable compromise. For reasons that she has seen in her wisdom the Church believes that Tony's views are not compatible with her teachings. On the other hand, Tony is not alive to defend his cause. The Caution in its present form at least allows the books to be published by authentic, recognized, and authorized publishers such as Gujarat Sahitya Prakash and not some pirate organization which could add statements which were not written by my brother. The Caution is similar to the Editor's Note one finds in the footnotes of some magazine articles: *The views of the author are not necessarily those of the Editor.*

I am very grateful that the song of the bird has not been stifled. The bird still sings.

CHAPTER ELEVEN

TONY'S RELATIONSHIPS: "DON'T CHANGE"[1]

Single-handedly (more likely, singly), Tony transformed the Church in India—and abroad—from the stodgy thing it had become to the personally liberated characteristic seen today.

—A TONY OBSERVER

THE REASON I HAVE quoted this Tony Observer is because it is the opinion of someone who was not a "blind" fan of Tony's but someone who respected him and tried to be as objective about him as possible. Secondly, I wish to clarify that just because I have quoted him it does not necessarily mean that what he says is true. No one person can make a major impact on a body as large and as universal as the Catholic Church. That generally takes a movement—and Tony was part of the movement.

The "old" Society was full of rules. These rules were adhered to without question. They formed a way of life that was never questioned. Jesuits from the old Society were men of uncommon stature and achievement and were surpassed by none in their love for God and the Church. The one thing they lacked though was the human

---

[1] "Like the others, my closest friend kept urging me to change. So I felt powerless and trapped. One day he said 'Don't change. I love you as you are.' Those words were music to my ears: 'Don't change. Don't change. Don't change . . . I love you as you are.' I relaxed. I came alive. And, suddenly, I changed!"—*The Song of the Bird,* p. 77.

touch. This is not to say they were inhuman. It was just that there was very little place in their formation or training for feelings and understanding. It was always intellect and formal relations, devoid of emotion or sentiment.

What I say above and in the rest of this chapter are my conclusions from absorbing and compiling what I have received from my many respondents, both Jesuit and ex-Jesuit.

Two small examples will demonstrate to you what I mean by "devoid of emotion or sentiment."

One of my respondents tells of a time when he was in a Jesuit school:

> I must have been in Std. VI when this happened. We had a new priest who had joined the school staff. Hardly a week later, an announcement was made during the school assembly. "Boys, please pray for the father of Fr. Furtado who expired last night." There was Fr. Furtado standing in front of the whole assembly with head bowed. We wanted to know what he was doing standing there. Wasn't he going for the funeral? Apparently not. Three days later there was another announcement. Incredulously we heard, "Boys, please pray for the mother of Fr. Furtado who died yesterday morning." And Fr. Furtado was standing right there in front of us, with head bowed as before!

Another respondent contributed the following:

> Our language group at Vinay (1971–1972) would celebrate birthdays in our group by getting each person to make a contribution of one rupee and having a small party. The fare here was not as important as the togetherness! There was an old lay brother in the House whom we had absorbed into our group. When Brother's birthday came round we made our usual arrangement and gave him a small party. His face registered his pleasant surprise at this unexpected gesture. Since he used to make the Mass wine at Vinay for the diocese of Bombay he brought us a celebratory bottle of wine. We realized this was one

party that we were going to enjoy for the fare as well—not just potato crisps this time. Then Brother said he wanted to speak. In a moving speech he told us that he had spent more than fifty years in the Society but never once had his birthday ever been celebrated; not once had anyone showered on him the kind of spontaneous attention that we young scholastics had paid him without making a big deal of it.

This is a brief look at how the "old" Society functioned in the matter of sentiment. The first incident was in the late 1950s and the second in 1971. Nothing wrong here. Just men dedicated to a higher and nobler cause. It was always dedication to God. There was no room for emotion and softness; definitely none for close friendships. The Society's Common Rules stated that there were to be no "particular friendships," i.e., no close or exclusive friendships between two Jesuits. The rationale behind this was that if there were a particular friendship then the two—or more—persons concerned would form an exclusive group and would be concerned only with each other rather than be thinking globally. This was the reason that Jesuits were human beings living in close proximity to each other and yet were strangers to each other.

Tony's deep relationships went a long way toward transforming his ideas and making him more human. Deep relationships became an integral part of his life and eventually his teaching. Toward the end of his life he had transformed the concept of deep relationships, beautifully integrating them into his relationship with God. He showed how it was possible to have a relationship and yet have no attachment.

Tony met his friend with whom he had his "first deep relationship" in 1971. It was a friendship that was to last for the rest of Tony's life and one that, far from making him closed and turned in on himself and his friend, in fact, opened him out to more and more people with whom he formed deep relationships. Deep relationships became part of the teaching at the Sadhana course and in Tony's talks to Jesuits and others.

I am indebted to those of Tony's friends who have shared details of the relationship they had with Tony, also sharing the relevant contents of letters that Tony wrote to them. Without these we would never have known the inside workings of a generous heart that loved so many and so well.

From this first close friend I was enabled to piece together this journey down a new road undertaken by Tony. This friend was there at the start and the two of them seem to have enjoyed a unique friendship, a friendship that overcame gaps in age, knowledge, understanding, and generations. Perhaps the most unique aspect of this relationship was the lack of jealousy and possessiveness in either party. Apparently things were not so smooth in the beginning and this relationship turned out to be a learning curve for both of them. While both were equally new to and tentative about such a relationship both had certain advantages and disadvantages. In Tony's case the disadvantage was that he was brought up in the old Society and had more to unlearn. His advantage was his knowledge of psychology and his experience of giving retreats as a result of which he had come to realize that many of the problems faced by priests and religious were caused by their lack of humanness.

I had best let his friend explain his side in his own words:

Till that eventful day when Tony called me to his room and explained to me the effect on him of my declaration of love for him I had always had an extremely low opinion of myself. I had always suspected I had certain abilities but had rarely received acknowledgement of anything positive in me. If any were ever given it was grudgingly so. What I had received in uncontrolled and generous measure both before and after I joined the Society was a lot of plain talk about what exactly people thought of me—and not much of it was positive. Tony was the first person in my life who not only seemed to appreciate me but actually voiced it. This was a novel experience for me and quite honestly for the first year of this new relationship I just did not believe I had even a tenth of the qualities that Tony seemed to see in me.

So in the beginning the relationship was not equal. I always felt "inferior" in the relationship and one day I could take it no more and had it out with him and told him exactly what I felt. This was at DNC in 1972. I believed I had gone too far but was feeling too stifled to care anymore. I fully expected Tony to tell me he was just sick and tired of my constant moaning and that that would be the end of our friendship. To my stunned discomfiture Tony told me that for the first time he understood where I was coming from. He admitted that he *had* been a bit overpowering in the relationship but that he had never done it deliberately and had never realized it till then. He was so gentle and understanding and apologetic that I was soon in tears— they come even as I write this. Tony added that something that he had always appreciated about me was that I would never feel jealous of his other friendships; that he could always talk about his new relationships with me and that I never seemed to mind; that he had always found me so secure about myself. I had to laugh through my tears and tell him that far from being a secure person I was very insecure. I had never felt jealous because I had never felt *worthy* to be his special friend in the first place and so never minded that he was going out to others so freely. He laughed and said, "This is exactly why I love you so much. You are so intensely lovable and you do not even know it!"

From that day on the relationship changed. We never ever needed to have a session like that again. I realized that it was not so much that he was overpowering as it was I who had been feeling inferior. In one short session Tony had "raised me up to more than I could be" (in the words of the song). The odd thing is I never did feel jealous ever. I knew he loved me and that was enough for me. Whether he loved me most or second or last did not matter. He loved me *enough*, as far as I was concerned.

Tony did have many friends and went about forming deep relationships with people. Just a few lines from different letters written by Tony to one of these new friends—a young Jesuit scholastic—show the trend. Observe how frankly Tony expresses his feelings; how he builds up the other and how humble he remains in his letters:

> You speak of missing me. Will it surprise you to learn that I am missing you? I am. . . . As a matter of fact, I am planning to come back earlier just for you. . . .
>
> I was thinking of you yesterday in the bus. I didn't miss you. I didn't feel the need for you. I just loved you and felt happy and contented that I had you for my friend. Then I suddenly realized that my relationship with you is a very unique one. I have never related with anyone in quite this way. My other relationships have been turbulent at times, full of storms, deeper occasionally, more vehement . . . with you it is peaceful, quiet, secure . . . yet deep and dependable and very satisfying to me.

The "turbulence" that Tony writes about was mainly in one particular relationship which was extremely stormy according to Tony's friend who told me:

> Tony loved that friend much but the latter would be unresponsive and moody. One part of me would be dismayed because Tony would humiliate himself and go and tell this friend *all* his feelings and the upheavals he was undergoing and the friend would remain unmoving and unmoved. Another part of me would admire Tony's courage and brutal honesty even if it showed him in a poor light. Those were indeed turbulent days for Tony and he struggled through them manfully. It was a stage not so much for Tony as for that friend and once the latter had achieved a certain maturity and security their relationship got on to a more even keel. In those early days it was very much a learning experience for Tony.

A Jesuit who later reached high places sent me a sharp observation of his regarding Tony and women:

> [Tony] was a very perceptive person and connected with women who may not have come across as attractive at first sight. He also subtly built their self-esteem and I think they added a softness to his life. There were some who adored him.

I am certain there were adorers aplenty but it was in 1975 according to one friend of Tony's that he began to sit up and take notice of one of these adorers. He told this friend that for the first time he felt inclined to form a deep relationship with a woman. She was a nun, he said, and he seemed very pleased and reported what he liked about her to his friend. This was the first of several deep relationships that Tony would have with women. As he himself always made clear, a deep relationship did not include sex.

About Tony and women, a lay woman from America writes:

> I found him understanding with women. I never found him critical or chauvinistic but he was truly self-assured and open. A great combination! I think some were intimidated not because Tony was intimidating but because they knew that he had something they did not. My guess is that he arrived at what he was by going very deeply into himself . . . where many dare not go! That is my read on it.

I know of some of these relationships because Tony himself told me about them and I have even met some of these women—including the first—when I visited Lonavala with my family in 1980, yet again in 1985 and alone in 1986. I again met a couple of women who were considered extremely close to Tony in December 1987. Their deep sense of loss and grief was plain to see. From what I could see Tony loved these women and they adored him. And there was always an innocence and simplicity about their love for him.

One of these friends kindly shared a few details of her relationship with Tony. Like others in a similar situation she had destroyed

Tony's letters out of a sense of detachment and has preserved only his last one, written before he left on his last flight to the USA and posted at Mumbai airport. She received it after Tony's funeral.

She wrote to me:

> My first meeting with Tony was in 1976 and was incidental. I was a young novice in the convent and had aspirations of becoming a missionary Sister. I did not know who Tony was and when I first met him I had no idea he was "the great Tony deMello." And he was so simple that I never suspected that he was anyone "great." Little did I know then how this man would change my life and how closely I would relate to him as the years went by.
>
> There were always women in his circle of friends who regarded him as very special. With women he was kind and soft hearted. He could be firm when he thought it was required but his approach was always gentle never brash or rude. However his love for women was not sexually oriented; nor did he ever regard women as sexual objects to satisfy his biological instincts. He was too steeped in his religious life to even think along these lines. Women were attracted to him and would always want to relate to him as special. I had the good fortune to be one of his very special friends and he always told me that I gave him life even though his mother had given him birth. He was such a special man and, above all, a humble wonderful human being.

One of Tony's many close friends told me that Tony had the exceptional quality of building a person up and transforming them and he would do it without any preaching or giving of advice. He just accepted them as they were and the unspoken message to them was that they need not change in order to be loved by him. As a result of this they did change—but only because *they* wanted to.

One sees this happening with the Sister just quoted above as well as the many people who interacted with him.

The same Sister continues:

For me personally, he was a changing force in my life. He caused a complete turnaround in my life and I always felt so protected by his constant presence even when we were not together. He pointed out my strengths and weaknesses and helped me grow. He taught me to be spontaneous and honest with myself and with others at all times. I don't believe I can compare him with anyone I have ever met, man or woman, because he was just such a very special, unique person. I will always treasure his memory and be thankful for getting the opportunity to meet and learn from him.

There certainly is something special about this woman and I say so with good reason. She made a gesture that showed me how secure she was in her relationship with Tony. She actually directed me to another woman who was, according to her, "very close to Tony too." I had had no idea about this new person till then and was thankful for the contact. In parenthesis I have to say that there seems to have been no dearth of people—men and women—whom Tony felt close to and with whom he shared his innermost thoughts. In this and other chapters the quotes from his letters to various friends demonstrate this point.

This other woman who was "very close to Tony too" was kind enough to write to me, among other matters, of her relationship with Tony:

Our first meeting was in 1979 at one of our Centers in Changanacherry, where he was giving a prayer seminar. I was one of the participants. I then went on to attend a midi-Sadhana in 1980. I liked him instantly and I was eager not to miss anything he said during the seminar. He had a special way of communicating through stories and humor and had a powerful way of expressing his insights. I found him a very human and spiritual person. . . .

He interacted with women with understanding. At times he was gentle and caring and at times he came across as hard, especially in therapy. He used to get annoyed when they did not get/receive the message he wanted to convey. Generally he was a warm-hearted person towards women. . . .

Not all Tony's relationships were deep ones. He did have many friends though and his ability to write to them and stay in touch with them was phenomenal. And whether the relationship was deep or not he always made the other person feel special. He had an uncanny ability to make the other feel "safe" or "bold" enough to discuss anything—even disagree—with him. Through it all he would always validate them as persons.

A Jesuit who was close to Tony for a long time has this to say:

I had a very long, personal and fruitful relationship with Tony, lasting seventeen years. I was in constant touch with him and had the privilege of even serving under him. I got to know and understand his nature very well. I did not always see eye to eye with Tony and had some huge arguments with him. Mostly though, they were of my initiation and Tony would always defuse the situation with his wisdom.

The same Jesuit who made the astute observation about Tony's relationships with women also speaks about his own relationship with Tony:

Initially he was a counselor and guide to me. But with time we became very close friends. I would share about myself and he would share about himself.

This is again confirmation of what I maintained earlier of how Tony accommodated everyone in his large heart and gave them genuine reassurance that they mattered to him.

I have been unable to contact many of the Jesuits who were Tony's close friends. In most cases they were younger than he. Many of them left the Society and now move in different circles and though I managed to write to or email some of them nothing much came of it.

From the contacts that I do have I have been able to pick up that Tony's concept of relationships was undergoing a major change toward the end of his life. In fact it is not so much his concept of relationships that is of special note here but his concept of life and its meaning. It is against this backdrop that one should read about his ideas on relationships. He was seeing relationships transformed into something pure and detached. He revealed much of this to a few very close friends.

One of these close friends wrote to me:

> As you know Tony had many friends, some of them very close to him. [Some other Sisters] and myself happened to be among those who were very close to him and he used to share his insights, feelings, inspirations and spiritual journey with us. He used to share with us directly (if we were with him) or he used to correspond if we were not nearby. Somehow he wanted to get our feelings and feedback about what he shared, and he valued it. For him it was part of being open to what he was going through. Part of what I have shared with you is from the letters he wrote and the others from the discussions we have had on different occasions.

It was Tony's extraordinary gift that he could make each of these close friends of his feel distinctive simply because he would genuinely see them as exceptional and unique. Whatever he said to his friends was always genuine and honest and from the heart.

The same Sister wrote to me about Tony's evolving concept of relationships:

> [Towards the end of 1986] Tony was talking about transforming his relationships with his friends into a phase of complete detachment and freedom. One time I asked him whether there was any place for writing to each other in his new-found mysticism; if he wished that we continue our correspondence. He replied, "Now let me make one thing absolutely and abundantly clear to you, my dear; mysticism or no mysticism, you are far too precious to me and far too much part and parcel of my being for me to be able to be detached from you. Can I be

detached from myself? When I speak of my detachment, I am not at all talking of 'giving up' Far from it. I am talking about loving you with a love that is much more pure without having to cling to you."

Then again in February 1987, I asked him in a letter if there was place for "memories and emotions" in his new way of thinking. He wrote, "Yes, of course there is, otherwise life would be so dull. But there is no place for negative emotions—all that kind of suffering is really a waste of time and a waste of precious life. Negative emotions always come from our wrong perceptions and wrong ideas. But for positive emotions there is plenty of place—however, positive emotions that are aroused by present reality, not by past memories, because to return to the past is to return to what is dead."

In Feb. 1987 when I told him that I fully accepted the path toward which he was moving, he wrote to me saying, "It brought me so much joy because the only slight pain I would have had in walking along this path (it isn't as if I can choose to walk along it or not, I am compelled to do so by some force within me) would have been if a couple of my closest friends like you were not to accept it. Now that I have the "blessing" from all of you, I can move along with a contented heart. And I love all of you even more for this, if that were possible."

One of Tony's close friends concludes her letter to me as follows:

Bill, you have asked me how I perceived Tony from a few angles. In reply, I can tell you that first and foremost he was a close friend of mine, my spiritual director and a person who was fully human and fully alive. Tony loved life and for him life was a celebration. He enjoyed it in the company of his friends and with people everywhere. Every time I was with Tony, it was challenging and energizing, triggering something new. It deepened my understanding and at times led me into deeper silence. I feel privileged and proud to have known him and been one of his close friends. I cannot compare him with anyone I know. He was very unique and, for me, there is no one like him.

Perhaps the last part of that last line—in the present tense, as something ongoing—is one that every one of his friends would say about him. Certainly it is the very reason why I felt moved to write this tribute to him. There were so many who were Tony's close and special friends and they were much closer to him than I was. I often mulled over this and had mixed feelings about it. Today I know that given the opportunity he and I too would have been close. And more uplifting than that thought is the fact that Tony in death is so much closer to me now than he was to me in life. Every time I read a book of his or hear him on my car stereo he speaks to me and I gain from him. The wonderful thing is that he shares a deep relationship now with thousands of people. I realize now that Tony was not created to belong to just one person or one family.

He was and is truly universal.

CHAPTER TWELVE

TONY, THE HUMBLE HUMAN BEING:
"LIFE IS MIRACULOUS"

MANY OF MY CORRESPONDENTS who read my e-biography of Tony have indicated to me that they only know Tony from his books. They see him as a larger-than-life figure and wonder what kind of *person* he was. Was he a happy person? Was he constantly in a state of elation? Was he ever depressed? Did he have quarrels with others? Were there misunderstandings? Did he ever stop talking to someone with whom he had had a disagreement?

So many questions and just a one-line answer would suffice. Tony was a man not a god. What I can say, from my limited personal contact with Tony and from all those with whom I have corresponded, is that Tony had no Ego. This he demonstrated in his speech, dress, and attitude to others. He was a humble human being. That is why everyone felt so comfortable and secure in his company.

If Tony the guru is best remembered for his incisive speeches that cut surgically and relentlessly through to the truth, Tony the man would be best remembered for his kindness and concern for others and for his jokes—many of them quite "off-color"!

While thinking of how best to portray Tony as a person I remembered a joke that he often told:

At Sunday School, Sister was at pains to explain to the children that "priests are special. They are the anointed ones of God. They make Christ present everyday at Mass" and so on and so forth. She was interrupted by Tommy who was waving his hand frantically. Tommy had a very profound question. He wanted to know, "Sister, do priests go to the bathroom?" Sister did not quite appreciate this "humanizing" of priests, but she also had to tell the truth. So she compromised with, "Yes! But not as often as other people!"

That would be a good description of Tony. Was he depressed ever? Did he have misunderstandings? Yes, but not as often as other people.

Tony was like any one of us. And he was different.

How people conduct themselves depends on how they perceive things; their philosophy of life. Tony had come to understand that life is miraculous and he expresses this in several of his books. Here is one example: *It isn't as if life is not full of miracles. It's more than that: it is miraculous, and anyone who stops taking it for granted will see it at once.*[1]

Tony would look at a person and see something different and exceptional in them. He would never hesitate to express this to them. It was as if he saw in them the miraculous. He would be struck by their spontaneity, their gestures, and their various qualities as if he were seeing something like these for the first time in his life.

In this connection one of my Jesuit respondents wrote to me:

He used to often mention how Christ loved little children and wanted us to be like little children because as he (Tony) put it, "Children have a sense of wonder; an immense capacity to marvel at a flower or a leaf which we adults take for granted." Tony had this same sense of wonder himself which would make him enjoy the inanest quality of a person and make that person feel extremely special indeed. In this sense he truly practised the Ignatian dictate of "finding God in all things."

Was Tony ever depressed? Of course he was; more often than we care to think. He walked around with that big broad smile and

---

[1] *The Prayer of the Frog—I*, p. 49.

indulged in boisterous laughter, but he had his fits of depression.

These occasions of depression became very few toward the end of his life. He would write to his friends when he was feeling low and he would pray. Here is a snippet from one of his letters to a friend who was a Jesuit scholastic:

> You will probably be surprised to receive this letter from me, particularly if you have already received the lengthy letter that I wrote you about a week ago. I myself am surprised I am writing this. Why am I writing it? For no other reason than that I'm feeling a little under the weather, so to speak, and having no one in particular to communicate with, my mind automatically turned to you. Oh yes, I did think of communicating with the Lord—quite a crazy kind of prayer it turned out to be.

Everybody goes through low times. The advantage for Tony of having close friends was that he had someone with whom to share the high moments as well as the low. The friends had the same advantage. Here is an excerpt from a letter to the same friend in response to the *latter*'s going through a rough patch:

> You know, I felt somewhat out on an ocean myself. I hired that boat that you use so frequently and sat in it together with you. And the overall feeling was, "What on earth would I do without you." I just felt intensely grateful that I have you. I am holding on to you, so to speak and it made me feel very safe and steadied.

Toward the very end of his life one sees that Tony had mastered the art of coping with depression. I have listened to his *Awareness* recordings numerous times. Each time he comes to the part about being depressed, I pick myself up and listen even more intently. He says, "People ask me if I ever feel low. Boy, do I get low feelings. Of course I do; if I had a dollar for every time I get a low feeling, I would be a millionaire. But you see, I don't identify with it. I observe it, I leave it alone and eventually, it passes. Like passing clouds. Clouds come and go."

So not only had Tony learned to cope better with depression (which we all experience from time to time) but typically he got his audiences to understand and follow suit.

In the *Awareness* and other tapes Tony comes across as accomplished. But when he writes to his friends you may have noticed that he is not the counselor, advisor, or retreat director. There is no sermonizing or drawing of lessons. He writes as one friend to another. He comes across as vulnerable and human. It is important to know this because he was so different toward the end of his life when such matters became of less and less consequence to him.

A letter to a friend written in 1975 shows this kind of vulnerability when Tony feels justifiably excited by the fact that he had won over a person who was indifferent to him:

> There are a dozen things I have to tell you. Let me begin with Khandala. While I was there I met with Fr. X—[a well-known, much loved, senior priest]. In the beginning I sensed some slight opposition, or rather some little coldness in him towards me or towards what I was saying. . . . I did not know what to do about it. But it wasn't long before I started to take a real liking towards him and he to me. We had a couple of intimate talks. When he got back he was praising me to the skies . . . saying things like, "We were like clay in that man's hands . . . I thought I knew many things, but after meeting Tony, I realized how empty I was."

It is consoling to think that a man as accomplished as Tony was even in those days would be thrilled by minor victories like these.

In a letter to yet another friend written in 1977 Tony shows a similar elation over personal changes:

> Everybody at Vidyajyoti [Jesuit Theologate in New Delhi], even the ones who had been in some contact with me last year, found me greatly changed! For the better, of course! The words they kept using most frequently to describe the change were confident, open, free and—this last from [a couple of Staff members]—

peaceful. I have noticed the change myself. . . . It is wonderful to be growing constantly and constantly exploring new paths, so you see we simply have to "foregather" as our friend P. G. [Wodehouse] would have put it so that you will see the change in me for yourself.

Tony was "an indefatigable talker" and so it is not surprising that he became a renowned *speaker*. How else could he otherwise have delivered his spiritual and counseling expertise to so many people? In the course of writing this book, some of my respondents have written to tell me that they met my parents. They believe that Tony inherited his sense of humor from our father and his ability to hold an audience spellbound from our mother. I was also told that I had inherited the same trait from Dad and I do agree. I love listening to and telling a good joke, some of them quite "off color" at times.

In Tony's case, I think speaking was a necessary asset but there were times when this irritated some people. Some Religious have been known to say things like, "If you want to go and listen to someone talk himself hoarse for hours on end, then go and listen to Tony. All he does is talk, talk, talk." I am amused by these comments because what they said was quite true. But when he talked people wanted to listen. Tony never forced people to come and listen to him—they voluntarily flocked to his discourses.

Earlier on in his life, Tony used to be affected by these comments. It saddened him that people held his talkative nature against him and that they could not "see" the meaning behind his discourses. I can also understand some of these people getting irritated by Tony and not wanting to listen to him. In his *Awareness* Conference, he speaks about waking people up. He says: *Most people are asleep. They don't want to wake up. They will tell you that they want to wake up. But don't listen to them. They don't want to wake up. All they want is for their toys to be repaired.*

Tony had a way of "waking people up" which upset some of them and they accordingly voiced their displeasure. He was known to shock people out of their "slumber" with outrageous comments which did not go down very well with some.

In turn, after hearing about their comments either second hand or sometimes directly from them, Tony used to try and make them understand. In most cases, they eventually saw what he was getting at and changed. In some cases they stubbornly resisted. I came across one such priest during my school days who used to make snide remarks about Tony. Given the circumstances I decided the best form of retaliation was to keep my mouth shut, something for which I am not renowned!

Toward the end of his life though, Tony fully accepted the fact that not everyone agreed with him. Moreover, he had reached such a point in his spiritual development that derogatory comments did not affect him one bit. He was wont to tell people, "If you benefit from me, that's fine and if you don't benefit from me, that's fine too." How does one draw a portrait of a man as many-faceted and talented as Tony was? I start to write about his kindness and generosity and find myself thinking of instances I have received of his honesty and forgiving nature. If I then decide to write about his honesty I find myself wanting to write about the effect he had on people—the Tony Effect. I then decided to let my respondents speak for themselves but even they are all over the map. There is just too much to Tony to put in any disciplined order.

So I shall give select responses from my respondents in some sort of nebulous pattern and hope that the reader will use these opinions as strands and weave it into the uncommon tapestry that was Tony.

There never was anything artificial or hypocritical about Tony. He was always up front and extremely honest.

A Sister wrote to me about his honesty:

I experienced Tony's transparency and honesty when dealing with people. He had a tremendous insight into people and was able to guide them, challenge them and help them. Truth Telling was his way of dealing with people, even with his own friends.

I know this to be true in his dealings with me. There never was anything deceptive about Tony.

Here is how one of Tony's very close friends, who was a religious Sister at the time, perceived Tony as a person:

> My very first impression of him was a good one. I remember thinking that he was not only a jovial and outgoing person but also a very mischievous one. I was taken by his caring attitude toward everyone he came into contact with. I did not have a clue about who he was and how well respected he was in religious circles. Tony had no ego so it was very easy to relate to and communicate with him. I only found out later that this priest who joked and laughed with us novices was, in fact, a very well regarded and respected retreat director. But the way he interacted with us did not leave us with the notion that we had to respect and bow to him. He put himself on the same level as us and made us feel equal to him.
>
> I cannot say that my first impression of him stayed the same as the years passed because Tony changed and grew along with his friends and associates. He was an open book for all to read. His charisma was magnetic without being clinging and he was always such a caring loving person, it was so easy to love him. In general, he interacted with people lovingly and tenderly. He was very talkative and vocal but his discussions never led to arguments. He stated his views clearly and soundly without offending people and always had a way of leaving people happy. He had a heart of gold with which to understand people.
>
> For me, Tony was the complete man, bursting with life, overflowing with laughter and kindness. He was a humble being, full of spirituality and understanding of others; brimful with love and one with nature. He was so intelligent and yet so simple and humble that he could relate to anyone, young or old, man, woman or child.

His Jesuit friend of many years states:

Tony was not only the best Jesuit I have ever known but also the best human being I have ever encountered. He was a generous, kind hearted, gentle human being and would never intentionally hurt anyone. Let me give an example of his generosity. When Tony started publishing his books, his community was receiving the royalties from the sales. A couple of people we knew had a desire to further their education but did not have the funds for this. I know that Tony personally requested the treasurer to use funds from these royalties to help these people. Tony did not consider this an act of great charity. He thought nothing of it. . . .

I know of countless people who came into contact with Tony who say that he changed their lives. He was honest, loving and loyal—not just with his friends but with his detractors as well. He had that special gift of understanding and forgiving any wrong doing even if he was at the receiving end of it. I have never had a friend like Tony and I don't believe I will ever encounter anyone quite like him.

The eloquent woman from America quoted earlier surpasses herself when it comes to giving an analysis of Tony the man:

Tony was a class act. He was gracious and kind. He interacted in a way that was respectful and always challenging. He challenged ideas that bound us with new ideas that freed us. In this way, he frightened some, especially those who came for the old stuff. I never heard him speak roughly to anyone but because he spoke the truth from such a deep place, he challenged people. He wanted people to see in a new way and he was very effective with that. . . .

The last time I saw Tony alive was probably in 1985/6. He was his usual self. Sometimes you could forget his humanity because he was such a riveting, delightful, intelligent, joyous, kind man. He seemed more than human at times. Tony was not just another retreat director he was a superb retreat director. He was exceptional. I have never met anyone like him. He was ever so impressive as a human being . . . so gifted, so bright, so compassionate, so aware and so willing to laugh at his weaknesses.

Perhaps the last word in this section belongs to a woman who felt so uplifted by Tony because she felt he showered so much love on her:

> There are no words to express what he did for me—it is something so unique which is why I always prefer not to discuss it because I can't put it in words. . . . For me he was such a great experience. No words can describe this. It is an experience that has left an imprint that will NEVER be forgotten.

No description of Tony would be complete without mention of his sense of humor and his jokes. He loved to collect jokes and apparently this habit went back to his early days in the Society.

His companion on the boat to Spain mentions this in his interview:

> Tony was a very jovial person and was full of jokes. He had a whole collection of jokes which he had written down . . . . On the boat trip he would entertain us. We travelled with a Monsignor—I can't remember his name—who later became the Bishop of Calcutta. . . . Tony used to relate the jokes to the Monsignor and we would all laugh heartily at them.

So Tony obviously started young. Apart from his jokes there were humorous incidents that took place during his various sessions. Anyone who has seen his DVDs or heard his audio tapes would know this. My respondents have given me a few incidents from Tony's sessions with the Jesuit scholastics. I summarize three of them below:

At the Ecstasy Course Tony would conduct Gestalt theory classes in the afternoon and occasionally demonstrate certain experiments like the Empty Chair Therapy and so on. One afternoon as Tony was talking he noticed one young man who was sitting in a peculiar manner with one leg crossed over the other and his hands in his lap. Tony called him forward to demonstrate that in Gestalt Therapy one never asks the question "Why." Instead you start a "conversation."

Tony: If your right leg could talk what would it say to your left leg? Express *feelings*.

Scholastic: "I am on top of you . . . And I feel good about it."

T: Be the left leg and talk to the right leg.

S: "I hate you, you're a pain. Get off me."

T: Say that again. Louder this time.

S: "I HATE YOU. GET OFF ME."

T: *Whom* are you saying that to?

S: (in awe) I just realized I am saying this to my friend.

T: (to the audience) You see? This is how we arrive at something.

Voice from audience: But Tony why was he sitting in that peculiar manner?

S: Actually I was sitting like that because the zip of my fly is broken and I had to hide that!

Loud laughter.

Tony: I hope you are wearing some decent underwear.

Even louder laughter.

Tony: You see what I mean? If you had asked right at the beginning *why* he was sitting like that, all you would have got from him is a broken zip . . . and possibly outrageous underwear!

Crash of laughter and applause!

In a Gestalt Therapy session at the same Ecstasy Course the group working with Tony singled out one particular person to sort out. Some of the remarks addressed to him were: "I hate the way you strut about like a peacock as though you are the greatest guy in the world." "You walk around like a roaring lion and you don't care for anyone. I resent that greatly." "I feel rebuffed and rejected by you. You are rude and brash and ride roughshod over people's feelings." They were piling it on. The group was also testing Tony to see if he would break his rule of "no playing Rescuer" and jump into the fray in defense of the "Victim" (who was one of Tony's close friends). Tony stayed out of it and remained silent. Someone said to Tony aggressively, "Tony, I resent the fact that you are silent and saying nothing." Tony responded with: "And I am angry with *you*! If you are upset with the way the group is treating him say so to the group. Don't suck me into your game. And anyway, to be honest, I know him only in some contexts. If this is how you all perceive him, go ahead and express yourselves. Let him speak for himself. I must add quite honestly though: I do not agree with your remarks that he struts like a peacock or walks like a lion. He has always struck me more as waddling like a duck!" The ensuing laughter broke the tension and brought a welcome though temporary reprieve for the one in the "hot seat."

In the Gestalt Therapy sessions that were conducted at Lonavala in the following year, Tony opened the session on the first day by announcing that anyone could say whatever they wished provided they expressed a feeling (not a thought) and it had to be their own feeling; they were not to express someone else's resentments etc. One participant decided this was his chance to express his rebelliousness. That entire day he said nothing at all in the sessions. By the end of the day he was beginning to make several group members uncomfortable. The next day his silence and complete indifference to everyone continued. Tony was unconcerned and let him be. By the evening of the second day this "indifferent" participant began to get reactions: "Look at him! Just staring at everybody and saying nothing." "He is just lying down there without a care in the world." Remark from Tony: "I thought I asked for feelings? Those are not *feelings*." Through all this the participant in question stayed silent. He would lie there on the mattresses which were arranged on the floor in lieu of chairs and occasionally fall asleep. His whole attitude was one of disdain. By the third day the group members began to get incensed. They began telling him that they were upset with him; that they resented him; they would prefer him to leave the group etc. Stoic silence from him. By the end of the third day Tony said in a stage whisper to him: "I say, even *I* am beginning to be puzzled by your behavior. What are you up to?" At this he broke into laughter; so did the rest of the group. Then he began to take an active part in the proceedings. At the end of the fifth day, Tony said to him in the group with a twinkle in his eye, "I say, you were silent for the first three days. But there is no need to make up for it so much now. Can you take it easy for a bit?"

Moments like these would release the high tension that these sessions could generate. By the end of the course many problems were resolved and everyone returned with healthier and happier attitudes.

Wherever Tony was there seemed to be laughter and fun. And sometimes Tony could be at the wrong end of a joke. When I was on my family visit to Tony at Lonavala in 1980, he was conducting a Sadhana course then with the help of his team and we were invited to share the house with them. While Tony and his team took care of all the participants' spiritual and counseling needs, there was a Jesuit lay brother who was in charge of running the house. Everyone who attended a Sadhana in Lonavala would well remember the efficient way their needs were catered to by Br. Mario Correia SJ. He ran the place to perfection, making sure the house was always stocked with adequate provisions and everything was in good order. Mario took very good care of us as well. My sons were quite young then and they both took a great shine to him. He catered to their every whim and there was nothing too difficult or impossible whenever they requested anything from him.

One evening, after the participants had finished their day, we all met in the "Refectory" for dinner. Tony arrived a bit late and immediately "took over" and started involving everyone in his conversation, talking and laughing and telling a joke or two here and there. Tony had instructed both our sons to call him by his first name. This was unusual at that time and particularly in India, where most children address elders as "Aunty" or "Uncle," irrespective of whether they are actually related or not.

Everyone was seated around the dinner table and listening intently to Tony talking. Much to the amusement and delight of all, my younger son, who was then not quite six years old, said during a pause in Tony's talking, "Tony, you are talking too much. Every time you open your mouth, a frog jumps out of it."

This comment brought the house down. Every person there without exception burst into loud laughter and some thumped the table in delight at this little fellow putting Tony in his place. Not to be outdone, Tony gathered his composure and once the laughter had died down, feigned seriousness and addressed the little fellow, "What do you mean I am talking too much? Do you know whom *you* are talking to? I am the Superior here."

Everyone expected the little chap to back down. Instead he replied, "Tony, you may be the Superior but Mario is the Boss!"

This brought another round of applause and much laughter, this time with Tony joining in with that big hearty laugh of his.

Maybe it needed one young deMello to sort out the older one? I wonder if Tony would have fared much better with the next generation of deMellos either. He often said he was not a writer but a story teller. He waxes eloquent about this in one of his books:

> The Spiritual Teachers of humanity, like Buddha and Jesus, created a device to circumvent the opposition of their listeners: the story. They knew that the most entrancing words a language holds are "Once upon a time . . . ," that it is common to oppose a truth but impossible to resist a story. Vyasa, the author of the Mahabharata, says that if you listen carefully to a story you will never be the same again. That is because the story will worm its way into your heart and break down barriers to the divine.[2]

Well, all I can say is that Tony had not met my five-year-old granddaughter and if he had I wonder how he would have dealt with her. One day, this granddaughter asked me to tell her a story.

---

[2] *The Prayer of the Frog*, Vol. II, pp. xxi.

Probably thinking of Tony and the magic of a story, I dramatically opened with, "Once upon a time, there was a little boy named Jack. . . . " "Papa," she said, rolling her eyes, "is this going to be a very *looong* story?" End of story! Then again, on reflection, I am sure Tony would have got away with the entire story, unlike me!

I was reflecting on how those who knew Tony would best remember him. From respondent after respondent I get instances of his great kindness and thoughtfulness. It is something that is so outstanding about him. A man who was a superstar, busy for every moment of his waking hours, unable to indulge in too much of leisure, always on the go for God—yet he always had time for others. He would show them he thought of them in a distinctive way.

A senior Spanish sister wrote to me to say:

> I saw Tony a few days before he flew to U.S.A. I did not notice him preoccupied but sometimes used to talk about death. He always called me when he was in Mumbai, and though he did not drink, he invited me to drink a beer because he knew I liked it. We talked a lot and how much we laughed together.

This would be a lasting memory in her mind whenever she thinks of Tony.

Tony would stick his neck out for someone out of sheer kindness. The Jesuit who had had a disagreement with Tony when the latter was teaching him in the novitiate later wanted very much to do the Sadhana course under certain conditions which were not easy to fulfill.

He remembers Tony's thoughtfulness in this regard:

> Since I was in formation, I felt a great desire to do Sadhana myself, the full nine-month one. But how was I to get leave from the Seminary to do it? However, I was due for Tertianship, and I asked Tony if I could do Sadhana as my Tertianship and Tony was all for that. But my Provincial gave a firm thumbs down to the proposal. However, it happened that during the year of the Second Sadhana, both Tony and my Provincial had

to be together for at least a couple of months at one of the Society's General Congregations in Rome [GC 32], and it was there that Tony used his immense powers of persuasion to convince the Provincial to allow me the privilege. I was then one of the very few lucky ones that combined Sadhana with Tertianship. . . .

Let me add here that any Jesuit reading this would understand the amazing implications of what transpired here. This Jesuit who did Sadhana in lieu of a "regular" Tertianship was not only the only Jesuit to do so but he was—arguably—the only Jesuit ever who skipped a regular Tertianship and yet got his Last Vows.

Another respondent tells me that when he was in a remote mission station Tony wrote to him and included in his letter an envelope with stamps so that he would be able to reply and not feel so cut off from the rest of the world.

A Spanish priest who did Sadhana recalls that Tony came to see them off at the train station when the course was over. Tony disappeared for some time and reappeared presently with a religious magazine in one hand and the latest *Newsweek* in the other. The magazine he gave to the home Jesuits and the *Newsweek* he gave to the Spanish priest telling him that it should entertain him on his trip. The latter was much moved by this thoughtful gesture.

One Sister who was in the first Sadhana group to admit women wrote to say that she got a letter from Tony two days before he died where all he said was that he would be returning to India on a certain date and that she should come and meet him without fail. It made her feel cared for. She adds:

> After reflecting on what Tony's impact on my life was I came to this conclusion. To put it all in a nut shell: Tony believed in me and that helped me to believe in myself. This is what I realized much later. This belief in myself helped me a great deal in the responsibilities entrusted to me later.

It is these little acts of thoughtfulness and kindness that all add up.

A Jesuit who had Tony as his Spiritual Guide for seventeen years writes:

> I loved him as I would my own father. Though he was my Spiritual Father, I never felt like that. I felt like I was his friend. I could confide anything in him and I knew for sure that he would understand and never condemn me for whatever mistake or wrongdoing I may do.

The same idea of non-condemnation and loyalty is conveyed by the Spanish priest who was Tony's companion right from the Spain days when he says about Tony that he would *"never abandon me."* I do believe those words are very significant and describe Tony so well. He had this tremendous loyalty to people and he would never judge them. Somehow he always conveyed love even when he was being firm with them. His was always the giving kind of love; never the wanting or demanding type.

How true it is that people do not remember what you say; they only remember how you make them feel.

My family and I have had two outstanding experiences of Tony that sum him up for me. Both instances took place in Australia. The first episode demonstrates for me Tony's willingness to leave the other person free and accept them unconditionally without passing judgment on them.

Tony had come to Sydney in early 1976 to give a retreat. Our second son was born in December 1975 and we timed his baptism to coincide with Tony's visit so that he could do the honors.

During his brief visit, he asked numerous questions about our life in Australia and how we were doing. I had sometimes thought (rather unfairly) that Tony may not have cared too much for the brother who had left India and adopted another country and that he had never shown much interest in what I was doing. (Could that have been the reason, I wonder, why in return I had not shown much interest in his activities?) So with all this sudden "interest" he was now showing in my life I recall thinking, "This is Tony subtly expressing his disappointment at my not having made my home in his beloved India."

But, as I was to discover later, I was quite wrong. He was really quite happy for me. In any case, we went on to tell him of the ups and downs in our new country. Featuring largely in our downs was our difficulty in getting a loan to buy our own home.

Tony listened attentively before asking me whether I believed in the power of prayer. Tony knew that I was leaning toward agnosticism. So I was taken aback by his question. But he went on to mention that if we were conducive to the idea, could we all pray together for a loan to be granted us? Amusing as this was—with my financial status no bank manager would have even entertained me—my wife and I agreed. After all, what did we have to lose by saying a simple prayer? Tony had us all sit at the dining table and join hands. Included were our first son and the baby in my wife's arms. Tony said a simple prayer to the Lord asking him to consider our plight and, if it were for our good, to grant us the loan. It really was that simple.

It was so simple that I forgot all about it! A couple of weeks later my wife reminded me that I had an appointment with our bank manager. I did so without any great hope. To my intense surprise—even consternation—we did get our loan! In retrospect, I realize, I should never have been surprised.

In 1978 Tony was en route to the Philippines via Sydney to give a retreat to Religious there. We had the pleasure of thanking him in person for his simple prayer in the very home we had prayed for!

What has always remained with me is not only the miracle of the granted loan but Tony's manner. For any other priest this might have been a heaven-sent opportunity to make his agnostic brother learn the error of his ways and read him a lecture. Instead Tony merely invited me to be open and made me feel totally comfortable as he prayed.

The second episode was a lesson on how to love. During that 1978 visit, both our sons hovered around Tony for his entire short stay. It was only for a weekend but they shadowed him wherever he went and he obliged them with plenty of hugs, conversation, and play. On the Monday I had taken the day off to drop Tony off at the Jesuit House in Sydney. Our older son wanted to stay home from school and be with Tony. We convinced him that Tony would be leaving shortly anyway. Reluctantly he packed his bag and dragged himself out the front door. We lived very close to his school and all he had to do was cross a major road at traffic lights a short distance away. Our little son was talking to some friends when one of the children yelled out that they should cross the road. In that moment he forgot what we had always taught him. Without checking the lights he darted across the road, only to hear the screech of car tires and see a car coming to a stop inches from him. The driver was hysterical. She grabbed him by the arm and dragged him to the Principal. The Principal, in his wisdom, first lectured the boy and then caned him. I received a call from him to tell me what my son had done.

I was livid. Tony was still at home with us and I narrated what had happened. Everything I had learned about discipline from my childhood manifested itself in my next statement, "Just wait till he gets home. He is going to get another dose of the cane from me. How stupid can a kid get to run across the road like that?"

I noticed Tony observing my reaction with a strange look on his face. Softly, he said, "Bill do you love him? Are you happy that he was not run over by that car and that he is safe?" When I replied in the affirmative, Tony went on, "Then, instead of caning him for something he did without realizing the consequences, when he comes home, why don't you take him in your arms and hug him close to you? Tell him that you love him and are happy he wasn't hurt. He has already received his punishment at school. Why would you want to further embarrass him and dole out another round of punishment when all he needs now is a reassuring hug from you?"

My parental instincts told me that Tony was right. I should be relieved and grateful that my son was not hurt. My conditioning told me otherwise. When was he going to learn to observe road rules? I needed to take drastic action to ensure his future safety. Tony's words, in that calm soothing voice of his, however, kept ringing in my ears, telling me there was another way.

When the little guy walked through the door later that afternoon, I could clearly see he was nervous. I must have had exactly the same look when I was facing my parents after one of my shenanigans. I did as Tony had suggested and took him in my arms and told him I loved him; that I was so happy to see he was unhurt and well. I could see his face changing from surprise to puzzlement, from confusion to relief, from relief to joy. That was priceless. In his gentle, unobtrusive way, Tony had taught me how to love. Sadly, after the incident, I went back to being the strict disciplinarian and my attitude led to much strife and stress.

So many men and women had the good fortune to have lived and interacted with Tony at close quarters. My meetings with him were limited and when we did meet, it was but briefly. Unlike many others, I cannot claim to have gained personal guidance from him during his lifetime except on a few occasions. I do now though—after my introduction to his recordings and books which I so thoroughly enjoy and from which I learn so much.

There is one thing which I will always remember and cherish most. I will always remember Tony's hugs. Tony hugging someone was the equivalent of a child hugging its teddy bear. Little children express their love so purely, so unconditionally, and with so much feeling. I used to feel a glow of warmth and comfort every time Tony hugged me. What a pity there were not as many as I would have wished for. The memory of those hugs are with me to this day.

As I draw near to the end of this chapter I mull over what I have received from so many respondents. One line sent by a Spanish Jesuit stays with me. It would probably be even more beautiful in the original Spanish but it is poetic enough in English.

It is absolutely true of Tony and reads like an epitaph:

"Tony was like a flowing mountain torrent—fresh, lively, powerful and changing."

EPILOGUE

On June 3, 1987, just before 4:30 in the afternoon, the bell of St. Peter's Church, Bandra tolled. It was tolling for a much loved and respected son of India.

Word of Tony's death had already reached thousands of people through the press and by word of mouth: *Anthony deMello SJ had died suddenly in New York eleven days earlier. Today his body was being brought home to rest.*

Mourners began filling the church rapidly and by the time Tony's body was carried in and placed before the altar, there was standing room only inside the church, with many more standing in the court-yard on either side of the church and out the front.

The Provincial, Fr. Lisbert D'Souza SJ had graciously consulted my sister Grace to seek her opinion on Tony's final resting place. She chose St. Peter's Church because she thought it would be more convenient for the many friends and admirers of Tony to attend the final farewell. The other alternative was Lonavala, which would have been a somewhat distant venue.

Some would disagree with this decision. They still think Tony's final resting place should have been in Lonavala, at the Sadhana Institute he established. I think not. There is enough evidence to show Tony had no attachments—not even sentimental ones. To Tony it would not matter at all where he was buried.

Among the mourners, there were a number of Tony's closest friends and many religious who had interacted with him, made retreats under his guidance or simply heard about this great man and read his works.

A woman, who was one of Tony's closest friends, sums up what many, many of Tony's close friends would have felt on that sad day. She mentions the atmosphere before the Mass had begun:

> It was one of the most painful days of my life. The church was overflowing with people as there weren't enough seats for all. Tony was lying still and the Laughing Saint was suddenly silent. Suddenly there came Tony's voice resounding from the walls of the Church. For a moment I really felt Tony was brought alive to meet so many hundreds of people who were sitting in silence. But it was only the recorded voice of him who was talking of life. There was a clear wave of loss and grief in the hearts of all present there.

The Mass was celebrated by Simon Cardinal Pimenta. The homily was delivered by Fr. Lisbert D'Souza. I wrote to Fr. Lisbert to ask him what he could remember of the funeral and his homily in particular.

Despite his busy schedule he was kind enough to reply:

> Yes I did give the homily at the funeral Mass. I had and have no practice of writing down a homily, so I have no text to share with you. But I do recall some of the kind of things I said as they are also the things I learnt from Sadhana.

Though he gives us the rest only in point form they are effective and appropriate. For those who have heard Tony or read his books these points need no elaboration. For those who haven't, these points serve as a sample of what to expect if they ever read or hear him.

Fr. Lisbert does mention in his letter to me:

> I don't want to say that I made all these points in my homily but I do recall weaving most of them in as experiences I had with Tony over the years:
> • Not to be afraid to question; to venerate no "sacred cows." As

Tony often said: if you meet the Buddha on the road, kill him.
- To believe that spirituality could be exciting and fulfilling.
- To be ready to be challenged and to have even my most cherished beliefs open to critique.
- To listen as much with the heart as with the head—something I found very hard as I am very much a "head person."
- Not to distrust emotions, mine or others, but to accept that they could tell me what the mind often failed to see.

What an excellent sum-up of much of what Tony stood for. Each of these points is tremendously rich and laden with meaning.

At some point during the ceremony the *Exultet* was intoned. Apparently this was one of Tony's favorite hymns. I was told this recently. This made me want to find out more about it. And I even listened to it on the Internet. Not being familiar with things Church I asked one of my respondents to elaborate on the *Exultet*.

Here is what he wrote:

"Exultet" (Let the earth rejoice) is the opening word in Latin of the Easter Proclamation. It is an ancient hymn sung by the deacon over the Easter candle which is lit at the start of the Easter Vigil. The Vigil takes place on Holy Saturday evening. It is a hymn of rejoicing that celebrates the resurrection of the Lord Jesus Christ. It serves as a short history of God's salvation of humankind.

I can see why this was among Tony's favorite hymns. In *Sadhana* he gives a fresh look at sin: "We can praise God even for our sins when we have repented for them, because he will draw good from them. And so the Church, in an ecstasy of love, will sing at the Easter liturgy, 'O happy fault . . . O necessary sin of Adam!'"[1]

The *Exultet* was sung on this occasion by Fr. John Baptist Fernandes SJ, the Music Director who had conducted the 600-strong

---

[1] *Sadhana—A Way to God,* pp. 164-165.

Choir that performed when Pope Paul VI visited Mumbai for the 38th Eucharistic Congress in 1964.

And so the Happy Wandering Sage was laid to rest. His coffin was lowered into a grave that was dug in a small alcove on the left side of the entrance to St. Peter's Church.

Some years after his funeral, my family and I visited his gravesite. It was unmarked and I was a bit taken aback at this non-recognition of a Jesuit as famous as Tony. So after having obtained permission from the parish priest, I arranged for a modest tombstone to be laid over his burial site.

Some years later this tombstone was removed on the grounds that if one Jesuit had a tombstone then the families of all the other dead Jesuits would request the same and there was simply not enough room to accommodate this. His name is now inscribed on a plaque, along with the names of other Jesuits buried in that alcove. When I heard of this removal of the tombstone I was rather upset at first.

But today I am a changed person thanks to Tony. I do realize now that this was not as important as I had made it out to be. I was, after all, thinking in the "regular way." I had seen all the other graves in that cemetery and was wondering why my brother did not have a tombstone on his grave whereas everyone else did. Today I realize that Tony would have laughed at my discomfiture. He would have said, "Bill, what does it matter where I am buried or who remembers me? I am no more special than any other human being."

More recently, in reading Tony's books, listening to his recordings, and watching his videos, I have rediscovered him. I found this very apt description of how Tony himself would have instructed his many followers on the disposal of his mortal remains:

> With the sky and the earth for my coffin; the sun and the moon and stars for my burial regalia; and all creation to escort me to the grave—could I desire anything more ceremonious and impressive?[2]

---

[2] *One Minute Wisdom*, p. 216.

I have had some people tell me that Tony had a premonition that he was going to die. A Jesuit, who worked with Tony for many years, had this to say:

> I took Tony to Lonavala train station on the day he departed for his last conference in the States. I had dropped him off at that station many times before and at every departure he always went straight to his seat and took his place on the train. This time however, he stood in the doorway of the compartment and waited till the train started to pull out of the station and waved to me. It never struck me then why he did this, but now I think he was waving goodbye to me forever. When I heard of his death, I was devastated and consumed by grief.

This Jesuit is only one of many who, in retrospect, imagined that Tony was giving them a sign of his final farewell. There are others who later read into things and assumed that Tony was trying to bid them a final farewell. They mention that in his last Prayer Seminar at JDV he spoke a lot about death. I asked a Jesuit who had attended that Seminar to comment on this. He told me that Tony spoke of death as he always speaks of death—putting it in perspective.

With due respect to all concerned, I don't believe that Tony was, for a single moment, thinking of his death. He was thinking of life in present moment freshness. His grieving friends and family are entitled to think otherwise. In their grief, his family and friends could well have imagined that Tony was saying his final goodbyes to them in subtle ways. I certainly did not get that impression on the occasion of our last meeting in New York. If Tony knew he was about to die he would most definitely have bid me a final farewell. Instead he told me how much he was looking forward to seeing my family and me later that year in Lonavala.

What is more, over the years, I have received many messages from people wanting to know what happened. How exactly did he die? How could he possibly die of a heart attack? And so on and so forth. For the time being, the death certificate provided by the New York department of health is all I have to go by.

Tony was human, after all, and while he never feared death, perhaps he would have been disappointed at not being able to continue his good work here among us. Personally, I am just a wee bit curious to know what exactly Tony would have been thinking, moments before he lost consciousness. I believe that there is only one person who could answer all these questions. That person is none other than Tony himself. Sadly, this answer will have to wait till we brothers meet again, who knows where, who knows when. By then, of course, it would still be a mystery for those who are alive and curious about the nature of his death.

I had returned to Australia in early June 1987 to grieve with my family. I was heavy-hearted and for many years I simply could not get over the fact that I was never going to see my brother again.

You see, Mum too had died suddenly albeit peacefully. We were all present at her funeral. I was not present for Dad's but Tony had called and told me of his passing. Dad too had died peacefully and painlessly. I was sad indeed to lose my parents but I accepted this as a fact of life. They were after all aged and "ready for death," so to speak.

But Tony's case was different! He was so young, so ready to take on the world, so vibrant and full of life. I just could not imagine that one so young and so full of life could be taken so suddenly and so early. This, in my opinion, was so terribly unfair and unjust. I brooded over his death for years.

This was the situation until last year, when I started "listening" to his *Awareness* Conference. After this I listened to *Rediscovery of Life*. And then I began to rediscover Tony!

And now I understand how to put his death in perspective. I understand a little better the meaning of life. And the meaning of death. And like all people who begin to get these insights I am quite unable to explain them adequately.

Since I began writing this book, friends of Tony who came

forward offered me such beautiful insights into his life and the meaning of his death as Tony himself would have wanted me to understand it.

More recently, I started corresponding with Fr. Miguel Lafont, who now resides in Japan and conducts regular Sadhana-type retreats there. He knew Tony well and had done several courses under Tony. He was generous enough to send me five articles he has written about Tony which he has not published yet. One article in particular explains, better than I can, my own understanding today of Tony's death.

I offer an excerpt from this article in the hope that it will help many a reader to understand life and understand death as Tony instructed his listeners to understand it.

Fr. Lafont writes:

During the [1986 Maxi-Sadhana] course of six months, we had several celebrations with a good dinner, beer and entertainment. This time we had planned another celebration but three days before the party Tony received news of his father's illness. Tony immediately began preparing for the trip to go to his father's bedside. He left at dawn. A few hours later we received the news of his father's death. We met to consider whether the party should go ahead or not. Most who were attending the Maxi-Sadhana, including me, thought it was better to postpone the party, although we knew that Tony did not think that way. Only a young Jesuit in the group opposed (the idea). He said he knew how Tony would feel and that he would be angry if he heard that we had cancelled the party. Three days later Tony arrived back in time for the celebration, and found that we had cancelled it. Tony was indeed angry with us for cancelling the party because he said we had not understood Sadhana. He turned to me in particular and said, "And you Miguel, at this point in your Sadhana, you do not understand? We are finishing the course and you have not yet understood Sadhana?"

Yes, indeed, we forgot what we were taught about death. In his book "A Call to Love" he writes: "What is death? A loss, a disappearance, a letting go, a saying goodbye. When you cling you refuse to say goodbye, you resist death and even though you may not realize it, that is when you resist life too.

"For life is on the move and you are stuck, life flows and you have become stagnant, life is flexible and free and you are rigid and frozen. Life carries all things away and you crave for stability and permanence.

"So you fear life and you fear death because you cling.

"When you cling to nothing, when you have no fear of losing anything then you are free to flow like the mountain stream that is always fresh and sparkling and alive."[3]

To us the death of Tony's father caught us by surprise. To Tony, it did not. Tony was not clinging to his father and learned to say goodbye at the funeral. Tony was not clinging to his father; he was not clinging to anything. He felt no fear of losing his father. He was ready to say goodbye.

To the above I would add a sentence which I read from a book on Tony. One of the contributors to this book quotes Tony:

If I die tomorrow *and I knew I was going to die*, the thing that would make me most happy is that I have helped so many people. My being on this earth has been of some use to humankind.[4]

I wonder if he knew how true this statement would prove to be after he died?

June 2012 marked the twenty-fifth year of Tony's passing. I had always imagined that when we die, we face the final curtain. That's it. No more encores, no more recitals or repeat performances. I do still believe in this theory. My immediate family and probably some of my friends may spend a moment of reflection and think of me

---

[3] *Call to Love*, Meditation 29, p. 113.
[4] *We Heard the Bird Sing*, p. 102.

with fondness. Maybe they will miss me. But, overall, they will get on with their lives.

In Tony's case though, this is not quite true. I am sure that those who personally knew and mingled with him also get on with their lives and have the occasional fond thought of him. They still cherish him in their hearts. What is amazing, from correspondence I still receive, is that more people who never met or interacted personally with this human being are attracted to his message and teaching. Tony continues to change lives! What a wonderful legacy he left behind. Twenty-five years after he died he continues to perform, to enlighten, to make people "come alive" through his books, audio, and video recordings.

In that fiftieth birthday recording, Tony ends the celebrations with a couple of hymns, accompanying himself on the guitar. He finishes the service with one song in particular, which he treats as a hymn. I have sung it myself along with others, on picnics and group outings.

I will quote Tony's words from that recording:

For our final hymn I invite you to join in the chorus. It's called "The Happy Wanderer." I like it because it nicely describes Sanyas. I felt quite flattered when one of you said you admired me for moving into the unknown, like moving from one thing to another; from one place to another, from one discovery to another. But it's a happy life. It's a wonderful life; so it's nicely depicted by this song. I will sing the verses and you must remember to join in in the chorus. I hope this guitar is in tune now . . . yes it appears to be.

He then begins to sing and when I listen to his happy clear voice, with all those present joining in the chorus, I can't help thinking how very appropriate it is and how well it suited my brother. I now see he is delivering another "freedom" message to all his friends:

I love to go a-wandering along the mountain track,
And as I go, I love to sing, my knapsack on my back.

I can almost hear Tony saying, "Isn't that the way to live? No encumbrances. No attachments. Just my knapsack on my back. I'm only passing through."

The last verse, which Tony sings very slowly and with meaning is as follows:

Oh may I go a-wandering until the day I die,
Oh may I ever laugh and sing beneath God's clear blue sky.

The Happy Wandering Sage continues, even in death, to sing his song and dance his dance to audiences from all over the world. May his song penetrate the hearts of many more after they have read this affectionate tribute I pay to my beloved brother.

THE FINAL WORD

WHEN I BEGAN WRITING this book, I had doubts aplenty. I had my moments of despair and anxiety. Some of the questions I asked myself were: Would I get it finished on time for the May 2012 deadline? Would I get all the material I needed to portray my brother as I really wanted to? Who would come forward with this information and when? My anxieties were completely unjustified. While I would have liked to receive much more information (like a starving person) most of what I needed to know just came, almost miraculously; as if it were meant to happen.

What transpired over the last twelve months has turned out to be a delightful, fulfilling experience. I have met so many wonderful, generous people, made new friends, and gained insights. What you have read is a compilation of memories—mine and those of persons who shared with me. I have heard it said that since Tony died there have been numerous articles, books, and Internet sites eulogizing him; but there has never been a single, honest, and comprehensive book detailing his life. At long last, this long-awaited book has now been completed.

It is not only homage but a tribute to Tony, who was such a wonderful, kind, sensitive, and humble human being. My recent discovery of his works have led me to examine my own life and begin to make changes to live better, in freedom, understanding, and harmony with humankind. This book has been painstakingly written, with so much love and admiration (thanks in large part to so many people who came forward to help me) for my wonderful brother. While we have all had our say and expressed our thoughts, lovingly and generously, my heart tells me that I should appropriately leave the final words of this book to Tony.

The story you are about to read was one of Tony's favorites, along with a sentence from which he derived much consolation.[1] I had read this story many years ago but only recently have I come to realize the full impact of its meaning. I hope it registers as well with you as it has with me:

There is a Chinese story of a farmer who used an old horse to till his fields. One day the horse escaped into the hills and when the farmer's neighbors sympathized with the old man over his bad luck, the farmer replied, "Bad luck? Good luck? Who knows?" A week later the horse returned with a herd of horses from the hills and this time the neighbors congratulated the farmer on his good luck. His reply was, "Good luck? Bad luck? Who knows?" Then, when the farmer's son was attempting to tame one of the wild horses, he fell off its back and broke his leg. Everyone thought this was very bad luck. Not the farmer, whose only reaction was, "Bad luck? Good luck? Who knows?" Some weeks later, the army marched into the village and conscripted every able-bodied youth they found there. When they saw the farmer's son with his broken leg they let him off. Now was that good luck? Bad luck? Who knows?

Everything that seems on the surface to be an evil may be a good in disguise. And everything that seems good on the surface may really be an evil. So we are wise to leave it to God to decide what is good luck and what bad, and thank him that all things turn out for good with those who love him. Then we shall see something of that marvelous mystical vision of Juliana of Norwich who uttered what for me is the loveliest and most consoling sentence I have ever read:

"And all shall be well; and all shall be well;
and all manner of thing shall be well!"
Anthony deMello SJ.
September 4, 1931–June 1, 1987

---

[1] *Sadhana—A Way to God*, pp. 167-168.

BIBLIOGRAPHY

Books by Anthony deMello

1. *Ah! These Jesuits!—The Inside Story* (Anand: Gujarat Sahitya Prakash [GSP], 1992).
2. *Ah! These Jesuits! —Going My Way* (Anand: GSP, 1992).
3. *Ah! These Jesuits!—The Man in the S.J. Mask* (Anand: GSP, 1992).
4. *Call to Love* (Anand; GSP, 1991); *The Way to Love* (New York: Image, 1992)
5. *One Minute Wisdom* (Anand: GSP, 1985; New York, Image, 1988).
6. *One Minute Nonsense* (Chicago: Loyola Press, 1992).
7. *Rooted in God—A Collection of Prayer Services* (Mumbai: St. Paul's, 2004).
8. *Sadhana—A Way to God* (Anand: GSP, 2005; New York: Image, 1984).
9. *The Prayer of the Frog* (Anand: GSP, 1982).
10. *The Prayer of the Frog—II* (Anand: GSP, 1982).
11. *The Song of the Bird* (Anand: GSP, 1982; New York: Image, 1984).
12. *Wellsprings—A Book of Spiritual Exercises* (Anand: GSP, 1984; New York: Image, 1986).

Other Sources

1. Anand Nayak, *Anthony deMello: His Life and His Spirituality* (Dublin: Columba, 2007).
2. *The Spiritual Exercises of St. Ignatius*, trans. Luis Puhl, S.J. (Mumbai: St. Paul's, 2006).

3. Aurel Brys, S.J., and Joseph Pulickal, S.J., *We Hear the Bird Sing* (Anand: GSP, 1995).

4. *Concilium* 159 (9/1982), *Learning to Pray,* pp. 77-81 (Edinburgh: T. & T. Clark).

Websites

1. Bill deMello:

   http://users.tpg.com.au/adsligol/tony/tony1.html

2. John Wataru:

   http://web.me.com/cyrilveliath/Site/Fr._John_Wataru_Uekuri_SJ
   .html

3. sadhana.jesuits:

   http://sadhana.jesuits.or.jp/e/sadhana/meditation.html

4. Sophia:

   http://pweb.sophia.ac.jp/jesuit45/Lafont.html

Appendices

I. Topics of Tony's Last Prayer Seminar at JDV, Pune

May 20, 1987 to May 26, 1987

DAY 1:

- Qualities needed to profit from life:
  1. Challenge old beliefs.
  2. Openness to see something new.
  3. Sincerity and honesty with oneself.
- Love—the foundation stone is forgiveness
- Misconceptions that need to be corrected:
  1. I am better than the other.
  2. They are totally wrong, I am totally right.
  3. The other is to blame and is responsible.

DAY 2:

- Q. Does awareness require effort or not?
  A. Depends on what you mean by effort. Suppose I am asked to sit on a hot stove. There will be an *early spring!* No effort needed.
- What is love?
  Love is SENSITIVITY —
  1. to the other;
  2. to creation;
  3. to all human beings.
  Love is clarity of perception, accuracy of response.

DAY 3:

- Negative emotions come from fear.
- Suffering and happiness.
- Attachments and craving cause suffering.
- Illusions create unhappiness.
- Our programming causes us suffering. All is in the mind.

DAY 4:

- Mystics are perpetually happy.
- God and Religion. Concept of God is not God. This is the biggest obstacle to experience God. God is UNKNOWABLE, UNINTELLIGIBLE, INEFFABLE.

DAY 5:

The aim of Meditation is to SEE, to Realize.

DAY 6:

Self is an ILLUSION. Get rid of "I" and you will be happy. You will experience the TIMELESS, ETERNAL, DIVINE.

II. Notification Concerning the Writings of Father Anthony deMello, SJ

Congregation for the Doctrine of the Faith

The Indian Jesuit priest, Father Anthony deMello (1931-1987) is well known due to his numerous publications which, translated into various languages, have been widely circulated in many countries of the world, though not all of these texts were authorized by him for publication. His works, which almost always take the form of brief stories, contain some valid elements of oriental wisdom. These can be helpful in achieving self-mastery, in breaking the bonds and feelings that keep us from being free, and in approaching with serenity the various vicissitudes of life. Especially in his early writings, Father deMello, while revealing the influence of Buddhist and Taoist spiritual currents, remained within the lines of Christian spirituality. In these books, he treats the different kinds of prayer: petition, intercession and praise, as well as contemplation of the mysteries of the life of Christ, etc.

But already in certain passages in these early works and to a greater degree in his later publications, one notices a progressive distancing from the essential contents of the Christian faith. In place of the revelation which has come in the person of Jesus Christ, he substitutes an intuition of God without form or image, to the point of speaking of God as a pure void. To see God it is enough to look directly at the world. Nothing can be said about God; the only knowing is unknowing. To pose the question of his existence is already nonsense. This radical apophaticism leads even to a denial that the Bible contains valid statements about God. The words of Scripture are indications which serve only to lead a person to silence. In other passages, the judgment on sacred religious texts, not excluding the Bible, becomes even more severe: they are said to prevent people from following their own common sense and cause them to become obtuse and cruel. Religions, including Christianity, are one of the major obstacles to the discovery of truth. This truth, however, is never defined by the author in its precise contents. For him, to think that the God of one's own religion is the only one is simply fanaticism. "God" is considered as a cosmic reality, vague and omnipresent; the personal nature of God is ignored and in practice denied.

Father deMello demonstrates an appreciation for Jesus, of whom he declares himself to be a "disciple." But he considers Jesus as a master alongside others. The only difference from other men is that Jesus is "awake" and fully free, while others are not. Jesus is not recognized as the Son of God, but simply as the one who teaches us that all people are children of God. In addition, the author's statements on the final destiny of man give rise to perplexity. At one point, he speaks of a "dissolving" into the impersonal God, as salt dissolves in water. On various occasions, the question of destiny after death is declared to be irrelevant; only the present life should be of interest. With respect to this life, since evil is simply ignorance, there are no objective rules of morality. Good and evil are simply mental evaluations imposed upon reality.

Consistent with what has been presented, one can understand how, according to the author, any belief or profession of faith whether in God or in Christ cannot but impede one's personal access to truth. The Church, making the word of God in Holy Scripture into an idol, has ended up banishing God from the temple. She has consequently lost the authority to teach in the name of Christ.

With the present *Notification*, in order to protect the good of the Christian faithful, this Congregation declares that the above-mentioned positions are incompatible with the Catholic faith and can cause grave harm.

The Sovereign Pontiff John Paul II, at the Audience granted to the undersigned Cardinal Prefect, approved the present *Notification*, adopted in the Ordinary Session of this Congregation, and ordered its publication.

Rome, from the offices of the Congregation for the Doctrine of the Faith, June 24, 1998, the Solemnity of the Birth of John the Baptist.

+ Joseph Card. Ratzinger *Prefect*
+ Tarcisio Bertone, S.D.B.
  Archbishop Emeritus of Vercelli
  Secretary

Explanatory Note

The writings of the Indian Jesuit priest, Father Anthony deMello (1931-1987) have circulated extensively in many countries of the world and among people of widely different backgrounds.[1] In these works, which often take the form of short anecdotes presented in an accessible and easy-to-read style, Father deMello collected elements of eastern wisdom which can be helpful in achieving self-control, in breaking the attachments and affections that keep us from being truly free, in avoiding selfishness, in facing life's difficulties with serenity without letting ourselves be affected by the world around us, while at the same time being aware of its riches. It is important to indicate these positive features which can be found in many of Father deMello's writings. Particularly in the works dating from his early years as a retreat director, while revealing the influence of Buddhist and Taoist spiritual currents, Father deMello remained in many respects within the boundaries of Christian spirituality. He speaks of waiting in silence and prayer for the coming of the Spirit, pure gift of the Father (*Contact with God: Retreat Conferences*, 3-7). He gives a very good presentation of the prayer of Jesus and of the prayer that Jesus teaches us, taking the Our Father as his basis (*ibid.*, 42-44). He also speaks of faith, repentance and contemplation of the mysteries of Christ's life according to the method of Saint Ignatius. In his work *Sadhana: A Way to God*, published for the first time in 1978, Jesus occupies a central place, particularly in the last part ("Devotion," 99-134). He speaks of the prayer of petition and intercession as taught by Jesus in the Gospel, of the prayer of praise and of invocation of the name of Jesus. His book is dedicated to the Blessed Virgin Mary, a model of contemplation (*ibid.*, 4-5).

But already in this work he develops his theory of contemplation as awareness, which seems to be not lacking in ambiguity. Already at the beginning of the book, the concept of Christian revelation is equated with that of Lao-tse, with a certain preference for the latter: " 'Silence is the great revelation,' said Lao-tse. We are accustomed to think of Scripture as the revelation of God. And so it is. I want you now to discover the revelation that silence brings" (9; cf. *ibid.*, 11). In exercising an awareness of our bodily sensations, we are already communicating with God, a communication explained in these terms: "Many mystics tell us that, in addition to the mind and heart with which we ordinarily communicate with God we are, all of us, endowed with a mystical mind and mystical heart, a faculty which makes it possible for us to know God directly, to grasp and intuit him in his very being, though in a dark manner . . ." (*ibid.*, 25). But this intuition, without images or form, is that of a void: "But what do I gaze into when I gaze silently at God? An imageless, formless reality. A blank!" (*ibid.*, 26). To communicate with the Infinite it is necessary "to gaze at a blank." And thus one arrives at "the seemingly disconcerting conclusion that concentration on your breathing or your body sensations is very good contemplation in the strict sense of the word" (*ibid.*, 29-30).[2] In his later works, he speaks of "awakening," interior enlightenment or knowledge: "How to wake up? How are we going to know we're asleep? The mystics, when they see what surrounds them, discover an extra joy flowing in the heart of things. With one voice they speak about this joy and love flowing everywhere . . . How to attain that? Through understanding. By being liberated from illusions and wrong ideas" (*Walking on Water*, 77-78; cf. *Call to Love*, 97). Interior enlightenment is the true revelation, far more important than the one which comes to us through Scripture: "A Guru promised a scholar a revelation of greater consequence than anything contained in the scriptures. . . . When you have knowledge you use a torch to show the way. When you are enlightened you become a torch" (*The Prayer of the Frog I*, 86-87).

"Holiness is not an achievement, it is a Grace. A Grace called Awareness, a grace called Looking, observing, understanding. If you would only switch on the light of awareness and observe yourself and everything around you throughout the day, if you would see yourself reflected in the mirror of awareness the way you see your face reflected in a looking glass . . . and if you observed this reflection without any judgment or condemnation, you would experience all sorts of marvellous changes coming about in you" (*Call to Love*, 96).

In these later writings, Father deMello had gradually arrived at concepts of God, revelation, Christ, the final destiny of the human person, etc., which cannot be reconciled with the doctrine of the Church. Since many of his books do not take the form of discursive teaching, but are collections of short tales which are often quite clever, the underlying ideas can easily pass unnoticed. This makes it necessary to call attention to certain aspects of his thought which, in different forms, appear in his work taken as a whole. We will use the author's own texts which, with their particular features, clearly demonstrate the underlying thinking.

On various occasions, Father deMello makes statements about God which ignore his personal nature, if not explicitly denying it, and reduce God to a vague and omnipresent cosmic reality. According to the author, no one can help us find God just as no one can help a fish in the sea find the ocean (cf. *One Minute Wisdom*, 67; *Awareness*, 103). Similarly, God and each of us are neither one nor two, just as the sun and its light, the ocean and the wave, are neither one nor two (cf. *One Minute Wisdom*, 34). With even greater clarity the problem of a personal Deity is presented in these terms: "Dag Hammarskjöld, the former UN Secretary-General, put it so beautifully: "God does not die on the day we cease to believe in a personal deity . . ."" (*Awareness*, 126; the same idea is found in "La iluminación es la espiritualidad," 60). "If God is love, then the distance between God and you is the exact distance between you and the awareness of yourself." (*One Minute Nonsense*, 266).

Following from a unilateral and exaggerated apophaticism which is the consequence of the above-mentioned concept of God, criticism and frequent irony are directed toward any attempt at language of God. The relationship between God and creation is frequently expressed with the Hindu image of the dancer and dance: "I see Jesus Christ and Judas, I see victims and persecutors, the killers and the crucified: one melody in the contrasting notes . . . one dance moving through different steps . . . Finally, I stand before the Lord. I see him as the Dancer and all of this maddening, senseless, exhilarating, agonizing, splendorous thing that we call life as his dance . . ." (*Wellsprings: A Book of Spiritual Exercises*, 200-201; *The Song of the Bird*, 16).

Who or what is God and what are men in this "dance'? And again: "If you wish to see God, look attentively at creation. Don't reject it; don't reflect on it. Just look at it" (*The Song of the Bird*, 27). It is not at all clear how Christ's mediation for knowledge of the Father enters into such a description. "Realizing that God has nothing to do with the idea I form of God . . . There is only one way of knowing him: by unknowing!" (*Walking on Water*, 12; cf. *ibid.*, 13-14; *Awareness*, 123; *The Prayer of the Frog I*, 268). Concerning God, therefore, one cannot say anything: "The atheist makes the mistake of denying that of which nothing may be said. . . . And the theist makes the mistake of affirming it" (*One Minute Nonsense*, 21; cf. *ibid.*, 336).

Nor do sacred scriptures, the Bible included, enable us to know God; they are simply like road-signs which tell me nothing about the city to which I am going: "I come to a sign that says 'Bombay.' . . . That sign isn't Bombay! Actually it doesn't even look like Bombay. It's not a picture of Bombay. It's a sign. That is what the scriptures are, a sign" (*Walking on Water*, 13). Continuing this metaphor, one could say that a road-sign becomes useless when I have reached my destination; this is what Father deMello seems to be saying: "The scripture is the excellent portion, the finger pointed toward the Light. We use its words to go beyond conceptions and reach silence" (*Walking on Water*, 16). Paradoxically God's revelation is not expressed in his words, but in silence (cf. also *One Minute Wisdom*, 118, 157, 191, etc. *Awareness*, 101). "In the Bible only the path is indicated to us, as in the Muslim, Buddhist scriptures, etc." ("La iluminación es la espiritualidad," 64).

Thus, what is proclaimed is an impersonal God who stands above all the religions, while objections are raised to the Christian proclamation of the God of love, held to be incompatible with the notion of the necessity of the Church for salvation:

My friend and I went to the fair. THE WORLD FAIR OF

RELIGIONS . . . At the Jewish Stall we were given hand-outs that said that God was All-Compassionate and the Jews were his Chosen People. The Jews. No other people were as Chosen as the Jewish People. At the Moslem Stall we learnt that God was All-Merciful and Mohammed is his only Prophet. Salvation comes from listening to God's only Prophet. At the Christian Stall we discovered that God is Love and there is no salvation outside the Church. Join the Church or risk eternal damnation. On the way out I asked my friend, "What do you think of God?" He replied, "He is bigoted, fanatical and cruel." Back home, I said to God, "How do you put up with this sort of thing, Lord? Don't you see they have been giving you a bad name for centuries?" God said, "I didn't organize the Fair. I'd be too ashamed to even visit it" ("The World Fair of Religions" in *The Song of the Bird*, 186-187; cf. *ibid.*, 189-190, 195).

The teaching of the Church on God's universal salvific will and on the salvation of non-Christians is not presented correctly, nor is the Christian message of God as Love: "'God is love. And He loves and rewards us forever if we observe His commandments.' "IF?" said the Master, "Then the news isn't all that good, is it?"" (*One Minute Nonsense*, 198; cf. *ibid.*, 206). Every concrete religion is an obstacle to arriving at the truth. Furthermore, what is said about the Scriptures is said also about religion in general: "All fanatics wanted to catch hold of their God and make him the only one" ("La iluminación es la espiritualidad," 65; cf. *ibid.*, 28, 30). What matters is the truth, whether it comes from Buddha or from Mohammed, since "the important thing is to discover the truth where all truths come together, because truth is one" (*ibid.*, 65). "Most people, alas, have enough religion to hate but not enough to love" (*The Prayer of the Frog* I, 104; cf. *ibid.*, 33, 94). When the obstacles that prevent one from seeing reality are listed, religion comes first: "First your beliefs. If you experience life as a communist or a capitalist, as a Moslem or a Jew, you are experiencing life in a prejudiced, slanted way; there is a barrier, a layer of fat between Reality and you because you no longer see and touch it directly" (*Call to Love*, 30-31). "If all human beings were fitted with such hearts people would no longer think of themselves as Communists or Capitalists, as Christians or Muslims or Buddhists. The very clarity of their thinking would show them that all thinking, all concepts, all beliefs are lamps full of darkness, signs of their ignorance" (*ibid.*, 94; cf. also *One Minute Wisdom*, 159, 217, on the dangers of religion). What is asserted about religion, is also said concretely about the Scriptures (cf. *The Song of the Bird*, 186ff; *One Minute Nonsense*, 19).

The divine sonship of Jesus is diluted into the notion of the divine sonship of all men: "To which God replied, 'A feast day is holy because it shows that all the days of the year are holy. And a sanctuary is holy because it shows that all places are sanctified. So Christ was born to show that all men are sons of God'" (*The Song of the Bird*, 189). Father deMello certainly manifests a personal adherence to Christ, of whom he declares himself a disciple (*Wellsprings*, 122), in whom he has faith (*ibid.*, 113) and who he personally encounters (*ibid.*, 115ff, 124ff). His presence is transfiguring (cf. *ibid.*, 92ff). But other statements are disconcerting. Jesus is mentioned as one teacher among many: "Lao Tzu and Socrates, Buddha and Jesus, Zarathustra and Mohammed" (*One Minute Wisdom*, 2). Jesus on the cross appears as the one who has freed himself perfectly of everything:

"I see the Crucified as stripped of everything: Stripped of his dignity ... Stripped of his reputation ... Stripped of support ... Stripped of his God ... As I gaze at that lifeless body I slowly understand that I am looking at the symbol of supreme and total liberation. In being fastened to the cross Jesus becomes alive and free. . . . So now I contemplate the majesty of the man who has freed himself from all that makes us slaves, destroys our happiness . . ." (*Wellsprings*, 95-97).

Jesus on the cross is the man free of all ties; thus he becomes the symbol of interior liberation from everything to which we were attached. But isn't Jesus something more than a man who is free? Is Jesus my Savior or does he simply direct me toward a mysterious reality which has saved him? "Will I ever get in touch, Lord, with the source from which your words and wisdom flow? . . . Will I ever find the wellsprings of your courage?'" (*Wellsprings*, 123). "'The lovely thing about

Jesus was that he was so at home with sinners, because he understood that he wasn't one bit better than they were' . . . The only difference between Jesus and those others was that he was awake and they weren't" (*Awareness*, 30-31; cf. also "La iluminación es la espiritualidad," 30, 62). Christ's presence in the Eucharist is but a symbol that refers to a deeper reality: his presence in creation. "The whole of creation is the body of Christ, and you believe that it is only in the Eucharist. The Eucharist indicates this creation. The Body of Christ is everywhere and yet you only notice its symbol which indicates to you what is essential, namely life" ("La iluminación es la espiritualidad," 61).

Man's being seems destined to dissolve, like salt in water: "Before that last bit dissolved, the [salt] doll exclaimed in wonder, 'Now I know who I am!' " (*The Song of the Bird*, 125). At other times, the question of life after death is declared to be unimportant: "'But is there life after death or is there not?' persisted a disciple. 'Is there life before death? —that is the question!' said the Master enigmatically" (*One Minute Wisdom*, 83; cf. *ibid.*, 26). "One sign that you're awakened is that you don't give a damn about what's going to happen in the next life. You're not bothered about it; you don't care. You are not interested, period" (*Awareness*, 42-43, 150). Perhaps with even greater clarity: "Why bother about tomorrow? Is there a life after death? Will I survive after death? Why bother about tomorrow? Get into today" (*Awareness*, 114). "The idea that people have of eternity is stupid. They think that it will last forever because it is outside of time. Eternal life is now; it's here" ("La iluminación es la espiritualidad," 42).

At various points in his books institutions of the Church are criticized indiscriminately: "My religious life has been completely taken over by professionals" (*The Song of the Bird*, 63ff). The function of the Creed or the Profession of the Faith is judged negatively, as that which prevents personal access to truth and enlightenment (thus with different nuances, *The Song of the Bird*, 36, 46-47, 50ff, 215). "When you no longer need to hold on to the words of the Bible, it is then that it will become something very beautiful for you, revealing life and its message. The sad thing is that the official Church has dedicated itself to framing the idol, enclosing it, defending it, reifying it without being able to look at what it really means" ("La iluminación es la espiritualidad," 66). Similar ideas are presented in *The Prayer of the Frog I*, 7, 94, 95, 98-99: "A public sinner was excommunicated and forbidden entry to the church. He took his woes to God. 'They won't let me in, Lord, because I am sinner.' 'What are you complaining about? said God. 'They won't let me in either!'" (*ibid.*, 105).

Evil is nothing but ignorance, the lack of enlightenment: "When Jesus looks at evil he calls it by its name and condemns it unambiguously. Only, where I see malice, he sees ignorance. . . . "Father forgive them, for they do not know what they are doing'" [Lk 23:34] (*Wellsprings*, 215). Certainly, this text does not reflect the entire teaching of Jesus on the evil of the world and on sin; Jesus welcomed sinners with profound mercy, but he did not deny their sin; rather he invited them to conversion. In other passages we find even more radical statements: "Nothing is good or bad but thinking makes it so" (*One Minute Wisdom*, 104). "Actually there is no good or evil in persons or in nature. There is only a mental judgment imposed upon this or that reality" (*Walking on Water*, 99). There is no reason to repent for sins, since the only thing that matters is to be awakened to an awareness of reality: "Don't weep for your sins. Why weep for sins that you committed when you were asleep?" (*Awareness*, 26; cf. *ibid.*, 43, 150). The cause of evil is ignorance (*One Minute Nonsense*, 239). Sin exists, but it is an act of insanity ("La iluminación es la espiritualidad," 63). Repentance therefore means returning to reality (cf. *ibid.*, 48). "Repentance is a change of mind: a radically different vision of reality" (*One Minute Nonsense*, 241).

Clearly, there is an internal connection between these different positions: if one questions the existence of a personal God, it does not make sense that God would address himself to us with his word. Sacred Scripture, therefore, does not have definitive value. Jesus is a teacher like others; only in the author's early books does he appear as the Son of God, an affirmation which would have little meaning in the context of such an understanding of God. As a consequence one cannot attribute value to the Church's teaching. Our personal survival after death is problematic if God is not personal. Thus it becomes clear that such conceptions of God, Christ and man are not compatible with the Christian faith.

For this reason, those responsible for safeguarding the doctrine of the faith have been obliged to illustrate the dangers in the texts written by Father Anthony deMello or attributed to him, and to warn the faithful about them.

Notes:

[1] Not all the works of Father deMello were authorized for publication by the author himself. Some were published after his death based on his writings, or on notes or recordings of his conferences. In this Explanatory Note, the following editions of his writings are cited: *Sadhana: A Way to God* (St. Louis, USA: The Institute of Jesuit Sources, 1978); *The Song of the Bird* (Anand, India: Gujarat Sahitya Prakash, 1982); *Wellsprings: A Book of Spiritual Exercises* (Anand, India: Gujarat Sahitya Prakash, 1984); *One Minute Wisdom* (Anand, India: Gujarat Sahitya Prakash, 1985); "La iluminación es la espiritualidad: Curso completo de autoliberación interior" in Vida Nueva (1987) pp. 27/1583—66/1622; *The Prayer of the Frog,* 2 vols. (Anand, India: Gujarat Sahitya Prakash, 1989); *Awareness* (London: Fount Paperbacks, 1990); *Contact with God: Retreat Conferences* (Anand, India: Gujarat Sahitya Prakash, 1990); *Call to Love: Meditations* (Anand, India: Gujarat Sahitya Prakash, 1991); *Caminhar sobre as águas: Quebre o Ídolo* (São Paulo, Brazil: Edições Loyola, 1992), Engl. trans. *Walking on Water* (New York: Crossroad, 1998); *One Minute Nonsense* (Anand, India: Gujarat Sahitya Prakash, 1992).

[2] The Letter of the Congregation for the Doctrine of the Faith on some aspects of Christian meditation *Orationis formas* (15 October 1989) seems to make reference to such ideas: "Still others do not hesitate to place that absolute without image or concepts, which is proper to Buddhist theory, on the same level as the majesty of God revealed in Christ, which towers above finite reality" (n. 12: *AAS* 82 [1990], 369). In this regard, it is also appropriate to recall the teachings on inculturation and interreligious dialogue in the Encyclical Letter of John Paul II *Redemptoris missio* (cf. nn. 52-57: *AAS* 83 [1991], 299-305).

III. An Eastern Christian Speaks of Prayer
Anthony deMello SJ

Tony's article "An Eastern Christian Speaks of Prayer" appeared in *Concilium* 159 (9/1982), *Learning to Pray*, pp. 77-81, published by T. & T. Clark.

Concilium is an international journal on Theology. It is reproduced in full with the kind permission of *Concilium*. Grateful thanks are due to Mr. Wilfred Felix, the current President of *Concilium*, and its Board of Directors.

1. The Seed

Why is God invisible? He is not. Your vision is blurred so you fail to see Him. The screen in the movie theatre becomes invisible when a film is projected on it; so, though you ceaselessly look at the screen, you fail to see it—you are too caught up in the movie.

The Hindu meditator sits and looks at the tip of his nose, symbolising the fact that God is right there in front of us, but our gaze is fixed elsewhere in the distance. There is no question of searching and finding the tip of your nose. Wherever you go, whatever you do, awake or asleep, whichever way you turn, it is right there before your eyes. You never lost it. You only fail to recognize it.

For centuries Hindu India has seen God as "dancing" creation. The extraordinary marvel is that men see the dance but fail to recognize the Dancer.

In one's quest for God, then, one must realize that there is nothing to search for or to attain. How can you search for what is right before your eyes? How can you attain what you already possess? What is called for here is not *effort* but *recognition*.

The disciples at Emmaus had the Risen Lord right before them, but their eyes had to be opened. The Scribes and the Pharisees excelled in effort and failed in recognition. And mankind on the Last Day will exclaim: "You were with us, and we failed to see you!" The quest for God then is the attempt to *see*.

A man sees a woman every day and she seems no different from other women until one day he falls in love with her. Then his eyes are opened and he is amazed that he could have been contemplating this adorable goddess for years and failed to see her. Stop searching, stop travelling, and you will arrive. There is nowhere to go! Be still and see what is before your eyes. The faster you travel and the more effort you invest in travelling, the more likely you are to go astray. People ask WHERE they will find God. The answer is HERE. WHEN will they find Him. The answer is NOW. HOW they will find Him. The answer is BE SILENT AND LOOK. (An Eastern tale tells of an ocean fish that sets out in search of the ocean; it finds no trace of the ocean wherever it turns, only water!)

2. The Rocky Ground

We seek to "see" God. But do we ever see anything? We look for a new flower and we ask, "What is that?" Someone says, "A lotus." All we have now is a new name, a new label, but we mistakenly think we have a new experience and a new understanding. As soon as we can tag a name on to something we feel we have added to our store of knowledge, whereas we have added only to our store of labels.

When God refused to reveal His name to Moses or to allow any image to be made of Him, he was not only proscribing the idolatry of the ancient primitive who identified Him with an image, but also the idolatry of the modern scholar who identified him with an idea. For our conceptual idols of Him are as pathetically inadequate to represent His Reality, as are idols of stone and clay.

The word "European" tantalisingly gives you some knowledge and absolutely no understanding of the individual standing before you. You would do him an injustice if you thought that the word "European" or any other word or group of words, for that matter, gave you any comprehension of his unique individuality. For the individual, like God, is beyond all words, ineffable. To "see" this tree, I must drop the label for it gives me the illusion that, because I have a name for it, I know the tree. More: I must drop all former experiences of other trees (as I must of all other Europeans if I am to be fair to this individual European here). Even more, I must drop all former experiences I have had even of this tree—we are all familiar, are we not, with the fact that we do not give this *present* individual a chance because we are constantly judging him by our past experience of him. Is it then surprising to learn that if I would experience God just now, I must drop all that others have told me about Him, all my past experiences of Him and all words and labels of Him no matter now sacred? Truth is not a formula. It is an experience. And experience is untransferable. Formulas are transferable material; so they are of little worth. What has value cannot be transferred.

The word, the religious formula, the dogma: they were meant to be pointers, indicators, helps to guide me in my approach to God. They frequently become the final barrier. As when I take a bus to go home and refuse to get off it when I have arrived. One thinks of so many people who go round and round in circles because they have never been taught to get off their conceptualising and theologising about the Divine; who refuse to abandon their discursive reflection in prayer and to enter the dark night, the conceptless cloud that the mystics speak of. They go through life collecting more and more labels, like the man who collects more and more material possessions that he will never use.

The river flows before your eyes and you are dying of thirst, but you insist on having a definition of water because you are convinced that you cannot quench your thirst unless you have the exact formula. The word "love" is not love and the word "God" is not God. Neither is the concept. Nobody ever got intoxicated on the word "wine." No one ever got burnt by the word "fire." Man is more interested in the reflection than in the real. So he lives in fiction. And when he reflects on God he lives on religious fiction. He is fascinated by his concepts because he thinks they mirror the Real. His mirrors must be broken. REAL food and REAL water are needed to satisfy a real hunger and thirst. Representations of food and water will not do. The formula H_2O will not quench his thirst no matter how scientifically accurate it is. Neither will his belief in God, however true. They may make him a religious fanatic, but they will not satisfy the need of his heart. (An Arab mystic tells of a man starving in a desert who sees a sack in a distance and rushes towards it in the hope that it contains something to eat, only to find it is full of precious stones.) Is it any wonder that, from having failed to understand this, the Christian churches have become exhausted mines? What is now quarried from the mines are words and formulas; and the market is glutted with these. But there is a scarcity of experience, so we Christians are becoming a "wordy" people. We live on words, like a man who feeds himself on the menu instead of the food. The word "God," the formula about God, is becoming more significant to us than the reality God. There is a great danger that when we see the Reality in forms that do not fit our formulas we will fail to recognize it, or even reject It is the name of our formulas. (A Sufi master says: "A donkey housed in a library does not become wise. So all religious knowledge has not improved me any more than a desert place made fertile by the presence of a treasure in it.")

3. The Good Soil

This attitude is best seen in the kind of divinity schools we Christians run. One would expect these schools to turn out persons who would cater to modern man's thirst for God. But they have become replicas of secular schools. They have professors instead of Masters and they offer scholarships instead of enlightenment. The professor teaches; the Master awakens. The professor offers knowledge; the Master offers ignorance, for he destroys knowledge and creates experience; he offers you knowledge as a vehicle, only to drag you out of it when the time arrives lest knowledge impede recognition.

Secular learning is acquired through reflection, thinking, talking. Religion is learnt through silent meditation. (In the east, meditation, "dhyan," means not reflection as it does in the west, but the silencing of all reflection and thought.) The secular schools turn out scholars.

The religious school produces meditators. Tragically most Christian divinity schools merely change the secular scholar into the religious scholar. The secular school attempts to *explain* things and creates KNOWLEDGE. The religious school teaches one to *contemplate* things in such a way that it creates WONDER. Man has deep-rooted Ignorance. His secular learning does not take away his Ignorance—it makes it more hidden, giving him the illusion of Knowledge. In the religious school the Ignorance is brought to the fore and exposed, for within it the Divine is to be found. But it is the rare Christian school that does this; all too frequently, the Ignorance is buried under further religious Knowledge.

The Christian religious school then must develop techniques to use Knowledge as a means to expose Ignorance, to use the word in such a way that it will lead to silence. Like the "mantra" or "bhajan" in India, where the word is first understood with the mind, then ceaselessly repeated till a silence is created whereby the formula is transferred from the mind to the heart, and its deeper meaning is sensed quite beyond all words and formulas. Religious students must be so trained that when they read or listen to the word, their heart is ceaselessly attuned to the "wordless" which resounds in the word. They must go through a rigorous discipline till their minds are stilled and they learn, in silence, to "ponder things in their heart." (A government official asked the great Rinzai for the secret of religion in one word. "Silence" said Rinzai. "And how does one attain silence?" "Meditation." "And what is meditation?" "Silence.")

Religious students will read their Bible. But every other page of that Bible will be blank, to indicate that sacred words are meant to produce and deepen silence, a silence that is enriched by the holy words, like a rich silence that follows the striking of a temple gong. They will devote as much time to the blank pages in their Bible as they do to the text because it is only thus that they become able to understand the text. For the Bible sprang from those blank pages, from men and women who were silent enough that they could experience the ineffable Truth which they could never describe, but which they struggled to indicate and point to in words that might lead others to experience the same Truth.

4. The Flower

The Bible teaches that no man can see God and live. When the mind is silenced, God is seen and the self dies. The Masters of the East agree: when silence enters the heart, the self dies. How? Not through annihilation, but through "vision." In the stillness of silence one "sees," experiences, that his self-as-center, his self-as-separate is "maya," illusory.

It is as if the dance were to come home to itself and "see" that it has no center, no being apart from the Dancer; that it is not a "being" at all, but an action. Only the Dancer is being. Only the Dancer is. The dance is not; it is-in-the-Dancer. God said to Catherine of Siena, "I am He who is. You are she who is not." When you enter into silence you experience that you are not; the center is no longer in you; it is in God; you are the periphery. One recalls those powerful words attributed to Meister Eckhart; "Only one Being has the right to use the personal pronoun 'I,' God!"

The one who experiences this becomes Awakened. He becomes a "nobody," an emptiness, an "incarnation" through whom the Divine shines forth and acts. The poet, the painter, the musician sometimes experiences inspired moments when he seems to lose himself and feels a creative activity flow through him of which he is more the channel than the source. What he experiences in his art, the Awakened man experiences in his life. He is active, but no longer the actor. His doings become happenings. He experiences himself as doing things which are simultaneously not done by *him*; they seem to happen through him. His efforts become effortless; his work becomes play, a "leela," a sport of God. Can it be otherwise when he experiences himself as a dance that the Divine is dancing, as a hollow flute through which God's music flows?

5. The Fruit

When silence produces the death of the self, love is born. The Awakened man experiences himself as different, but not separate, from other men and from the rest of creation. For there is only one Dancer, and all creation constitutes only one dance. He experiences them all as his "body," his self. So he loves all men as he loves himself.

He does not necessarily go out in service. He knows that anyone who seeks to serve, is in danger of becoming like so many "charitable" people who are not religious at all; they are *guilty*; do-gooders who are always interfering with the lives of others. It is, alas, possible for you to give your goods to feed the poor and your body to be burnt and to still not have love. The best way that you can be of service to the world is that YOU disappear. Then you become a vehicle of the Divine. Then service will spontaneously occur, but only if the Divine impels you to it. It might just as possibly impel you to sing songs or retire in the desert, and the whole world will be enriched by your songs or by your silence.

Instead of being harmed by your service. ("Pardon me," said the monkey as he placed the protesting fish on the branch of a tree, "I am saving you from drowning." Service can kill!)

In whatever you do, be it service or silence or song, you will be totally absorbed, for your "self" will no longer be in the way and you will give with your whole being. This is religion at its highest. Not sitting in solitude, not chanting prayers, not going to church, but going into life. Your every action now flows from silence, from a silenced self. Your every action has now become meditation.

Christian action today is in danger of flowing from TALK and REFLECTION rather than from SILENCE. Christianity is in danger of becoming a TALKING and a THINKING religion. The Eucharist is spoken of as being a CELEBRATION but has become mostly a CEREBRATION; the priest talks to the people, the people talk back to him, and priest and people talk to God. If we would make religion a celebration again, we must lessen the THINKING and the TALKING and introduce more SILENCE and DANCING. (A guru on being asked by a disciple how he had attained God replied, "Through making the heart white with silent meditation, not through making paper black with religious composition.")

Nor, we might add, through making the air thick with spiritual conversation.

Index